URBAN
MINISTRY

URBAN MINISTRY

David Claerbaut

Zondervan Publishing House
a Division of The Zondervan Corporation
Grand Rapids, Michigan

URBAN MINISTRY
Copyright © 1983 by The Zondervan Corporation
Grand Rapids, Michigan

Library of Congress Cataloging in Publication Data

Claerbaut, David.
    Urban ministry.

    Bibliography: p.
    Includes index.
    1. City clergy. 2. City churches. 3. Cities
and towns—United States. I. Title.
BV637.5.C58   1983   253′.0973   83-14743
ISBN 0-310-45961-3

Edited by Diane Zimmerman
Designed by Louise Bauer

Printed in the United States of America
83 84 85 86 87 88 / 9 8 7 6 5 4 3 2 1

To

Erwin Claerbaut
and
Bill Leslie,

one a layperson and the other a pastor,
each of whom has been a pioneer
in urban ministry

Contents

Foreword

Urban ministry evokes many different images in the 1980s. This is so partly because conceptions of the city vary so much, even among scholars, and partly because the nature and mission of the urban church leave many confused. A good bit of contemporary research, such as that of Franz Schurmann at the University of California at Berkeley, shows that the fate of cities is inextricably bound up with international movements and economies. The visible dynamics of that trend mean that our large cities are growing richer and poorer at the same time. Urbanization then becomes a very complex subject, and the mission of the church on that matrix becomes even less clear to many urban church leaders.

David Claerbaut does a great service in this book by cogently defining a city by its functions and effects and then showing in specific examples how those make an impact on us and the people to whom we minister amid a variety of social contexts and structures.

As a sociologist, Claerbaut speaks with competence, as might be expected. And because he lives, works, and worships in the city, he speaks also with credibility.

In a previous book, *The Reluctant Defender,* Professor Claerbaut describes the pilgrimage and remarkable ministry of an urban lawyer, Chuck Hogren, who founded the Cabrini-Green Legal Aid Clinic. The writing of that book, like this one, required both a theoretical and a working knowledge of urban persons and urban systems. Few, it seems, know both.

Urban ministry books with few exceptions tend to slight either the city or the church. Some have been heavy sociological tomes of good classical systemic analysis but with little passion for the church except as a front for ecumenically based, highly funded programs. Other literature has spoken of urban ministry from the other extreme, with virtually no contextual analysis and with programmatic case studies that happened in cities but were contextually inconsequential. They were called urban but did not address the city.

Another genre of urban ministry books calls the church to come back to the city, completely unaware of or insensitive to the fact that only the white middle- and upper-class institutional churches left, but that the Spirit did not leave and neither did the church. Its poly-chromed existence remained, more than ever, an urban fact of life.

Professor Claerbaut's book fills the need for a contemporary, socially, personally, and spiritually sensitive book that makes urban theory intelligible for practitioners by putting names and handles on sociology so we can actually hope to help people and move systems for the glory of God and the building up of His urban kingdom.

David gives us this hope and help in the book by lifting up some cases and resources from many called and committed urban servants who are making a significant difference on the urban world. May their tribe increase.

Ray Bakke
Chicago, Illinois

Preface

Some time ago when I was involved in teaching several seminary courses on urban ministry, I discovered a dearth of textbooks on the subject. The few in existence were heavy on theology and ministry but rather light on an understanding of the city itself and its impact on ministry. This book, in part, is a response to that problem. Though titled *Urban Ministry*, the text focuses more specifically on the effects of the city on ministry.

Having examined a number of urban topics at length for a previous work on social problems,[1] I had some ready research from which to draw. In this work, however, the urbanological material has been augmented, developed, and focused to fit an urban-ministry perspective. I have attempted to make the book applicable—conceptually and practically—to pastors who lack background in urban sociology, seminarians, parachurch workers, and other "first-entry" people. Though much of the material may be familiar to urban veterans and particularly to black church people who have a rich heritage of effective urban ministry, I trust that some of the concepts, models, and strategies will be helpful to that audience as well. Moreover, I have been careful to present the materials in such a way that they will be useful regardless of the reader's position on any liberal-conservative theological continuum.

The book contains a number of references to Chicago's LaSalle Street Church and its pastor, Bill Leslie. There are several reasons for drawing on this ministry. First, I have rather extensive knowledge of this church and pastor. Over its two-decade commitment to truly urban ministry, LaSalle has managed to confront, through trial and error as well as careful study, an impressive variety of urban challenges. Secondly, Leslie and the church have regularly kept abreast of the current models, theories, and practices extant in urban ministries nationwide. Finally, the church's location in a community within the nation's second largest city, a city that has undergone a series of ethnic and economic changes, makes it a valuable model and resource.

Before ministry in the city can be discussed, several terms need to be defined. One of these is *city*. Amos Hawley provides a brief definition in viewing the city as a "permanent, relatively densely settled and administratively defined unit of territory, the residents of which gain their living primarily by specializing in a variety of non-agricultural activities."[2]

In reality, no single definition of a city is sufficient. With some generalizing, it could be said that there are two dominant approaches to the study of the city.[3] One is the *ecological approach*.[4] Drawing from the fields of biology and botany, this approach focuses on spatial distribution and growth—geographical form. The concentric-zone model, discussed in chapter 3, is an example of the ecological approach.

The other view can be called the *sociocultural approach*.[5] This approach focuses on cultural, psychological, and social processes and functions among city dwellers—their distinctive styles of feeling, thinking, and acting and the unique patterns of their relationships. George Younger calls the city "a social organism, a way of living together."[6] Lewis Mumford viewed the city as the point of maximum concentration of power and culture.[7] The sociocultural approach regards the city as a collection of personal and impersonal groups. The latter generate interacting institutions—political, educational, economic, and religious.[8]

A subcategory within the sociocultural approach derives from the field of anthropology. This approach emphasizes the origin and development of various urban migrant people. It stresses practical measures for dealing with such problems of urban life as poverty, deviance, majority-minority relations, and institutional failure.[9] The anthropological approach is much used among some schools of missiology, such as the one at Fuller Theological Seminary in Pasadena, California.

The second term that needs to be defined is *urban ministry*. This term encompasses the urban church and ministry. Although the urban church can be defined in a variety of ways, a good working definition is "a community, usually organized formally, of God's people in the city." Ministry is carried on both within to the members and without to the world. Ministry has six facets: (1) worship—adoration to God; (2) evangelism—reaching those on the outside with the gospel; (3) discipleship—developing mature followers of Christ; (4) fellowship—care and intimacy among the members; (5) stewardship—responsible earthly citizenship aimed at advancing justice and improving the quality of life in the neighborhood, city, and world; (6) service—addressing immediate physical, social, and spiritual needs of those within and without.

These six facets of ministry are stressed in different proportions in various churches. Traditional churches have tended to envelop all six ministries. Growing churches, however, tend to focus primarily on one or two of the facets, thus developing a distinctive identity. These churches can often be divided into three categories. *Experiential* churches highlight worship and evangelism through creative and conventional approaches. *Relational* churches emphasize discipleship and fellowship. *Task* churches focus on stewardship and service.

Urban ministry is an exceedingly broad topic. Although this book deals occasionally with experiential and relational categories as well as ministries of worship, evangelism, discipleship, and fellowship, its chief focus is on the task church and its ministries of stewardship and service. In addition, it emphasizes life and ministry among the poor of the inner city, where the problems are the most severe and the challenge to ministry is the greatest. However, with the explosive increase in the number of mainline denominational churches in changing neighborhoods and urban processes permeating all of society, I trust the material discussed in this book will be applicable to ministry in a variety of contexts.

I wish to give a special acknowledgment to Diane Zimmerman and Estelle Zelner for their help in editing the manuscript.

Note: In order to avoid a ponderous style, the masculine (he, him, his) is used rather than combinations (he/she, him/her, his/hers) in gender-indefinite cases. Nonetheless, no attempt at chauvinism is intended.

1 | Urban Ministry— Biblical Mandate

It has been said that Christianity has failed to make an impact on three major areas: the Hindu culture, the Islamic society, and the major cities.[1] Our concern here is the city: the gospel must penetrate the city if it is really to penetrate American society, for the city is the soul of the society. Cities determine the destiny of nations. They are, as Roger Greenway says, "centers of communication, commerce, cultural life, and government."[2] To remove the cities is to excise the central nervous system of the American society. There is, then, a very practical mandate to serve the city.

THE CITY—THE WAVE OF THE FUTURE

Urbanization is an irreversible trend. In fact, about one-half of the world's population now lives in urban areas, and the number continues to grow. Mexico City, for example, is the world's largest city, with 17 million inhabitants. Presently it is growing at the rate of 6.2 percent—a million per year. America is becoming a nation of "strip cities," metropolitan areas that extend from Boston to Washington, D.C., and from San Francisco to San Diego.[3]

The city is not, however, just a place with certain structures and forms; it is a set of processes that flow out through suburbia and into rural communities. Farmers, who once viewed themselves as self-sufficient, are caught up in the process of urbanization. For example, when the federal government established sanctions against the sale of wheat to the Soviet Union because of its involvement in Afghanistan, the backing up of the futures market could be felt in the harvest field. In addition, an ever greater proportion of the farmers' crops feed city dwellers. People in small towns also feel the effect of urbanization as major food chains replace corner grocery stores. Moreover, in every locale, urban or rural, formerly urban problems such as drug abuse, housing shortages, unmarried cohabitation, unemployment, care for the elderly, and poverty are now felt.

To understand the city is to understand the future. A world-class city is a microcosm of the world. A city dweller has the opportunity to become truly international and crosscultural. Lewis Mumford puts aside the old separation of urban from rural, arguing that the entire planet is becoming an interrelated village. He says that beyond place, the city is an organ for developing and expressing the new human personality—the "world person." [4]

Major cities do indeed mirror the world's population. Take Chicago, for example. There are more American Indians living in its Uptown community than anywhere else in the country, with the possible exception of some reservations. Only Warsaw contains more people of Polish extraction. Its Hispanic population is nearly as large as the entire population of Seattle, Washington. There is explosive growth among Koreans, Vietnamese, Cambodians, Laotians, and other "new Asians" as well. There are, in addition, about 1.5 million black people living in Chicago. [5] The population of Los Angeles, already heavily Hispanic, includes increasing numbers of Asians, with nearly three-fourths of its residents nonwhite.

People in these cities, especially the inner cities, are suffering. They experience crowded conditions, poverty, powerlessness, and ill health. They are in spiritual need, for their inner lives—their souls—are dying. But they also have social, physical, and political needs. They need whole-person care. Hence, the church in the city faces an awesome challenge. This challenge—to extend service to the social as well as the spiritual realm—is a most appropriate one, for it is biblical.

Yet urban ministry has faced controversy. For decades Christians, especially evangelicals, have battled over the issue of evangelism versus social concern. These two ministries have often been viewed as opposed to one another. Those who espoused evangelism felt that to care for temporal needs was to be concerned with the part of the person that will die anyway. What was needed was concern for the eternal soul. Those who espoused social concern argued that soul-winning may be of value, but in a world in which people are not eating properly, are housed in substandard conditions, are jobless, and do not receive adequate health care, presenting Christ as the answer remains only an abstract. David Moberg states that when the church remains silent on difficult social issues, "it renounces its claim that it ministers to 'the whole man.' " And yet, as he unconditionally warns, social services should not be used as "bait" to win souls.[6] And so the debate has continued. Many conservatives see social activists as apostate, while those who have social concerns are tempted to become aspiritual in their efforts.

This is a sad situation for all involved. According to John Perkins, neither the liberal nor the evangelical church has functioned as a complete church. Much of their energy has been drawn away in criticizing each other, and the result has been less-than-effective spiritual ministries.[7] In fact, resistance to social concern among some Christians has had a large part in the tendency of churches to abandon the city. Greenway laments that "by their locations, their architecture, their liturgy, their sermons, and their entire program, urban Protestant churches have conveyed the message to the masses that these churches are not for them."[8]

Humans were created to be whole persons, with physical, mental, and spiritual dimensions. Deprivation in any of these dimensions has a deadening effect on the others, since all parts are interrelated and interactive. Suffering physically makes it difficult to function well psychologically. Severe emotional disabilities are sometimes translated into physical disabilities. A spiritually sterile life is often revealed in depression and a low energy level. Just as theologically we cannot divide people into component parts, so also in ministry we must not dissect but rather serve whole persons. The soul without the body is a ghost; the body without the soul is a corpse. In fact, Greenway claims that only a holistic approach to ministry can satisfy biblical directives and the needs of the city.[9]

BIBLICAL MANDATE

The biblical mandate for urban ministry can be seen in two topics. First is the Scripture's appeal to the city itself—with all its institutions—by the Old Testament prophets and New Testament apostles.

Second, and far more weighty and complex, is God's concern for justice for the poor and oppressed. His concern that the powerless members of society be treated fairly and with compassion is seen in numerous passages in both testaments and in the practices of the Israelite culture and the early church. Finally, and most powerfully, God's concern has been demonstrated fully in Jesus Christ.

The Concept of the City in Scripture

The city with all its institutions is treated as a single entity in many scriptural passages. Raymond Bakke claims to have found 119 cities mentioned in Scripture. In the Old Testament the prophets were involved not only in evangelizing but also in urban planning. Jonah called Nineveh—as a city, including its king—to repentance. Babylon, the symbol of collective evil, was such a successful target of evangelism that its lifestyle and even its government were affected.[10] Joseph and Daniel did key urban planning while occupying powerful political positions. Jeremiah modeled sainthood in an alien city. Nehemiah was the architect of true urban renewal in Jerusalem.

In the New Testament the early church made evangelism in the city one of its highest priorities. Paul's epistles as well as the Book of Acts indicate this. Their example was Christ who Himself grieved over Jerusalem. Barnabas developed a missionary church in Antioch, and the apostle Paul proved to be an urban strategist in evangelizing cities.[11] In fact, the faith and the church grew in the cities of the ancient world. Ancient Rome, for example, was characterized by apartment living with units almost as densely situated as in present-day New York City. The majority of Rome's 1.6 million citizens lived in five- and six-story apartment buildings, and the early church evangelized the area effectively.[12]

The prophets and apostles involved themselves in the life of the city and its institutions without compromising their faith or values. They are examples of urban involvement rather than exodus.

Concern for the Poor and Oppressed

The theme of justice for the poor and oppressed is of particular import in Scripture. Over four hundred verses indicate God's concern for the poor, and over eighty verses underscore divine concern for justice.[13]

God commands that we care for the poor and rewards those who do.

God blesses those who are kind to the poor (Ps. 41:1).

Anyone who oppresses the poor is insulting God who made them. To help the poor is to honor God (Prov. 14:31).

He who shuts his ears to the cries of the poor will be ignored in his own time of need (Prov. 21:13).

If you give to the poor, your needs will be supplied! But a curse upon those who close their eyes to poverty (Prov. 28:27).

The good man knows the poor man's rights; the godless don't care (Prov. 29:7).

And if you do good only to those who do you good—is that so wonderful? Even sinners do that much! And if you lend money only to those who can repay you, what good is that? Even the most wicked will lend to their own kind for full return.

Love your *enemies!* Do good to *them.* Lend to *them.* And don't be concerned about the fact that they won't repay. Then your reward from heaven will be very great, and you will truly be acting as sons of God: for he is kind to the *unthankful* and to those who are *very wicked.*

Try to show as much compassion as your Father does (Luke 6:33–36).

But if someone who is supposed to be a Christian has money enough to live well, and sees a brother in need, and won't help him—how can God's love be within *him?* Little children, let us stop just *saying* we love people; let us *really* love them, and *show it* by our *actions* (1 John 3:17–18).

The evidence of God's concern for the poor is overwhelming, leading Greenway to say, "God is on the side of the weak and suffering,"[14] and Ronald Sider to claim, "God is on the side of the poor."[15]

In the spirit of this concern for the poor, Senator Mark Hatfield of Oregon introduced a resolution in 1975 urging the Congress of the United States to assert that every person has a right to a nutritionally adequate food supply. The basis for this resolution is that God, who possesses the earth and its fullness, regularly proclaims in Scripture the high value He places on human life.[16]

Justice for the oppressed is also a major scriptural issue. God commands that justice be done. He shows His concern particularly for the powerless. [17]

> For the Lord loves justice and fairness; he will never abandon his people (Ps. 37:28).
>
> Happiness comes to those who are fair to others and are always just and good (Ps. 106:3).
>
> Evil men don't understand the importance of justice, but those who follow the Lord are much concerned about it (Prov. 28·5).
>
> You should defend those who cannot help themselves. Yes, speak up for the poor and needy and see that they get justice (Prov. 31:8–9).
>
> Learn to do good, to be fair and to help the poor, the fatherless, and widows (Isa. 1:17).
>
> He saw to it that justice and help were given the poor and the needy and all went well for him. This is how a man lives close to God (Jer. 22:16).
>
> [God] has told you what he wants and this is all it is: *to be fair and just and merciful, and to walk humbly with your God* (Mic. 6:8).
>
> "When you put on a dinner," he said, "don't invite friends, brothers, relatives, and rich neighbors! For they will return the invitation. Instead, invite the poor, the crippled, the lame, and the blind. Then at the resurrection of the godly, God will reward you for inviting those who can't repay you" (Luke 14:12–14).

Both in the law of Moses and later through the prophets, God warned His people that judgment would result from their refusal to show justice to the poor, the oppressed, and the powerless. [18]

> You must not oppress a stranger in any way; remember, you yourselves were foreigners in the land of Egypt. You must not exploit widows or orphans; if you do so in any way, and they cry to me for my help, I will surely give it. And my anger shall flame out against you, and I will kill you with enemy armies, so that your wives will be widows and your children fatherless (Exod. 22:21–24).

Isaiah castigated the city of Jerusalem for its corruption. [19]

> Jerusalem, once my faithful wife! And now a prostitute! Running after other gods! Once "The City of Fair Play," but now a gang of

murderers. Once like sterling silver; now mixed with worthless alloy! Once so pure, but now diluted like watered-down wine! Your leaders are rebels, companions of thieves; all of them take bribes and won't defend the widows and orphans (Isa. 1:21–23).

And he foretold God's judgment on Judah.[20]

Woe to unjust judges and to those who issue unfair laws, says the Lord, so that there is no justice for the poor, the widows and orphans. Yes, it is true that they even rob the widows and fatherless children.

Oh, what will you do when I visit you in that day when I send desolation upon you from a distant land? To whom will you turn then for your help? Where will your treasures be safe? (Isa. 10:1–3).

Jeremiah warned the people that their only hope for escape was to change their ways.

You may remain under these conditions only: If you stop your wicked thoughts and deeds, and are fair to others, and stop exploiting orphans, widows and foreigners. And stop your murdering (Jer. 7:5–6).

Through Amos God inveighed against not only the oppression of the poor (Amos 2:6–7) but also the exploitation of the dispossessed by the rich (6:1–7), calling rich women "cows" (4:1). He noted the injustice in the court system as well (5:10–15), and God made His anger known about this evil (5:21–24).[21]

With some irony the writer of Ecclesiastes notes that the evil of oppression is perpetuated by bureaucracy and that no one is willing to take responsibility.

If you see some poor man being oppressed by the rich, with miscarriage of justice anywhere throughout the land, don't be surprised! For every official is under orders from higher up, and the higher officials look up to their superiors. And so the matter is lost in red tape and bureaucracy (Eccl. 5:8).

In the New Testament James cautions the powerful about the outcome of their exploitation.[22]

The value of your gold and silver is dropping fast, yet it will stand as evidence against you, and eat your flesh like fire. That is what

you have stored up for yourselves, to receive on that coming day
of judgment. For listen! Hear the cries of the field workers whom
you have cheated of their pay. Their cries have reached the ears of
the Lord of Hosts.

You have spent your years here on earth having fun, satisfying your every whim, and now your fat hearts are ready for the
slaughter. You have condemned and killed good men who had no
power to defend themselves against you (James 5:3–6).

Standing idly by is not acceptable. There is no evidence that the
rich Dives oppressed Lazarus the beggar. He just ignored him (Luke
16). Clark Pinnock, in observing the eternal destiny of Dives, feels the
story "ought to explode in our hands when we read it sitting at our
well-covered tables while the third world stands outside."[23] Harvie
Conn says that injustice is "apostasy; the rejection of the poor, the
rejection of God."[24]

So obvious is God's concern for justice that the Israelite culture
and the early church were to be characterized by egalitarianism and
human rights. There was to be no special regard for status groups and
class distinctions.

In the Old Testament no elite class was to control the real estate,
nor was there to be a system of riches for a few with only crumbs for
the masses. Legal statutes were designed to protect criminals from
excessively cruel and inhuman treatment, and to protect minorities,
widows, orphans, and slaves. Industry was to be furthered and
slothfulness condemned. Slavery was restricted so that savage and
dehumanizing forms of furthering economic ends were minimized.[25]

The principle of stewardship in the protection of the poor and
disadvantaged was so pervasive that it was unlawful to charge the poor
interest on loans (Exod. 22:25; Deut. 23:20). Every seven years all
debts were forgiven (Deut. 15:1–6), and the fields were left fallow so
the poor could go out and gather the increase (Exod. 23:11; Lev.
25:6). Moreover, the poor were allowed to glean fields after a harvest
and eat anything in the field the harvester was unable to take with him.
Every fiftieth year was the Year of Jubilee when all land was returned
to its original owner. This principle underscored the point that God's
people are stewards of all—even land—but God is the owner (Lev.
25).[26]

The principle of service was found in mandatory almsgiving.

Almsgiving was classified as a form of justice and 10 percent was expected to be given to the poor every third year (Deut. 14:28).

There is evidence that the moral law of Moses was not abrogated in the New Testament (Matt. 5:17–20; Rom. 8:4). The disciples shared a common fund (John 12:6) and received resources from the women who followed Christ (Luke 8:3). The early church shared everything (Acts 2:43–47; 5:1–11; 6:1–7), and Paul regularly emphasized caring for the poor (Rom. 15:22–28; Gal. 2:10); in fact he was arrested while sharing financial aid with the saints in Jerusalem (Acts 24:17).[27]

The most powerful example of God's concern for justice is found in the ministry of Jesus Christ. Christ spent large amounts of time feeding the hungry, healing the sick, and delivering the demon-possessed. He defined His own mission by saying,

> The Spirit of the Lord is upon me; he has appointed me to preach Good News to the poor; he has sent me to heal the brokenhearted and to announce that captives shall be released and the blind shall see, that the downtrodden shall be freed from their oppressors, and that God is ready to give blessings to all who come to him (Luke 4:18–19).

In these words He is referring to Isaiah's prophecy and the social tyranny of the Old Testament days.[28]

Christ's humble social status indicates God's understanding of and deep concern for people of every stratum.[29] According to Sider, Christ's parents were very poor and Christ was a refugee and then an immigrant entering Galilean society (Matt. 2:19–23). He was not paid for His public ministry and had no home of His own (Matt. 8:20). He also placed His disciples in poverty (Luke 9:20; 10:4).[30]

Jesus referred to His identification with the have-nots in answering the messengers of John the Baptist when they asked whether He was the Christ (Matt. 11:2–6). Paul emphasized this identification when he wrote, "Though he was so very rich, yet to help you he became so very poor" (2 Cor. 8:9). John says, "We know what real love is from Christ's example in dying for us. And so we also ought to lay down our lives for our Christian brothers" (1 John 3:16).[31]

Any comprehension of the biblical command for love as expressed in Mark 12:28–31 and John 13:34–35 convinces us that

Christians must be actively involved in their neighbors' lives. To imitate Christ necessarily involves concern for all the aspects of one's fellows (Eph. 5:1–2). In fact, acts of compassion done to others are viewed by Christ as acts of worship to Him. And neglect of the needy and oppressed is regarded as abandoning Christ (Matt. 25:31–46).[32]

If the incarnation of Christ is taken seriously, then the church must see itself as continuing the Incarnation. Rene Bideaux claims that a church does not become missional until, by risking change and destruction, it accepts its own death and resurrection for the sake of the gospel.[33] The Christian church must act as Christ's hands, feet, and eyes in the world. It must both preach a message and perform a ministry—just as Christ did.[34]

Spiritual and Social Reconciliation

Christianity is relevant when its love ethic is infused into all spheres of human existence. When a person enters into a relationship with Christ, he is to be Godlike in all his relationships. This makes a Christian an evangelist, reconciler or peacemaker, prophet, reformer, and agent of relief and ministry. The Christian is called to a vertical relationship with God and a horizontal relationship with his fellow creatures. The calling to horizontal and vertical relationships is inseparable. These relationships are twin dimensions of the Christian experience. This is evident in the prophets (Isa. 1:12–17; Amos 5:21–24; Mic. 6:6–8), in Christ Himself (Matt. 25:31–46; Luke 10:25–37), in Paul (Rom. 13:8–10; 1 Cor. 13:4–7; Gal. 5:22–23), in James (James 2:8, 14–17), and in John (1 John 1:3–4, 7; 3:14–18; 4:20–21).[35]

A key mandate in Scripture, then, is spiritual and social reconciliation: bringing alienated people back into harmony vertically with God and horizontally with others. Because human beings are cast in the image of the divine, it is only natural that they be completed by a relationship with God. Even if churches were successful in elevating the standard of living of every one of its people to a middle-income status, there would remain a gnawing hunger for a sense of completeness. The evangelical mandate is the spiritual glue that holds the church together. It is the stuff of commitment and dedication to discipleship, of living out the Christian life in fellowship and likemindedness.[36]

Social concern—stewardship and service—complements evangelism in that it helps people understand the love of God. In addition, social ministries remove temporal barriers such as hunger and emotional problems. Quests for justice and peace overturn oppressive forces that destroy people's lives and reduce their ability to respond to the person of Christ. But again, most importantly, social concern exemplifies the caring love of God.[37]

If the church is to take its mandate seriously, it will have to transcend social barriers—racial, economic, linguistic, cultural, sexual, and age—in order to meet the challenge. To do this reconciling, the church must go to people where they are. Howard Rice stresses this by saying that if we really believe God dwells with people, then we have to go to the cities where most of them are.[38] For the church in the city this means locating in and among the poor. All too often, however, middle-class Christians move out as the poor move into a community. Then, several years later, those same Christians go back to try to evangelize the present inhabitants. It is no wonder that the poor have little respect when those doing missionary work did not want to live with them in the first place.[39] When the church does demonstrate genuine social commitment, however, its spiritual message gains credibility.

In summary, the scriptural mandate is both spiritual and social reconciliation. In fact, evangelism undergirds social concern. Social improvement alone leaves a person incomplete without knowing Christ. Moreover, people who are spiritually transformed are able to make commitments toward transforming their society. A Christian commitment can provide spiritual power and energy necessary to endure in advancing social justice. And a Christian commitment encourages the believer to live like Christ, who modeled social concern and care in His daily life and ministry.[40]

IMPLICATIONS FOR MINISTRY

Once convinced of the divine mandate favoring social justice, it is important to reflect soberly on how that social concern should be made manifest and to work out a set of principles that should guide these stewardship and service ministries.

Types of Social Concern

Social concern is often of three general kinds. One is *social reconciliation,* or peacemaking. Both a stewardship and service ministry, reconciliation focuses on healing attempts to reach across the barriers of economics, race, and community to love and care for people regardless of social category. It means, especially, identifying with the poor and oppressed. It may involve being a lightning rod for many of their frustrations and angers as the church seeks to alleviate alienation and separation among peoples.

Bideaux says that a missional church may have to break out of its own tight fellowship to embrace the poor and dispossessed who are just outside the door, to reach out to heal the individual and social hurts in their community.[41] Jacques Ellul states that the Christian must be on the side of the poor. He must identify with them, and the best way to identify with them is to listen to them. Claude-Marie Barbour, a Presbyterian minister, advocates "mission in reserve," mingling among the people and having them explain where their needs are. Barbour used this method in Gary, Indiana, and his Shalom Ministries program has spread to other urban areas.[42] Nicholas Wolterstorff, in referring to Ellul, emphasizes the importance of Christians siding with the cause of the oppressed. It is only if Christians make the cause of the poor and oppressed their cause that they can feel they are loving their neighbor and seeking a condition of genuine peace.[43]

The second kind of social concern is *social relief.* This service ministry includes such deeds of mercy as giving the "cup of cold water." It can take the form of working with senior citizens, tutoring neighborhood youth, providing legal aid or psychological counseling, and so forth. In Trenton, Michigan, St. Paul Lutheran Church encouraged service ministries among its members by first administering a Spiritual Gifts Analysis questionnaire. Administrators in various areas then contacted the members, encouraging them to experiment with the use of their discovered gift in some service area.[44]

The third kind of social concern is the stewardship ministry of *social reform.* Relief deals with the symptoms of society's malignancies. Reform addresses the basic unjust conditions and systems that oppress and dehumanize people. Its emphasis is on institutions. Reform is necessary if social progress is to be made, and, even more importantly, if Christ is to be seen as Lord over social institutional life and activity as well as over individual lives.[45]

In Miami, where the exodus of Anglos and the influx of Hispanic refugees is a major concern, Msgr. Walsh tells of the activist role of the Church of Miami. Not without controversy, the church has worked at the development of a refugee policy at various levels of government and has taken leadership in the community on social questions. It has demonstrated its advocacy stance by adapting itself to the new culture and language of the refugees.[46]

Institutions and systems are virtually important. The apostle Paul writes of the age being dominated by principalities and powers that oppose Christian ideals. In our time, examples include: a society that tolerates poverty and denigrates those who are poor; a two-track justice system that provides one route for the rich and powerful and another for the poor and indigent; a nation that is, on one hand, experiencing an unparalleled explosion of knowledge and, on the other, allowing millions of inner-city youth to drown in a Dark Ages–like abyss of illiteracy.[47]

God's directive through Jeremiah that the Israelites work for the welfare of the alien city, Babylon, because their own welfare as exiles was tied to that of the city (Jer. 29:7) reminds us that we need to do this reconciling, relieving, and reforming in the city. The urban policy of the Presbyterian Church in the U.S.A. states that to those who are hungry, God's grace is food; to the powerless it is justice; and to those who are alienated it is love. We need to reach the city with the love of God's grace.[48] Such a perspective moved an elderly Jesuit priest in India to say, "I bring God to the people in the form in which God is absent. Here it is water."[49]

Implementing Social Ministries

The work of the individual urban church is facilitated when there is a commitment to urban ministry on the part of a larger body. There are a number of examples of this. The Kansas City Metropolitan Lutheran Ministry, an alliance of thirty-eight Lutheran churches, provides a means for coordinating social ministries as well as encouraging one another through a larger fellowship.[50] In Tulsa, Oklahoma, a Presbyterian Urban Ministry Council has formulated an urban strategy for the metropolitan area.[51] The National Division of the United Methodist Church provides consulting, educational, and funding services to various Methodist Annual Conferences. In North Fort Worth, Texas, four severely declining churches were helped when an ecumenical church cluster worked at meeting community needs. The National Division is involved in such ventures as these.[52]

Dennis Shoemaker suggests that denominations entering urban ministry focus their resources on no more than three critical urban churches. Shoemaker points out several ingredients for maximum future effectiveness. First, careful evaluation. Next, careful statistical research. Then the results should be practically applied to urban strategies. Finally, a plan that will garner the support of both urban and suburban churches should be developed. Measurement of success should be determined on the basis of meeting people's needs rather than increasing numbers.[53]

The beginning for any urban church is a commitment to turf. The Central Presbyterian Church in Atlanta exemplifies this. Since 1858 it has been involved in its community. Over the years it has opened its doors to everyone—from mourners at the funeral of Martin Luther King, Jr., to protesting farmers. The key is that Central remained central as it stayed in the city.[54]

Simply staying in the community is not enough. According to Frye Gaillard, if a church does not meet the opportunities for ministry around it, that church has "moved." Pointing to the First Presbyterian Church in Charlotte, North Carolina, as model, he says evangelism must go beyond works to caring deeds. Realizing the love of music in the inner city, the church began providing music lessons for neighborhood children. Their effort was so blessed that now the church has a Community School of the Arts with 850 students, about half of whom are from welfare families.[55]

Turf commitment must generate turf awareness. This means getting to know the members of the community, the agencies located there, and those who have power in it. Realistic assessment is imperative. Once such knowledge is obtained, the church needs to determine where it can align with other institutions to bring about change and where it may have to act independently. In either case, the prior issue of accurate diagnosis, based on possession of the facts of the turf, cannot be overestimated.[56] The Diocese of Oakland, for example, used a census tract map and other census data to assess the demographic nature of each parish. Often community organizations and associations will be happy to provide up-to-date information on a neighborhood.[57]

Resources for beginning urban ministry are available. The Southern Baptist Convention publishes a booklet that shows churches how to analyze their circumstance and suggests ideas for gathering pertinent data and formulating objectives.[58] A *Strategy Workbook for St. Louis, 1978,* produced by the United Methodist Church, can serve as a model for urban programming.[59] Our Savior's Lutheran Church in Minneapolis developed a packet that includes their urban outreach plan. This guide is especially helpful because it shows what worked, what did not work, and what the plans for the future are.[60] A United Church of Canada Task Group in Toronto put together a *Workbook on Mission and Ministry in the Metro Core.* This report intersperses biblical quotations so that it is a working theology for urban ministry.[61] Finally, an excellent source for the local church developing its mission in the context of social change is *150 Plus Tomorrow,* available from the Presbytery of Chicago.[62]

Two of the best clearinghouses for urban ministry materials are SCUPE and ICUIS, both in Chicago. SCUPE stands for Seminary Consortium for Urban Pastoral Education. ICUIS is the Institute on the Church in Urban-Industrial Society.[63]

Conclusion

Tragically, the unchecked materialism of our age engulfs the church as well as the larger society. Biblical injunctions against materialism seem to go largely unheeded. Yet, as Bakke disturbingly points out, Ezekiel 16:49 declares that the major sin of Sodom was its insensitivity to the poor and deprived within that decadent city.[64] A reading of Matthew 18–20 is both unsettling and illuminating in its presentation of what God's standards are in contrast to those of the prevailing culture.[65]

Although the business of breaking away from the status quo is a thorny one, it must be confronted. For the church, to be effective, must model what society should be rather than occasionally critiquing what it is.[66]

In a society that affirms the separation of church and state, it is perhaps most prudent if the church attempts to accomplish reform by regularly reminding the institutions of power of their obligation to dispense justice. There must be regularized vigilance here, such that the church knows how to encourage those political forces that affirm justice and rightness, and how to oppose those that seek only manipulation. This does not mean being a naïve pawn of a political party or candidate. Rather, it means studying the issues and problems and affirming positions and programs that bring justice and reconciliation. Often there may be no clear road to take, as the issues may be muddied and the political choices a matter of Tweedledee and Tweedledum. If so, the church should be aware of that, too, and see what alternatives are available. In short, although it may be wise not to align oneself officially with any mainline party or candidate, preserving apolitical integrity, it is important that the church educate itself on key issues, advocating social justice and human rights.[67]

To carry out the biblical mandate of social concern, it is important that church members study significant social and community issues and confront the congregation with the data. Such investigations and reports will likely give rise to debate, but they should also produce ideas for creative actions to be taken. Study groups should report and speak to, not for, the church. They are not the church but informers of it. Nonetheless, such lay activity builds consciousness among attenders that the church is concerned about social issues and that it is the obligation of the members to become active in efforts to bring reconciliation, relief, and reform.[68]

2 | The City and the Inner City

American cities grew in response to economic forces rather than through rational urban planning. They tended to shoot up where natural resources such as waterways and raw materials made industrial expansion most attractive. Early opportunities for unskilled labor brought floods of immigrants into the rapidly growing American cities. Cities continued to grow because they became centers of industry, transportation, and communication. In short, they became the nerve centers of society. Cultural refinements—art, drama, music, and literature—followed after the urban seeds, as Donald Benedict says, had shot well out of the ground.[1]

Today American cities are declining in response to changing economic forces. Industrial cities of the North are no longer thriving, and the explosive growth in the Sun Belt seems to be slowing. Problems of poverty and unemployment are on the rise. One out of every six American families is on welfare, with one of three on the brink. Many of these indigent people are located in urban squalor.[2]

DECLINE OF THE CITY

Carl Dudley sees social decline and transition in the city as the result of pulls and pushes in the American economy. More spacious and desirable opportunities open up in the suburbs or urban fringes, and the affluent head in that direction, while a poor class of urbanites pushes into the vacant area. There is an ongoing process of exit and entry such that neighborhood and community transition is simply an urban fact of life.[3]

Jim Newton describes the overall transition process within a community as taking place in five stages: (1) the construction of single- and multiple-family dwellings; (2) a stable and homogeneous resident population; (3) a pretransition phase with a socially different group moving in—this group need not constitute even 10 percent of the community's population; (4) a transition stage during which the new group comes to represent from 10 to 50 percent of the population; (5) the posttransition stage when the new group becomes the majority.[4]

The process of recent urban deterioration follows a pattern. As the affluent move out, businesses head for suburban developments and malls. The absence of businesses and a strong middle class erodes the tax base so that, without governmental aid, cities head for bankruptcy. Although some urbanologists detect some movement back to the city because of high energy costs in commuting and the desirability of "rehabbing" older dwellings, this trend does not suggest socioeconomic integration. If anything, economic segregation looks to become more stark as affluent communities create walled sub-cities around themselves amid the hungry slum dwellers.

In addition to the erosion of the tax base caused by the exodus of the affluent and businesses, the tax structure itself kills urban communities. In Philadelphia, for example, the schools stayed closed one September, while the city sank its money into measures that actually benefited the suburbs. This practice is true of many cities. It is primarily city money that pays for sports stadiums, airports, art centers, and theaters. Yet it is the suburbanite population that has the money to go to the ball park and travel on the jets; and it is to satisfy more affluent tastes that art exhibits and professional theaters exist. Cultural refinements and entertainment opportunities are important—but their value is tarnished when they reflect economic exploitation. According to Anthony Campolo, "We have two names for welfare, don't we? When white suburbanites are on the receiving end, it's called 'public service.' God is not mocked."[5]

In the same spirit as Campolo, the outspoken Michael Harrington, in *The Other America,* claims that what we have is socialism for the rich and free enterprise for the poor.[6] By this he means that whereas middle-class Americans regularly complain about "socialist'' welfare programs for slum dwellers, the fact is that the more affluent receive the thumping majority of the tax dollars. That the poor receive very little can be observed in how much of each tax dollar goes into highway construction, higher-education facilities, salaries of governmental employees, and maintenance and renovation of parks and other recreational facilities used by the larger society. Although some argue that the middle class should receive more tax benefits because they pay the preponderance of the taxes, the point is that they do.

In fact, political pressure from power brokers is such that it is almost impossible to get legislation that will deliver benefits to the needy without skimming the cream for the rich. In California, the hazard insurance legislation directed at the burned-out Watts area was written in such a way that the nonpoor could get low-cost insurance as well. The result was that insured Bel Air mansions were built on mudslides and hills that had been burned regularly. Hence, benefits ostensibly for the poor enriched the wealthy.

In addition to erosion of the city's tax base and unjust allocation of tax benefits, the city's finances are affected by the fact that earnings are taken out of the city by many suburbanites who make their living in the city. They drive in on public expressways and city streets that are paid for by city taxes, drink city water, flush city toilets, and walk city pavements, but they pay taxes and acquire goods and services in a suburban municipality. All the while the poor remain in a colony of misery, walled in by poverty and a lack of opportunity.

F. K. Plous, Jr., claims that 85 percent of urban decline can be traced back to three pieces of legislation.[7] The first was the Homeowner Loan Act of June 13, 1933. Along with the Federal Home Loan Bank Act of July 22, 1932, this Act replaced the five-year renewable mortgages with fifteen- to thirty-year mortgages. This legislation made the privately funded building and loan entities into predecessors for the present quasi-socialized savings and loan associations. Though the purpose of the Act was to help the housing industry mired in the Depression, the effect was to sponsor the building and sale of free-standing, owner-occupied dwellings while ignoring the needs of multiple-family rental housing. Because available land for free-standing dwellings tended to be in the suburbs while the large rental housing was in the city, the legislation had a suburban bias.

The second piece of legislation was the Serviceman's Readjustment Act of June 22, 1944. The GI Bill financed the suburbs by having the government guarantee money lent by banks and savings and loan associations to GI's. Housing starts, almost all suburban, zoomed. No comparable program, involving owning or renting, existed for the city.

The Federal-Aid Highway Act of June 29, 1956, was the third factor. This Act led to the bankrolling of the 42,500-mile Interstate Highway System and other highway projects. Federal transportation planners damaged the city by cutting up city neighborhoods and paving them over, thus lifting valuable land from the tax rolls. The effect was a simplified transportation into the city for suburbanites who held city jobs while stifling mass transit, a key to urban health.

With suburban growth and urban decline, Plous says that the middle class "smelling the meat acookin' elsewhere, wisely left, and refugees from rural poverty and Southern discrimination flowed in to occupy what was already abandoned territory."[8]

EMERGENCE OF THE INNER CITY

According to Ed Marciniak, the city can be studied as an urban layer cake.[9] The first layer consists of family-associated people. Layer two involves the neighborhood. The third layer is the larger community: the police, the fire district, the school district, the political division or ward, library, local newspaper, citizens' organizations, and perhaps a Kiwanis association. Beyond the community level is the city as a whole. These layers are interdependent: if any one layer does not function, the whole cake will ultimately collapse. The first two, however, are probably the most important, for they form the foundation.

Marciniak argues that cities never have worked; they are in constant transition and restructuring. In fact, the great cities tend to be rebuilt every one hundred or one hundred fifty years. What can work are the neighborhoods. When they decay, inner cities emerge and the city at large becomes shaky. Vitality is at the micro rather than the macro level.[10] This topic is discussed at length in the next chapter.

Characteristics of the Inner City

Since the inner city is the major focus of this book, the concept requires definition. The inner city does not necessarily refer to the geographic center of the city. In fact, it is probably more accurate, when describing a given city, to speak of its several inner cities. An inner city can be defined as a poverty area in which there is much government activity and control but little activity by the private sector. Often, merchandisers, businesses, and churches have left the area. The usual urban amenities, such as dry cleaners, barber shop, camera store, appliance shop, and the like, are in limited supply. But governmental agencies, public housing, and social institutions are visible. Private institutions of this type—both for-profit and not-for-profit—are absent.[11]

Besides "poverty area," there are a number of other synonyms for the inner city: low-income community, central city, or ghetto. Although technically referring only to a place of isolation, the term *ghetto* has come to suggest a predominantly black community. Inner cities are not always black. They can be inhabited by almost any racial or ethnic group. Blackness is common because blacks are the most urbanized of all ethnic groups and a sizable proportion (about one-third) are trapped in poverty.

Regardless of ethnic makeup, the inner city can often be characterized as "the other world." It is the other side of the American fence, opposite the side on which grass is green. A black college student once wrote a term paper for one of my classes in which she described that other-world feeling she had had when she was younger. The young, black, inner-city child, she wrote, feels that he must live in the worst place in the entire world, for nothing that goes on in school or his textbooks, from reading class to geography, is in any way related to life in the community in which he lives.

Almost invariably inner cities, by United States standards, are crowded. If, for example, the entire Chicago metropolitan area were as crowded in residential density as its three major black areas, there would be 135 million people living in Chicago. That is about 60 percent of the population of the United States. Chicago's infamous Cabrini-Green had over eighteen thousand residents in its 5×8 block borders during the turbulent sixties. New York's Harlem and Spanish Harlem are also teeming with people.

Overcrowdedness can have nerve-shattering consequences, especially for people with rural roots. Misery and degradation are packed together. Experiments with laboratory animals indicate that when rats are confined to an overpopulated space, they begin killing each other off until their numbers reach manageable size. Social scientists continue to debate the likely human implications of these types of findings.[12]

At any rate, building is lined up against building, or in the case of high-rises, floor is stacked upon floor as the misery heads skyward. With exploding numbers comes limited space, limited privacy, and the omnipresence of noise from voices, stereos, cars, and people themselves. Eight may live in a three-room apartment. "Go to your room" is a disciplinary statement that would be simply preposterous to an inner-city child.

Overcrowdedness, of course, points to as critical a physical characteristic of an inner city as any—inadequate housing. Quality housing in the inner city is in such small supply that the 1960s saw the emergence of a new cabinet department—Housing and Urban Development. The poor are, by virtue of their poverty, herded into central-city communities where land and, more particularly, housing are at an absolute premium. Where housing does exist, the buildings are old and crumbling. A ride through an inner-city area invariably reveals this phenomenon to the curious onlooker, who will see either ancient and deteriorated or gutted and burned out buildings.

The only other housing available is public housing such as the federally sponsored high-rises—high-rises because limited space demands vertical rather than horizontal construction. One of the problems contributing to the decay of the inner city is that the poor do not own property. The welfare system allows recipients to rent dwellings but not buy them. To qualify for low-cost housing a person must not earn in excess of a given, rather paltry amount (often about $8,000 annually). This works against the care of property that results from pride of ownership.[13]

While the rest of society laments the absence of moderately priced housing and reasonably sized lots on the urban fringes and in the suburbs, the poor look for shelter of any kind.

Causes of Inner-City Conditions

A number of causes contribute to the conditions of overcrowdedness and inadequate housing in the inner city. The first cause is the transition from a stable neighborhood to a changing neighborhood. As people move away, vacant housing develops, followed by entry of people socially different from the dominant residential group. The more different the incoming group is, the quicker the residents flee. Hence, stability is gone. No one is certain when the "tipping point" in any community will occur, but when it does, the community quickly turns over. Some realtors unscrupulously come in and prey on the fears and stereotypes of the anxious residents. They may plant fears of plunging real-estate values and imminent violence in order to buy up resident housing cheaply, only to turn around and sell that same housing to incoming residents at a booming profit. This practice is called *blockbusting,* and though grossly unethical, it is very common.[14]

The second cause is fiscal dysfunction. Many neighborhood functions reflect personal income, which in part is turned into taxes to maintain semipublic enterprises such as schools, libraries, public offices, and hospitals. As income accumulates, the residents put it into banks and savings and loan associations. In turn, these financial institutions lend money in the form of credit to neighborhood residents to enable the community to grow and develop. If, however, the demand for housing decreases in the neighborhood, trouble ensues. Since the housing supply is fixed, this dip will drop prices, which will alarm financial institutions and cause them to cut back on loans. This cutback is called *redlining.*[15]

Redlining begins with bank officials outlining an area that they feel will decline over the next twenty years (the length of many mortgages). As a result of this prediction, the bank chooses not to lend any mortgage money to anyone wishing to purchase land in the redlined area. Though illegal, this practice is used to protect the bank against high-risk lending. What is happening, however, is that the bank, ostensibly a servant of the community, becomes its killer. People who desire to purchase in the inner city and then rehabilitate the dwelling are summarily ruled out of such an enterprise, while current owners become increasingly aware that they are literally stuck with unsellable property. This encourages *management toward demolition.*

The result of these practices is that the inner city takes on the appearance of a ghost town as the area becomes dotted with burned-out, abandoned buildings, surrounded by open space. In spite of inadequate housing and this available land, there is no building going on. In every case the community and its residents lose because the bank, by virtue of redlining, has made its prophecy of community doom self-fulfilling.

A study of the redlining practices of a savings and loan association in Toledo revealed a distinct pattern of lending. Inner cities received little or nothing in mortgage loans while rapidly growing suburban areas got much higher amounts. The closer families lived to the S & L, the less they received. Areas that received the least were characterized by old, inexpensive housing, a largely black population, and a high percentage of female-headed, poverty-level families.[16] In Chicago's South Shore, about three hundred housing maintenance jobs were lost in a redlined area. Owners had managed toward demolition.[17]

In stable communities, with deposits going into banks and with loans coming out, a dollar will turn around about seventeen times.[18] In a redlined area, however, the money flows steadily out, with the neighborhood financial institution sending the money to larger downtown banks. In the meantime, nothing is built or developed, and the community deteriorates. Such a shipping out is evident in a Chicago west-side area where three hundred thousand black people live without a single financial institution to serve them.[19]

City money is flowing to the suburbs. The South Shore residents have $31 million on deposit in two major Chicago banks and have received only $76,000 in loans. A recent estimate revealed that the amount of capital necessary to turn the South Shore community around equalled almost exactly the total amount the residents had on deposit. All they needed was a recycling of their own money. This stands in sharp contrast to the $1 billion cost the government would have to meet to tear down the community and rebuild it in the suburbs. Yet the government does this, as approximately twenty-five thousand living units are built annually in the suburbs while an equivalent number in the city are destroyed.[20]

The importance of investment in a community cannot be overestimated. William Ipema points out that in Chicago, for example, thirty-six of its seventy-six communities are nearly dysfunctional fiscally. With community fiscal health much determined by green flow—credit and capital funding—some of these communities are dying, as less than one percent of savings money is making its way back into the community in the form of loans.[21]

In addition to the conditions created by blockbusting and redlining, there is also the problem of *slum landlording*. An owner of a dilapidated dwelling will manage it toward demolition. The first step is to fill the building with as many ''rents'' as possible. Rents are then received without any attempt to keep the building in repair. The aged nature of the building, coupled with its heavy usage by children and young adults, results in rapid deterioration. City inspectors, whose task it is to check the quality of urban structures and insure that they are ''up to code,'' are easily bribed into not reporting housing-code violations. The inspector's conscience is assuaged because he feels that the city grossly underpays him and that reporting building violations will simply set off a lengthy legal procedure, sometimes as long as four years, which will likely end with either the landlord minimally repairing the building or abandoning it entirely and leaving the people shelterless.

One of the reasons the owner does not make repairs is to keep overhead and real estate taxes at a base level. Rents are picked up until the building is so badly worn that it either begins to collapse or the city demands repair. At that point the building is often ''torched''— burned to the ground. The torching marks the end of both the structure and the legal problem of the owner, who will probably collect fire insurance money since that is one premium he will keep paid. Torchings often occur with the inhabitants still in the building, destroying much of their goods as well as imperiling their safety. Such fires appear more accidental and raise less suspicion. They are extremely common, however. During 1974, for example, there were fourteen thousand fires in the South Bronx.[22] In urban areas nationwide, literally thousands of such torchings of buildings occur in old white, black, and Hispanic sections.

In addition to failure to repair buildings, slum landlords neglect utility needs of the renters. A not uncommon practice is to fail to heat a building in the dead of winter. So prevalent is this problem that city television stations regularly flash the city hall telephone number where help can be obtained. Colds, influenza, pneumonia, and frostbite are common health problems in inner-city winters. From the standpoint of the slum landlord, who is aware that the court process is slow and few poor city dwellers have any knowledge of it, ignoring the needs of a building is a low-risk, high-profit enterprise.

Blockbusting, redlining, and slum landlording are outgrowths of greed and prejudice. This greed and prejudice will almost certainly be

felt by the pastor who truly desires to minister to an urban neighborhood. As such, it is of utmost importance that he learn as much as
possible about the institutional policies and processes attendant to
high density.

THE RESPONSE OF THE CHURCH

Churches in the city have had to respond to both the decline of the city
and the emergence of inner-city areas. Some churches, as Carl Dudley
points out, pass through several stages as they respond to their
changing community, eventually relocating or closing. Other
churches, however, have sought ways to revitalize the community by
dealing with conditions of inadequate housing, fiscal dysfunction, and
government control.

The Church in Transition

Although churches and denominations like to affirm integration and
may even assert that a minority group would be welcome to take over a
church if it becomes dominant in the neighborhood, churches do not
usually respond that way. Dudley describes the series of responses
churches make to a changing community.[23] They are strikingly similar to the stages through which terminally ill patients pass.

After initially ''going indoors'' to reaffirm what is really left of
their notion of community culture, a congregation discovers that some
of their families have moved out of the neighborhood. The usual
reaction to this is regionalism—attempting to keep these families in
the church by making the church a metropolitan rather than a neighborhood enterprise. They seek to affirm their initial culture while in a
psychological state of denial.

This usually collapses after funds are drained and the exhausted
pastor leaves. Expansion thus gives way to contraction. A smaller
church admits it is undergoing changes but is determined to prevail.
There is increased giving and activity as the parishioners, rather than
simply the pastor, become the church. Spiritual faith increases in this
phase and there is a sense of genuine zeal. Stresses do build, however,
and on occasion people will explode for seemingly inexplicable reasons, leaving the church. There is much suppressed anger in this
response as the church attempts to manage its way through the
transition.

When the church runs out of money, the accommodation stage emerges. The church expands its outlook, seeking to perform ministries in the changing community and being willing to share whatever resources they have with other groups in order to raise money. Church buildings will be rented out, federal monies sought, the pastor allowed to work in a secular job on the side, and so on. Bargaining characterizes this stage as the church lives in tension. Interestingly, Bill Leslie of LaSalle Street Church, perhaps out of concern for this accommodation mentality, has always maintained that a congregation should pay its own way for all conventional ministries, seeking outside dollars only for supplementary efforts such as legal aid or counseling.

Dudley observes that accommodation congregations will even lend their facility to other small ethnic and minority churches. However, they tend to draw the line when it comes to black congregations. Koreans, Chinese, Hispanics, and other non-English-speaking groups are accommodated, but blacks who speak English are expected to join the host church and take on its culture. Dudley says he knows of not a single black congregation sharing a facility with a white church in a changing community.

The accommodation phase ends with the younger, upwardly mobile families moving out and leaving the older parishioners behind. The resultant phase is one of grief. The grieving period gives way to death. The church may fade gradually by reducing its activity or it may relocate. Regardless of the style, it is in its last phase.

On occasion, out of the contraction stage evolves a new type of church—one dominated by an ethnic or racial minority group with a faith expression congruent with its nationality. The whites in these churches find it alien, however, for their formative experience with God is not rooted in Spanish or some other non-Anglo pattern.

In 1979 Dudley claimed that about 10 percent of mainline denominational churches are facing transition currently, with an additional 10 percent likely to confront it in the eighties. He further pointed out that it costs roughly $10,000 per year for about ten years to weather transition. This can be compared with the $300,000 cost of starting a new suburban church.[24]

Revitalizing the Community

The church that chooses to be involved in revitalizing the community must seek creative answers to the problems of inadequate housing and fiscal dysfunction. These answers may include such ideas as sponsoring rehabilitation organizations, offering courses in building maintenance, founding banks, using investment portfolios judiciously, and working with community and governmental agencies. There are a number of examples from around the country.

Before a church becomes involved in dealing with the issue of inadequate housing and the practices of redlining and slum landlording, it would be good to do some necessary research into local community housing. Alderman Richard Mell suggests ten checkpoints.[25] Many of these issues can be checked out at a knowledgeable social agency. The social service agencies are all listed in the Social Service Directory available from the United Way.

1. Determine which way credit or money flows in community institutions. Does the money come from the residents, go into community institutions, and then flow out of the community? Or do these institutions reinvest the money to developing a stronger community? What about redlining by banks or insurance companies?

2. Check into institutions outside the community. Which ones are sensitive to inner-city needs and which are notorious for exploitation?

3. Find out who owns the community property. Is it privately owned? Slum landlorded? Government sponsored? How dense is the area? If there are vacancies, find out why.

4. What is the condition of the buildings? Why are they in that condition?

5. What kinds of aids are available in the public sector for housing development?

6. Have there been any redevelopment attempts? What aids for rehabbing are available?

7. What are the going tax rates? Is there massive tax delinquency and corruption?

8. What community organizations are concerned about housing?

9. Are there industrial and commercial job opportunities? If there are, they show evidence of concern for the community because these entities have a vested interest in their location. If there are not, the community has become more blighted.

10. What is the future of housing in the community? Is the area becoming less residential or more so? Does the community have plans for the area?

Once armed with the answers to these questions, the church can proceed with greater confidence. There are a variety of responses churches can make. A church should look first at what social agencies may be doing in the community before embarking on some costly, alienating, overlapping effort.[26] Knowledge of such simple matters as key helping institutions in the community, city agency phone numbers, and other urban areas where housing can be obtained at low cost can be very helpful to confused residents who do not know which way to turn.

To effect change in a community it is necessary to organize. Without organization there can be no coherent voice. It is important also to find local, indigenous leadership and build from that base. The revitalization of an inner city requires partnerships, alliances, and coalitions rather than just money. Coalitions are important because of the interconnectedness of the community involved. Once there is a concerned and articulate community force, there can be effective negotiation with city hall. Moreover, it is crucial that positive relations are maintained with government at all levels. Despite the fact that the government may sometimes be the adversary, without cordial relations little progress can be made.[27]

Ipema has some ingenious suggestions about how to work with, rather than against, social agencies.[28] First it is important that they be approached in a positive way. A climate of cooperation is very helpful. To have maximum effect, however, it is important that the church know the mechanics of a given agency, i.e., what services the agency offers, how one makes application, and what procedures the organization follows.

Ipema suggests that a pastor develop a relationship with a middle-level official. Lower-level officials may provide unsatisfactory service, while upper-level officials may be enmeshed in the bureaucracy. In initiating a relationship, it is very helpful to begin by asking how the church may be able to help the agency. An enterprising pastor can identify needs and problems that his parishioners can help to solve. Such a cooperative approach opens doors and builds relationships.

Philip Amerson suggests that churches consider taking advantage of available consultation services. Such services can help set a focus, discover resources, and develop a workable plan aimed at reaching important and realistic goals.[29] Ipema cites three such organizations that can aid community development efforts: the National Training and Information Center, which helps community organization; the Center for Neighborhood Technology, which solicits federal research and development dollars for urban use in addition to stimulating community self-help activities; and the Center for Community Change Consultants, which is also involved in self-help efforts.[30]

Stanley Hallett also presents some ways of impacting on "the system." For example, the federal government spends billions of dollars on research and development. Church and community groups could begin to discuss how to put pressure on this part of the federal budget. In Chicago, the Center for Neighborhood Technology has built a community coalition aimed at making demands for some of that money.[31]

A pastor is wise also to get involved in his local community organizations. These alliances can be powerful forces in combating everything from pollution to prostitution, redlining to residential neglect. Such involvement is risky because the issues are controversial. However, community organizations by their nature are nonpartisan and people-oriented. According to P. David Finks, community leaders are open to contemporary theologians who will grapple with and act on problems affecting community. A conference of the Oakland Community Organizations, a coalition of 150 neighborhood alliances affirmed this. Moreover, if a pastor is genuinely interested and helpful, he may find himself serving on a community organization's board of directors where he can have a real impact at the policy level.[32]

If a church's research into housing conditions and community housing uncovers redlining practices, it would be helpful to join with other ministers in the neighborhood and approach the local lending institutions on the matter. In Chicago, one church found a number of Christians in high places in an urban bank and invited them to tour the community one morning to show them the results of redlining. Consciences were pricked and eyes opened; this large bank is now turning its policy around.

In Cleveland, a group of business leaders met regularly with Rev. Henry Andersen of the Fairmount Presbyterian Church for prayer and Bible study. Out of these meetings emerged a set of goals that included encouraging business leaders to remain and invest in Cleveland, affirming pluralism, and formulating long-range plans for the city's development.[33]

In Philadelphia, Campolo and some of his associates bought stock in a large Philadelphia bank. In order to combat redlining, they designed a plan to invite some of the members of the press to a stockholders' meeting at which the group would present policy proposals aimed at ending any redlining practices. The presence of the press made voting against such human resolutions very uncomfortable.[34]

A group of churches in Chicago's South Shore also invested in a bank. The bank now has $15 million in loans in the South Shore community with a lower default rate than the average at the downtown First National Bank.[35]

Hallett urges churches to reassess their portfolios. If they are doing business with financial institutions that are less than sensitive and concerned about the community, pressure can and should be brought to bear on them. In addition, churches can organize neighborhood groups to confront lending institutions concerning their community responsibility. If credit is not being extended, the people can demand data justifying the nonlending policy. Often no such data exists; decisions are made ad hoc on the basis of racial or socioeconomic bias.[36]

Vincent Quayle encourages individual churches as well as denominations to take an advocacy stance on behalf of low-income victims of housing shortages and to affirm that position through portfolio investments in Christian nonprofit housing efforts or private lending institutions that will agree to extend low-interest housing loans.[37] In this same line, John Perkins suggests that public housing become cooperative housing. The inhabitants would be given a deed and the opportunity of paying in equity. The interest rate could be one percent over the first five years, 2 percent during the next five, and 5 percent after that. This would yield immediate equity and, of course, pride of ownership.[38]

There is no limit to what a visionary, stewardship-oriented church can do. The Fairfield Avenue Baptist Church in Chicago, for example, has worked effectively in their community by forming block clubs and organizing a community cleanup. In addition, they have held dinners, inviting aldermen, local police, school personnel, garbage collectors, and public aid attorneys, in order to thank them for helping in the ministry to the neighborhood. By recognizing and helping them they can confront them effectively when accountability is low. Moreover, the same church has opened a series of accounts at a local bank and has made other efforts to reverse the bank's tendency not to invest and lend in the neighborhood.[39]

In 1979, Chicago's Bethel Lutheran Church decided to tie the life of the church to that of its community. In response to that commitment, Bethel responded to the severe housing needs in the community with a project called the Bethel Cooperative Housing, Inc. They have completed several multiple-family dwellings and have been working toward the completion of a sixteen-unit "sweat equity" building.[40]

In Detroit, the Church of the Messiah sponsors a painting company, hoping it will eventually become a rehab organization. The church also owns several buildings, including the six-flat Mustard Seed Apartments.[41]

In Harlem, St. Philip's Episcopal Church has renovated three housing complexes, providing the community with over six hundred new apartments. Believing that housing is critical to family life and that the family is life's core unit, the church plans to rehab another thirty-seven hundred apartments.[42]

The St. Ambrose parish in Baltimore worked at helping community members become homeowners. Calling themselves housing counselors, people from the church started to perform real estate functions such as appraisal, sale negotiation, drawing up contracts, and arranging financing. Because of their conscientiousness and persistence, local lending institutions cooperated. At one point, St. Ambrose was counseling two thousand families a year. Since the economy tightened and interest rates skyrocketed, housing counseling has slowed, but the commitment to residential ownership continues. St. Ambrose has also done rehabbing. Using local workmen and neighborhood unemployed, the church has renovated over four hundred houses and converted an abandoned school into a twelve-unit apartment house.[43]

New York's Cathedral Church of St. John the Divine has been involved in similar efforts. Under the leadership of the Very Reverence James Parks Morton, the Urban Housing Assistance Board (UHAB) was founded. UHAB is not only involved in rehabbing but also offers courses in building maintenance and management and acts as a liaison between housing partnerships and governmental agencies. Its liaison efforts include help with paperwork and financing as well as guaranteeing that contract terms are met and a stable management is set up. UHAB has been so successful that recently the New York Housing Development and Preservation department turned over five buildings to groups developed and supervised by UHAB. Like St. Ambrose, the Cathedral Church employs and trains people virtually off the street. It operated a stone-working apprenticeship program, a woodworking skills training term, and other crafts programs to teach marketable skills. In this way, neighborhood people not only help the church but also work toward individual economic self-sufficiency.[44]

Conclusion

These are some of the many ways an enterprising congregation can be instrumental in revitalizing the community. As the church responds with creative approaches, the problems of inadequate housing, red-lining, torching, burned-out areas, freezing conditions in winter, and the like can be met. The church can have a part in encouraging financial institutions and private enterprises to invest in the community. Most of all, the church can weather the transitional stages and continue to minister in a changing city.

The effectiveness of these approaches is greatly enhanced when the pastor and as many members of the congregation as possible live in the community. Although such a residential commitment to turf is not always possible because of family, safety, or other important considerations, it is a powerful statement in the eyes of the community itself.

3 | Urban Stratification and the Neighborhood Church

Stratification refers to the arrangement of a society into a hierarchy of layers that are unequal in power, possessions, prestige, and life satisfactions. More importantly, however, stratification provides unequal opportunities to accrue the most necessary and desirable commodities of earthly existence. It always generates differences in lifestyles, or living patterns. In short, stratification separates groups of people.

Stratification within cities is often related to regional boundaries. One of the more common conceptualizations of this stratification involves the use of the concentric-zone model of urban areas.[1]

The central zone contains the business district where civic, commercial, and governmental functions take place. Next comes the transition zone that includes the slum neighborhoods. Oddly enough, the land here is very valuable because of its proximity to the business district. However, because the buildings are aged and in decline, much work is necessary to make the area suitable for the expanding industrialists. The next zone contains working-class homes. In this area live people whose parents were able to escape the transition zone. The fourth region is a residential zone containing single-family dwellings and apartment hotels. On the border is a commuter zone in which people seeking more desirable living spaces reside.

The socioeconomic status of the residents generally rises further from the center of the city. Communities are more stable and organized, street crime is less frequent, and the quality of education and city services improves. Hence, upward social mobility means outward geographical mobility.

Understanding the larger or macro American stratification system, especially as it applies to the city, is of paramount importance in coming to terms with the dynamics of the more immediate micro system—the neighborhood. The bulk of this chapter is devoted to discussion of the larger system. This is then applied to the neighborhood and, more specifically, to the neighborhood church.

STRATIFICATION AND SOCIAL CLASS

The purpose or function of stratification, according to Kingsley Davis and Wilbert Moore, is to motivate individuals through the inducements of wealth, prestige, and power to assume positions that the society deems important and that require much talent.[2] An example of such a position is that of physician. Being a physician requires considerable talent. Because physicians deal with the critical issues of defining and treating health disorders, the position is of great import to the society. Hence, being a physician is lucrative. Entertainers and professional athletes are similarly rewarded because what they do requires a good deal of talent and the society, having more and more leisure time, demands to be entertained.

The Bases of Stratification

The primary bases of stratification are occupation, income, and education, with occupation being by far the most important. When sociologists determine position in the social structure, they often use these three as the criteria for placement. Occupation is especially important because in America you are, as Robert Kennedy said, what you do.[3] That is, your social identity is premised on your occupation. Moreover, to know a person's occupation is already to know a good deal about his income and educational status.

Joseph Kahl presented a more expanded view of the bases of stratification, listing seven major dimensions that underlie the American stratification system.[4]

1. *Prestige.* Some members in the society are granted more respect and deference than others.

2. *Occupation.* Occupations differ in prestige, importance to the society, or rewards associated with them.

3. *Possessions.* This dimension refers to the varying amounts of property, wealth, and income.

4. *Social Interaction.* Different classes develop different patterns of interaction, and because people tend to associate with others at their same level, these patterns markedly separate the classes.

5. *Class Consciousness.* People are very aware of a social structure and their status in it, hence reinforcing its importance.

6. *Value Orientations.* There is evidence that different social classes have somewhat different value systems, which in turn motivate them to seek different lifestyles.

7. *Power.* Power is differentially distributed and those at the top of the social structure have greater leverage in controlling and directing the actions of others than those below them. Indeed, this power differential is as important as any criterion, for it not only refers to the ability to control the flow of wealth and political advantage, but also the ability to maintain an unequal status quo.

Stratification and Societal Dysfunctions

Sociologically, stratification has certain societal dysfunctions. Four in particular stand out. First, because people are born into a given stratum, they do not have equal opportunities at birth. As a result, *the full spectrum of society's talent is not discovered.* Where one is slotted into the stratification system at birth has very real consequences for the size of one's family, the amount of interaction with one's parents, and the amount and quality of education one is likely to receive. If there were true equality of opportunity, it is altogether possible that a cure for cancer might have been discovered by now—or a host of other achievements might have occurred earlier. However, the poor are all but lost to society as a result of various factors: the poor quality of education they receive, higher rates of infant mortality, motivation undercut by the anguishes of poverty. A large sector is unable to contribute to the society.

Second, because of gross inequities in reward distribution, *there is a lack of unity in the society.* When some receive better health care, education, police and fire protection, and so on, there is bound to be discord and unhappiness over these inequities. The society disintegrates into interest groups, factions, and other divisions. These further divide the society and weaken it.

Third, with some in the society being granted greater deference and respect than others, *loyalty to the society is destroyed.* "Who you are" and "who you know" are very important in America. Having wealth and a powerful position guarantees no waiting in restaurants, better service on airlines, quicker contact with important officials, and greater expressions of social respect. The rich and powerful have the greatest ease in getting services of every kind—even free tickets to the major events. The result is that those who are not respected, who have to stand in line and be asked insulting questions when requesting public services, lose respect and allegiance for the system. It is little wonder that patriotism does not flourish in the inner city. It is difficult for a person to become teary-eyed over the national anthem when it celebrates a society that does not really respect and value him.

Fourth, stratification affects self-image, which in turn is related to creative development. This issue is of special significance for children. Children who grow up well fed, respected, and loved, and who attend schools in which students are made to feel important and valued, develop more positive self-concepts than children who realize that they are not deemed of much worth in the society. The result, more often than not, is that those who are made to feel positive are more likely to actualize their potential and develop their skills than those who feel they are not of much worth and who are discouraged from feeling they have anything to contribute. Where creativity and industriousness are depressed, *the society suffers from a loss in its collective reservoir of talent.*

These are but four of stratification's dysfunctions. It should be noted that they are societal; in other words, they hurt society as a whole. Some individuals may benefit from these societal dysfunctions, for they are advantaged by others' disadvantages; however, the society as a whole is still the victim.

It is interesting to note that the very terms used to describe the American class system—upper, middle, and lower—convey subtle notions of superiority and inferiority that may also be dysfunctional to the well-being of the society as a whole.

The Social Class System

The American social class system can be analyzed in a variety of ways. Some simply posit an upper, middle, and lower class. Others add what is called working, or blue-collar, class, sandwiched between the middle and lower classes. A more detailed approach cuts the social structure into six sectors—upper-upper, lower-upper, upper-middle, lower-middle, upper-lower, and lower-lower. What follows is a rather brief outline of the six social classes. For the urban pastor, who may find himself working primarily with the last two groups, knowledge of the structure as a whole can be valuable in understanding the social context in which his parishioners live.

Upper-Upper Class. Often referred to as "old money," these people are those who have possessed truly super riches over a number of generations. They are usually identified by family rather than as individuals. The Vanderbilts, Rockefellers, and Mellons would fall into this group. These people keep very much to themselves and associate within their own circles. Their elitism is protected and perpetuated by the tendency to marry within their own stratum.

Lower-Upper Class. Often called "new money," this group differs from those in the higher status primarily in the length of time the wealth and prestige have been in the family.

In general, relatively little is known about the upper classes because they have a thirst for privacy and so escape the usual data-gathering efforts by sociologists. Moreover, most sociologists are middle class and so are not conversant with the lifestyle of the elite.

However, certain traits characterize the upper classes in general, and the upper-upper class in particular. Family reputation is very important. The upper class is identified by families and it is the family name that must be advanced and protected at all costs. Individual members of the upper class gain social standing by virtue of their family background and so are socialized to make family reputation a matter of high priority.

Expenditures are often made to magnify and elevate the family name. Many upper-class families, for example, have foundations bearing the family name, and upper-class individuals frequently lend themselves (and their names) as chairpersons of charity drives and socially respectable fund-raising efforts.

Women are very influential in social matters. Upper-class females are often pursued by the fashion media, are the subjects of newspaper features, and often become social trendsetters. The upper-class people are often referred to as "society," largely because of their social prestige.

Perhaps most important of all is that the upper class is truly super rich. Their wealth is tied up in the major American industries and business enterprises, and hence, whenever the wheels of American commerce are turning, these people are making money. As long as capitalism survives, these people survive.

Upper-Middle Class. The upper classes constitute roughly 2 percent of the society, while the upper-middle includes about 8 percent. The upper-middle class consists of the upper and middle levels of business and management in addition to the major professions. Reputationally, they are viewed as "highly respectable," not because they are actually more moral than other classes, but because their moral values are the most dominant in the society and their thirst for respectability is probably the most intense among the strata.

It is the upper-middle class that takes the lead in civic affairs, including public education. In fact, it could be said that whereas the upper classes own and control the major corporations and institutions, the upper-middle class tends them on a day-to-day basis from administrative and executive posts. Because of this institutional dominance of the upper-middle class, it is imperative that those who wish to succeed in the American mainstream be able to communicate with members of this class. For that reason, it is the upper-middle class clothing style and social demeanor that is taught as "proper" in most public schools.

Lower-Middle Class. These "good common people" comprise about 30 percent of the American society. They come from the ranks of small businesspeople, clerical workers, and low-level white-collar workers. These people are often rather conservative politically out of a desire to hold on to their middle-class status. They conduct their lives in a very ordered, patriotic, respectable, and self-improving fashion.

Upper-Lower Class. The largest of the social classes at 40 percent, this group is often difficult to distinguish from the lower-middle class. Their values and lifestyle are very middle class out of a desire to be viewed as middle rather than lower class. Considered "respectable," this sector includes skilled and semi-skilled (blue-collar) workers as well as small tradesmen. Moreover, policemen and firemen are often placed in this group. They often live in less desirable but nonslum urban neighborhoods, and they strive for a reputation of respectability. Male chauvinism is often rather overt here, with a tendency for women to remain subordinate.

Economic status is not very important in identifying the upper-lower class, for in many cases their annual income will equal or exceed that of the lower-middle and even upper-middle classes. The differences lie mainly in *how* they earn their money. They usually are paid by the hour and hence experience affluence through overtime and second jobs. Their economic status is rather tightly tied to the national economy; therefore, in boom times employment and money are plentiful, while during a period of recession their lifestyle can become rather austere.

The upper-lower class is often rather unsympathetic toward the poor, in part because of their wish to be associated with the middle rather than the lower class. There is also a rather strong "I fight poverty, I work" doctrine operative in this group. Frequently, they will oppose public aid of almost any sort, as they feel its funding is coming from their hard-earned, blue-collar income. In short, although they are socioeconomically closest to the poor, attitudinally they are at a considerable distance.

Lower-Lower Class. This group—the poor, about 20 percent of the society—suffers from a negative reputation in the eyes of the rest of the society; they are often viewed as opposites of good, middle-American virtues. Probably the most painful aspect of being poor is the psychological assault it carries. The poor are considered the least worthy in a capitalistic system. They are viewed as takers rather than givers, burdens rather than blessings, contemptible and dirty rather than respectable and clean. The process of receiving public assistance is particularly humiliating.

The lower-lower class includes unskilled laborers with sporadic and unstable jobs, poor farm workers (especially those in the southwestern portion of the United States), the chronically unemployed and unemployable, and those on public assistance.

When white Americans think of a lower-lower class person, there is a tendency to conjure up the image of a black face. Such a notion is false; the largest number of those in this class are white (although poverty strikes nonwhites harder by percentage).[5] In fact, this class is made of many disparate groups. Every ethnic, age, and religious group has representatives in the lower-lower class.

Poverty is most apparent in the cities. As more and more affluent whites leave the city limits in quest of a comfortable suburban lifestyle, they are either not replaced, causing city populations to dwindle, or their place is taken by poor people, whether they be Mexican-

American migrants, Puerto Ricans in search of better job opportunities, blacks from the South, or white European immigrants.

Some sociologists include among the poor all those in the lower fifth of the income distribution. Others use less arbitrary definitions and set the poverty population at forty to sixty million Americans. The official government criteria for determining poverty are based on region of residence and family size. In 1981, poverty income was set at $9,287 for a nonfarm family of four. By this definition, approximately thirty-two million Americans were poor. Considering what is required to feed, house, and clothe an urban family of four today, such a figure is appalling. The number one priority among the poor is obviously survival—little wonder, considering the economic deprivation in which they live.

Such tension and concern over survival issues tend to bring about a strong present, rather than future, orientation. The future is not something to look forward to if the economic and social horizon is not bright.

Lower-lower class status often has adverse effects on family life. Anxiety over acquiring the necessities eats away at intimacy and harmony within the family. Social life, especially in urban areas, is often not rooted in the home. While in the larger society the home is a place of peace and surcease from the pressures of the workaday world, among those at the bottom of society home is often a nerve-jangling, noisy, overcrowded place. Because homes are not owned by those who live in them and are often not kept up by slum landlords, there is little pride taken in the residence, and hence, little emotional attachment to it.

Pleasures and enjoyable leisure are in short supply in this sector. If one is unemployed, there may be a great deal of free time, but it is often not very relaxing or personally enriching. Pessimism and hopelessness corrode the spirit.

Despite all the problems of poverty and inner-city living, there are genuine strengths evident among the poor. Although family life is often under stress, there are many vital marriages in poverty communities. Moreover, many solid citizens and battle-tested mature Christians emerge from single-parent and intact families in inner cities. Dr. William Pannell, alluding to his Detroit experience, noted families in which one child may run afoul of the law and become drug dependent, and yet another in the same family may become a lawyer or a teacher.[6]

Even in the areas of crime and drug abuse the statistics can be read from two points of view. On one hand, rates do tend to be higher in inner cities and among the poor in general; on the other, they are not so high as to obscure the fact that amid all the deprivation, the majority of inhabitants of poor communities remain "straight."

Out of the crucible of poverty come impressive psychological strengths. The survival mentality gives rise to a resilient form of mental toughness, a courage bred of enduring a difficult existence. Coping skills are highly developed so that crises do not cause panic and the insults of prejudice do not destroy character. More study needs to be made of the strengths among inner-city populations so that strategies can be developed that maximize these skills.

Conclusion. The social-class system is perpetuated by the unequal distribution of power. While the upper class tends to "own" the society, the middle class dominates and operates it. The result is that the system (whether it is economic, educational, or political) is governed by middle-class rules and styles of operation. For those at the lower end of the system, the middle-class method of operation imposes a dual burden. The poor not only have the usual worries about succeeding, a concern at all levels of society, but they also have to learn rules of the system in which the success game is played. This dual burden produces a great deal of tension among society's "outsiders," tension which many "insiders" neither understand nor notice.

The consequence of this overall power disparity is conflict. It accounts for cleavages between labor and management, the poor and the rich, the government and those governed, and on and on. This is by no means an attack on the capitalistic system, for all political systems have their flaws. The point is that stratification produces winners and losers, and urban pastors are wise to understand the dynamics of the socioeconomic system as a whole, for it accounts for how the winners and losers are determined.

Perpetuation of Social Strata

The self-perpetuating nature of the stratification system is a critical element in understanding its inequitable aspects. Sociologists estimate (and this is a liberal estimate) that only about one in every four Americans moves up the social structure in the course of a lifetime. In

MODEL FOR THE PERPETUATION OF SOCIAL STRATA

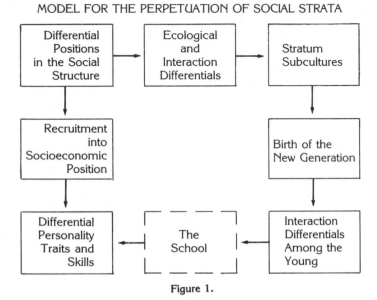

Figure 1.

other words, stratification is usually a "womb to tomb" phenomenon. Perhaps the best way to dramatize how self-perpetuating the system is, is to use an adaptation of Mayer and Buckley's Model for the Perpetuation of Social Strata (see Figure 1).[7]

Differential Positions in the Social Structure. The model begins with the adult socioeconomic status. Beyond occupational position, income, and level of education, this status has implications for individual political power, community influence, access to the media, and personal satisfaction.

Ecological and Interaction Differentials. The adult socioeconomic status is related to the social and physical environment. Depending on what socioeconomic stratum a person is in, he will be located in a community of the upper, middle, or lower class. Furthermore, the physical nature of this community—size of the lot, whether buildings are single- or multiple-family dwellings, recreational space, upkeep of the buildings and streets, age of the structures, residential density (people per square mile)—will also differ according to social class. These social and physical elements are powerful in shaping and socializing the individual. Spending time with a certain class of people shapes a person's thinking, and no matter how unpleasant the physical aspects, regularized contact with it brings a certain degree of acclimation.

Stratum Subcultures. This socialization gives rise to classes as subcultures. Each socioeconomic layer develops its own particular ways of thinking, feeling, and acting, distinguishable from the other classes. In short, each stratum constitutes a subculture—a mini-way of life.

With regard to subcultures among the poor, there is a debate as to whether the poor hold "poverty values." The prevailing position, the one this author is most comfortable with, is that although the poor are forced to make certain lifestyle adjustments as a result of their scarce means, these adjustments constitute adaptations rather than genuine value differences. As Charles Valentine points out, to posit a true "culture of poverty" may suggest, however subtly, that the poor choose to be poor and enjoy a culture founded on deprivation.[8]

Birth of the New Generation and Interaction Differentials Among the Young. Within each stratum children are born and the differences in strata give rise to differences in socialization of these children. Lower-class children become accustomed to large families, limited space, poverty, and insecurity. Few of them will take vacations with their parents. Instead they will develop local "street savvy." Physical toughness and the ability to endure personal deprivation and hardship will likely be fostered. Upper-status youth will associate with other such young people, who have large homes and big yards. They will have their own rooms, stereo equipment, and television. They may travel with their families across the country and perhaps around the world. Food will be in plenteous supply and contact with adults within the nuclear family will be more frequent. They will lack few material possessions or creature comforts.

Differential Personality Traits and Skills. These socialization differences will, as already implied, have consequences for the development of personality traits and skills. What is crucial is that personality—that organized matrix of behaviors, attitudes, values, beliefs, and motives characteristic of an individual—is much determined by early socialization experience. Hence, the poor youngster is likely to develop a lifeview congruent with his social background. Street savvy, a job, a car, and freedom from the oppressive burden of poverty are likely to be more immediate goals than a first-rate education, a white-collar job, or travel.

Although the lower-status youth may well value the same things other children value, his sense of realism, coupled with his limited exposure to a life in a more privileged setting, will likely cause him to act on a different set of values. Exposure to poverty, violence, drunkenness, and police harassment is likely to spawn political and social attitudes consistent with having viewed the effects of these problems. The more affluent youth, who has spent his time among people whose economic and occupational destiny are pretty much under their own control, is more likely to develop a set of attitudes that emphasize individual achievement, along with economic and occupational security.

In terms of skills, the poor youngster is likely to develop abilities vital to surviving the physical and emotional traumas of life. Other children are likely to learn verbal skills, such as reading, writing, and speaking standard English, as well as how to present themselves favorably to the white-collar professionals who determine who will be employed. In short, although the skills learned by those at the bottom are valuable, if not absolutely critical, they will not aid the person in adjusting to or succeeding in the middle-class institutional network, beginning with school and leading to the job market.

Recruitment Into Socioeconomic Position. Once preadult socialization is complete and personalities are shaped and skills developed, the individual is ready to assume his status in the adult structure. And, because of the markedly different set of influences and influencers, according to status at birth, the odds are overwhelming that the person's adult socioeconomic status will be the same as that of his childhood.

The School. The school is placed between the socialization differences and personality traits and skills because its entrance into the child's life occurs at that chronological point. Theoretically, the American school system is designed to equalize opportunity, that is, make certain that success or failure is a function of ability and effort. In short, it is intended to compensate for or eliminate the effect of socioeconomic status at birth. However, the overwhelming bulk of studies conducted by educators and sociologists indicates that, if anything, the school reinforces rather than removes status differences.[9] In fact, the most powerful determinant and the best predictor of an individual's achievement in school is his socioeconomic status. This should be no surprise when it is considered that the social and academic skills most rewarded and nurtured by the schools are those highly valued and almost religiously taught in the middle class.

Conclusion. An overall view of the whole self-perpetuating system makes it obvious that instead of every person having an equal likelihood of spending his adult life in any of the classes, one's status at birth largely determines one's adult future. At birth, one is already set in motion—the train is on a track, on a route headed toward an identical adult status. Only a dramatic intervention en route somewhere will move the individual off the track and headed toward a different status.

Perhaps the most powerful of American myths is that we are what we are (socioeconomically) because of achievement rather than because we were born that way. It is this myth of self-congratulation and other-degradation that drains away empathy for those who find themselves at the bottom of the American socioeconomic system. It is this myth that makes it difficult for urban pastors to get help in the form of money or time from affluent congregations and denominations. People are thought to be poor because of their own deficiencies, not because of any inherent, self perpetuating qualities of the socioeconomic system. This is not to say that individual effort and achievement are unimportant. It is to say that they are by no means the only dynamics involved. In the final analysis, if urban pastors can overcome this and related antipoverty biases, they will be more likely to gain support and involvement for urban parishes.

NEIGHBORHOODS AND THE NEIGHBORHOOD CHURCH

A knowledge of the societal stratification system provides insight into smaller systems such as neighborhoods. In fact, Paul Peterson emphasizes the point that even cities themselves should not be viewed as ''nation-states,'' or autonomous entities. On the contrary, understanding a given urban policy requires a knowledge of the wider socioeconomic and political climate. Factors in the state or nation at large, external to a given city, can be determinative of strategy.[10] Likewise, an awareness of the stratification of a city and the society at large is vital in diagnosing a neighborhood.

The importance of neighborhood is seen in the fact that people often think in terms of the neighborhood rather than the city in which they live. Richard Coleman, in his work for Massachusetts Institute of Technology and Harvard, writes that neighborhoods serve a variety of functions, including influence on children, adult social comfort, physical safety, and harmony with the surroundings.[11] According to Hahn and Levine, even government services are shifting toward a neighborhood focus because effective delivery of services requires client cooperation and local governments will not accrue the desired political benefits without gaining cooperation from receiving neighborhoods.[12]

In this work, the concept of the neighborhood necessitates expanded treatment because it is the direction urban ministry is going. Defining a neighborhood as a stewardship and service area provides the urban church with a manageable turf on which to do its work. Greenway asserts that "the principle which needs emphasizing is that of the neighborhood church."[13] Moreover, such a geographical approach, based on church resources, increases effectiveness of programs, which can then be replicated elsewhere by others. Our Savior's Lutheran Church, a downtown Minneapolis congregation of nearly a thousand members, took this approach, believing it was more practical to work in their own neighborhood than to spread itself thinly across the city.[14]

Types of Neighborhoods

Before looking at examples of what some urban churches are accomplishing by a neighborhood approach, it is necessary to understand what a neighborhood is and what types of neighborhoods can be found in a city.

Warren and Warren, who do perhaps the best job of showing how to define, organize, and even change a neighborhood, use three basic principles in studying a neighborhood.[15] The first principle is *identity:* To what extent do the people feel they belong to a neighborhood, sharing a common destiny with their fellow residents? The second is *interaction:* How frequent and in what numbers do people visit their neighbors in the course of a year? The third principle is *linkages:* What and how effective are the channels people use to funnel information in and out of the neighborhood?

These three principles are criteria for determining the social structure of a neighborhood. They cut across economic and racial lines and so can be used in any urban neighborhood. On the basis of these criteria—identity, interaction, linkages—six basic types of neighborhoods can be differentiated.

The first and strongest type is the *integral neighborhood*. Here identity, interaction, and linkages are all positive, with the people cohesive and active. They are involved both on the local turf and in the city at large.

The *parochial neighborhood* is second. There is evidence of sound identity and interaction, but such a neighborhood receives a minus in linkages. These neighborhoods are self-contained, are often very homogeneous ethnically, and are cut off from the larger community.

The *diffuse neighborhood* has a sense of identity, but little in the way of interaction or linkages. Such a neighborhood is homogeneous in the sense that it can be a new subdivision or inner-city housing project. However, the neighborhood lacks internal vitality and is not closely related to the larger region. There is little involvement with neighbors.

The *"stepping-stone" neighborhood* lacks identity, but receives a plus in interaction and linkages. People here are upwardly mobile and involve themselves with neighbors not out of shared interest but in order to get ahead. There is a musical-chairs quality about these neighborhoods: people move through on their way up.

The *transitory neighborhood* has little identity or interaction. It does have linkages, however. Here population change is evident and the neighborhood breaks into clusters. Often long-term residents are separated from newcomers. There is little joint activity or organization.

The sixth type is the *anomic neighborhood*. This has little identity or interaction and few linkages. It is hardly a neighborhood at all because there is no cohesion and there is great social distance between its members.

A parish outreach program by the Diocese of Oakland used an interesting approach to analyze their neighborhood. Core church families were each given fifteen to twenty nearby families to visit. The purpose of the visit was to develop friendships and build bridges. From these visits, neighborhood and community needs were defined.

After all the information was gathered and discussed, a parish convention was held in which needs were openly discussed and strategies for action were developed and voted on. Out of this process neighborhood problems were addressed; the church was renewed through prayer, reflection, and action; and bridges were built within the parish between the church and the residents.[16]

Neighborhood Empowerment

As can be seen in the Oakland example, analysis of the neighborhood is one of the precursors to effective ministry. In fact, such analyses leads to the real focus of contemporary urban ministry: empowerment.

Empowerment involves the transfer of control and neighborhood determination from downtown administrative centers to neighborhood residents. Neighborhood empowerment is an effort at the decentralization of power, enabling neighborhood residents to control their own situation. As certainly as individuals in therapy start improving once they realize they can do something about their problems, so also neighborhoods are revitalized when self-determination is in evidence.

Hallett makes the case for empowerment when he says that neighborhoods should be examined in terms of whether their residents can move from a survival level in which there is dependence on public aid of some sort, to marginality in which they can barely make it on their own, to initial accumulation where there is down-payment money for a house or car, to moderate accumulation with savings accounts and planning for the future, up to rapid accumulation in which money begins multiplying itself.[17] Samuel Acosta, at a conference of churches-in-transition held in Philadelphia, emphasized empowerment among Hispanics, claiming that what is vital are methods of empowering Hispanics to control the forces that affect the quality of their lives.[18]

Unhooking a neighborhood from dependency on outside programming and resources is basic to empowerment. What is necessary is public investment in neighborhoods rather than public aid maintenance dollars that assure barely a survival level.[19] Too often public aid monies earmarked for needy city dwellers never reach them. For example, over 50 percent of government monies targeted for the poor is funneled through Medicaid and Medicare, so that much of it goes into the pockets of professional distributors. Sometimes the professionals are less than ethical. In Detroit, one physician had a mobile office. He operated out of the trunk of his car, cruising the neighborhoods, giving superficial checkups to indigent holders of "green cards," and billing the government. A bit of unpublished research in Chicago indicated there was enough dollar-flow into one low-income community to keep two suburban neighborhoods alive. Unfortunately, because those dollars were filtered through bureaucracies, most of the money wound up in the hands of white-collar personnel. Public schools and fire and police departments often receive special funding for work in inner-city neighborhoods, but they rarely make an effort to hire neighborhood residents who know their immediate needs and could use gainful employment.

Neighborhood empowerment requires organization and planning. It means addressing issues on a variety of fronts. Such issues include influencing institutions and businesses to hire neighborhood residents; gaining a voice in the administration and operation of schools; gaining control by means of property ownership; demanding proper and responsive political representation; improving health care, perhaps by developing an organization such as a health maintenance organization that yields benefits for staying healthy; obtaining greater commitment and improved services from financial institutions. In addition, with the rise of modern government administration systems, to impact urban political structures requires dealing with appointed bureaucrats rather than elected officials.[20] Thus a key neighborhood empowerment issue is gaining bureaucratic accountability.

Marciniak, a veteran of urban revitalization, suggests twelve strategies for improving and empowering neighborhoods.[21]

1. Mobilize voters to clean out political figures who prey on neighborhood misery.

2. Work toward eliminating or reforming day-labor organizations through competition. Day-labor organizations hire unemployed residents on a day-by-day basis to do contracted work. The workers are paid in cash at the end of the day. The profits are raked in by the organization, which, in some cases, encourages willing workers to bribe the officials in order to get a job for a day.

3. Work with the electorate to rid the area of undesirable liquor establishments and other trouble spots.

4. Deal head-on with the neighborhood's concern about street crime.

5. Provide escort service and other moral support for witnesses to appear in court in cases dealing with street crime and intimidation.

6. Work at cutting through bureaucratic barriers in removing abandoned autos.

7. Approach public officials to stop licensing any more sheltered care facilities such as nursing homes or half-way houses for the mentally disturbed until the community has had time to deal with the ones already there.

8. Encourage local institutions to remain and adapt to changing populations and lifestyles.

9. Promote investment in older, multiple-family dwellings in order both to renovate neighborhood housing and avoid the development of a slum.

10. Urge new "urban pioneers" to take residence in the neighborhood and work toward its continuing revitalization.

11. Demand that city officials not inundate the neighborhood with public housing, but rather allocate such developments on a "fair share" basis.

12. Capitalize on the power of local institutions whose own futures are linked to the well-being of the community for support and strength.

A Stewardship Ministry

Working toward empowerment is a stewardship rather than service ministry. The church must get beyond the old missionary model in which a missionary goes into an area with all his expenses and salary paid by outside sources and then performs a relief ministry. In the urban church that kind of approach is seen in using the church as a clubhouse for activities and as a dispenser of services to the needy. As important as relief ministries are, the church must go beyond being an ecclesiastical version of the welfare system.

Many churches are making this move. The community garden program in Kansas City is a creative example of empowerment and self-determination rather than dependency and receivership. Community gardens produced over $750,000 worth of fresh food.[22]

In the South Bronx, the Local Initiatives Support Corporation aims at revitalizing neighborhoods through empowerment. The LISC is based on the assumption that there are usually surprisingly strong sources of community strength even in the most depressed areas and that outside developmental efforts need to be tied to neighborhood sources of self-help. The LISC also affirms the importance of the private sector as financier and fellow problem solver in efforts toward neighborhood revitalization.[23]

Efforts at neighborhood revitalization are greatly enhanced by building coalitions. In Chicago, four churches worked in concert to develop Atrium Village, a multimillion dollar housing venture attempting to build a bridge between an indigent and superaffluent community. This same Chicago-Orleans Housing Corporation hopes to experiment with the use of solar energy and other conservation measures in city housing. This church coalition has members on a community board working on a new park system, on the local high school board, and on a neighborhood alliance focusing on transportation and streets.[24]

Coalitions abound. The Archdiocese of St. Paul and Minneapolis has developed the Christian Sharing Fund, which supports a variety of community-based efforts. Projects that request funding must be of a social-change nature, dealing with institutional causes of poverty and powerlessness.[25]

In the South Bronx, seventy-nine black churches from a variety of denominations joined together to form the Shepherd's Restoration Corporation, which supports housing, economic, and other social activity in the Bronx.[26]

In Buffalo, thirty-eight Protestant and Catholic churches merged, developing the United Citizens Organization, believing that churches represent potential strength to deal with the massive institutions that dominate society.[27]

In Kansas City, Missouri, the Linwood United Ministries—a coalition of fifteen church-related organizations—has been involved in assisting low-income families in their efforts to buy or rent housing, combating redlining, and a host of other social efforts.[28]

Empowerment efforts are aided by strength of unity. This is especially important because these efforts often mean dealing with institutions, the topic of the next chapter.

4 | Poverty From an Institutional Perspective

The truths of stratification and self-perpetuation of the socioeconomic system are not widely known or accepted. As a result, negative attitudes toward the poor persist.

The perpetuation of poverty by society results partly, as Harrington points out, from its invisibility.[1] It is very difficult for people to become concerned about problems with which they are not confronted. In cities, the poor are so severely segregated that a person can live for years in an urban metropolis without ever driving to a poor neighborhood. When poverty is an abstraction, it is exceedingly difficult for many middle-class people to believe that there can be as many as thirty-two million people in this country living below the poverty level. This invisibility is exacerbated by the immobility of the poor. Many are unable, because of physical illness or financial deprivation, to leave their neighborhoods. So just as the middle class do not go into poor neighborhoods, neither do the poor make their way into middle-class neighborhoods.

To argue that poverty is a self-perpetuating condition in a capitalistic society is to attack the nation's sacred civil doctrine of the self-made person. To suggest that one is poor because of an unequal distribution of opportunities is to suggest that riches are as much a matter of good fortune as virtue.

Ironically, a middle-class person has no feelings of inferiority about not being truly rich, for if asked why he is not more affluent, he will be quick to tell of his roots and how these precluded the opportunity for acquiring great riches. Yet this same individual cannot accept the similar accounting for poverty. Elliott Aronson says we are rationalizing rather than rational entities.[2] Never is that more in evidence than in our being critical of the poor while excusing our own failure to reach the economic heights to which we would aspire.

INSTITUTIONS AND THE POOR

In spite of the many poverty myths, poverty means much more than absence of money. It is powerlessness and alienation from the key institutions of society. The importance of the lack of integration of the poor in the major institutions of the society is highlighted by Oscar Lewis.[3] Although, as Lewis rightly contends, urban and rural poverty share many characteristics, urban poverty is distinctive in that the city's poor feel a heightened sense of powerlessness and confusion as they deal anonymously with massive, impersonal bureaucracies, bureaucracies in which size and officialdom have an intimidating effect.

In many communities multistoried government buildings are filled with middle-class personnel whose main task is to orient aimless poverty victims to the prevailing system, referring them to employment centers, health clinics, neighborhood mental health offices, special school programs, city services pertaining to public aid and building maintenance, legal aid agencies, and on and on and on. Probably no characteristic of urban poverty stands out more than this lack of experience and familiarity with basic urban services and agencies.

Sociologically, institutions are abstract collectivities that meet basic human needs. In America, six major institutions are often defined: *p*olitics, *r*eligion, *e*conomics, *f*amily, *e*ducation, and *r*ecreation. The acronym for this institutional system—PREFER—itself clearly reflects the relationship of the inner-city poor to each of these institutions—the fundamental human needs of the people are barely met in any of them.

The urban poor are almost completely cut off from the wider society and yet are oppressively controlled by it. They are usually geographically separated from ''polite society,'' but the power figures of the city hold tight control over what are euphemistically called ''poor neighborhoods.'' The police are ever-present, the politicians regularly ''ride herd'' in the ghetto areas, the schools teach a mainstream lifestyle, large denominations constantly dictate policy to their "urban missions," and the welfare system keeps tight rein on the lifestyle of public-aid recipients. The feeling of oppression—of a noose around a poor neck—often creates a volatile climate in the inner cities.

Politics

Politically, the poor are all but without representation. Not a single senator or congressman is noted for championing the cause of the poor. In fact, almost every well-known figure who is viewed as an advocate of the poor is outside the prevailing system. Jesse Jackson and Cesar Chavez are two examples. The poor are minimally represented because in a capitalistic society they produce little in the way of goods and services. What is more, with mass disorganization and estrangement, coupled with little stable community leadership, they vote in low numbers, making them almost irrelevant to well-dressed, high-powered political candidates.

In poverty areas can be found the classic example of political reversal. Instead of the political system depending on the support of the people, the people depend on it and so become the pawns of the political system. A housing issue in a Chicago inner-city community illustrates this.

A mass meeting over a housing grievance was held in one of the neighborhood's churches. City officials, neighborhood residents, and community workers were present to hear the matter. The conflict was resolved, the city officials assuring the citizens that they would make good on their vows to provide and maintain adequate housing. A subsequent meeting was scheduled for a month later to check on the officials' progress toward honoring their promises.

A month passed and the day of accountability arrived. Much to the surprise of the community workers, neither the aggrieved neighborhood residents nor the city officials showed up. The church hall was nearly empty. A bit of investigation revealed a political coup. Apparently an official from his downtown city office called the tenant council in one of the high-rise buildings and stated that he was privy to a rumor that if the meeting were held as scheduled, the welfare checks, due on the third of the month, would be late in arriving. Faced with a choice between improved housing or food, the residents quickly capitulated to the threat and the meeting was boycotted. For the city, it was the perfect squelch. They claimed publicly that they had obviously done their job well, for the community, by virtue of their nonattendance at the meeting, showed that the matter required no further attention.

Often people wonder why inner-city citizens who do vote, vote for the same political regimes that are said to have held them down. There are several reasons for this trend. One is a lack of alternatives. A known half-loaf is better than no loaf at all. However, more importantly, the voters are often intimidated. It is common for local political organizers to roam the streets and subtly but clearly warn the citizens that if candidate ''X'' does not receive adequate support at the polls, he will have little reason to serve the community well. Translated, that means that fire protection may be even more lackadaisical than before, police service will become increasingly oppressive and decreasingly protective, project buildings will be ignored, slum landlords will be under even looser control, and garbage may continue to pile up, making the rat and roach epidemic even worse.

Little political organization and savvy and a resulting lack of power account for the reason so few changes are made in the inner city. An urban church worker learns quickly that the people are not only beset with ineffective governmental programs and policies but, even worse, are without realistic grievance mechanisms to ameliorate these problems. In fact, many welfare-oriented government programs exist simply because of political powerlessness, and although they may be designed with the best of intentions, they are just substitutes for what is really needed: an equitable share of political power in a representative democracy.

Religion

Religion, as an institution, is also tainted by poverty. In many inner cities the church is the only really caring agency of any enduring value. It is a meeting place, a fellowship center, and a source of support. However, these churches almost invariably exist on a hand-to-mouth basis. This problem is growing. For example, according to Richard Gary's research, by 1987 half of all Episcopalian churches will not be able to support a full-time pastor.[4]

Urban church staffs are small, with many positions filled by volunteers. There is a great need for professionalism and urban expertise, but there is simply no money to fund the programs that could use trained personnel effectively. If the church is nondenominational, it lives off the income garnered from the collection plate. Such a budget would provide only for the minister, if even that. In many cases, an indigenous pastor is only a part-time professional, spending most of his time working in a factory or a store in the neighborhood. If the church belongs to a mainline denomination, it is most likely on that denomination's home missionary budget, receiving a monthly pittance to carry on the awesome task. In short, another reversal is in operation. The churches that need the money for comprehensive and effective whole-person ministry receive the least support, while other congregations debate whether to purchase a new organ or better sanctuary carpeting.

Economics

Poverty in economics connotes much more than simply a lack of money. High unemployment and underemployment mean a dearth of opportunities to acquire money.

Much of the insensitivity of middle- and upper-class people toward the poor is an outgrowth of the Protestant work ethic. The Protestant work ethic in its oversimplified form suggests that if one works hard, one will attain success. It is a strongly procapitalistic religious doctrine, emanating from the notion that God blesses those He favors and, therefore, if one is living in God's favor and laboring faithfully, success will result.[5] Much of the Protestant ethic is valid, for one would be hard-pressed to find many truly successful people who have not worked very hard at achieving that success. In that respect, its endorsement of hard work and attention to duty is sound. The problem comes with the Protestant ethic's unwritten corollary: If one is not successful, one has not worked hard.[6] Once that corollary is accepted (and it is subtly taught throughout the nation's schools and churches) the seeds of prejudice toward the poor are well planted.

One aspect of this problem is that many people cannot understand why there is so much unemployment in the inner cities. A look at the daily papers reveals legions of job opportunities.

This issue merits examination. If one takes a close look at those want ads, it becomes apparent that there really are not very many jobs for the poor. First, many of these jobs require a substantial amount of education. Even those jobs that require less formal education still require well-developed literary skills. These requirements eliminate most of the poor. Second, many of the factory jobs listed are not located close to poverty areas. Many industries, and hence jobs, have moved to the suburbs. Third, of these jobs that remain, many pay the minimum wage. At the minimum wage times forty hours, the vast majority of low-income families earn below the federal poverty level. In addition, job-related expenses such as travel, perhaps baby-sitting, clothes, and other mundane items, make it even less economical to accept such employment.

In the early seventies, a large candy manufacturer felt compelled to do something to relieve the pain of unemployment in Chicago's Cabrini-Green. The company offered plant jobs to those who needed them. There were two problems. One was that they offered the then minimum wage of $1.75 per hour, and the second was that the jobs were fifteen miles away in a western suburb. What is especially poignant about this example is that it is typical of well-meaning attempts to redress poverty through employment opportunities.

Though less talked about, underemployment is also a problem. There are a myriad of poor who work, but less than full-time or at jobs well below their capabilities. For those who work part-time, there are sharp financial effects, making it doubtful whether it is economically wise to be working at all. For those who work at jobs below their abilities, there is a morale-deadening factor, one that robs labor of all sense of satisfaction and accomplishment.[7] This widespread under-employment is not unemployment and is therefore not included in the monthly unemployment rates. It is obvious that work is not a guaranteed route out of poverty.

In addition to employment problems, the poor also face exploitive consumer practices. The poor spend a greater proportion of their income for necessities in the form of food, shelter, and health care than do the middle class, although the quality of their investment return is much less.[8]

The poor pay more for less.[9] Inner cities are teeming with exploitive money hounds who prey on helpless residents. Because there are often no large grocery stores in the neighborhood and no transportation to stores outside the community, the people often buy their goods at small, neighborhood establishments. A walk through almost any such store will reveal inflated prices and inferior merchandise. The proprietor takes advantage of the patrons' lack of shopping alternatives. If the people do not do much looking elsewhere, they are often unaware of how badly they are being exploited anyway.

However, the presence of a larger chain store is no guarantee of fairness either. In Chicago, one A&P store "serving" an inner-city community was taking the spoiled fruits and vegetables from the suburban stores and selling them at increased prices. When confronted by a group of concerned citizens, the store simply closed down rather than rectify this or any other of its exploitive practices.

Moreover, with inadequate funds, the poor cannot take advantage of sales on food or other goods sold in volume. This means that poor shoppers invariably pay much higher prices for the staples of life.

Exploitation is most rampant in consumer fraud in the form of corrupt car dealers, furniture stores, and most importantly, finance companies. Usually the dealer will sell a gullible consumer an item for a very small downpayment and then sell the contract to a neighborhood finance company. The interest rates on the merchandise are exorbitant, but the purchaser, who lacks awareness about installment buying and is dazzled by the acquisition of a bit of luxury amid the squalor of poverty, eagerly signs on the dotted line. Frequently, the purchaser simply defaults on the payments because of unexpected financial catastrophes or misunderstandings related to credit payments, or for some other reason. The result is the repossession and resale of the merchandise. The finance company is cut in on this bonanza through contracts laden with outrageous interest. These contracts prove extremely lucrative when fully paid, and even if the loan is in default, a good deal of interest money is usually pocketed. The victim is always the consumer. Such capers are pulled off again and again because the people are not aware of their rights, are lied to concerning them, or do not understand the legal channels open to them to redress these inequities. [10]

There is exploitation even in financial transactions. The poor cannot turn to banks for their dealings. One reason is that few if any banks are located in inner cities. Moreover, because of their middle-class aura, banks are very threatening to many of the poor. Also, with little income, who can be concerned with opening a savings account or a trust fund? [11]

With few inner-city residents having bank accounts, either for checking or savings, almost all transactions are done in cash. In order to do business, one must have checks cashed and obtain money orders. Such dealings are executed at the currency exchange, which is notorious for legally stealing from the poor. The currency exchange has a monopoly on cashing checks, supplying money orders, and paying utility bills (electric, telephone, and gas bills are regularly handled at these places). The result is that the currency exchange demands ridiculous service charges for almost every conceivable activity. Thus the poor, who need to pinch literally every penny, watch dollars needlessly slip away.

On top of the problems of employment and consumer exploitation, there is little economic and consumer knowledge. Perhaps the most basic reason is lack of experience. Those who have been raised in poverty have never had much money to be handled in the first place.[12] Consequently, such childhood socializers as allowances, toy purchases, and junior savings clubs are all but nonexistent, giving the people little or no conscious socialization into money management. Adults do not have charge cards, checking accounts, tax accountants, and itemized deductions on which they sharpen their fiscal acumen and pass it along to their youth. There are simply no models. In female-headed families, the oldest child is often saddled with the shopping duties. Because such persons often have no knowledge of how to handle money shrewdly and have little cash to begin with, they are often the victims of economic exploitation.

Family

Sociologically, there is no more critical institution than the family. It is the chief agent of socialization and the transmitter of basic values. Nowhere are families more frequently broken than among the poor. There is no shortage of reasons for this. Poverty itself is among the most important. The very economic system that operates in poverty communities breeds family destruction. For years, many states required that a family be broken before it could receive any public aid. As a result, many marriages broke up simply because the family could not survive with an intact marriage "headed" by a jobless and perhaps unemployable male.

Despite recent changes in the welfare restrictions in some industrial states, the rigors of poverty eat away at the marriage bond. In

America, a man's identity and worth are determined largely by his occupation. If one is either terribly impoverished or, worse, unemployed, one's identity and self-worth are under intense assault. Frustrated wives, exhausted by the ravages of poverty and slum living, are tempted to carp at their spouses about the squalor in which they and their children are forced to live. These forces wreak havoc on male egos and exert pressure on couples to "split."

As a result, in addition to the extremely high divorce rate in almost any inner-city community, often an equivalent number of marriages end in desertion or separation. In the case of desertion, the wife may never know the whereabouts of the departed husband. She is left with only the anguish of rejection. There is no contact, no resolution of the problems, no visitation with the children. Nothing. For the departed male, this may seem the only sane option. Facing an alienated wife, hungry children, and a slum dwelling is only a reminder of personal failure.

Often in the case of desertion divorces are obtained through legal-aid clinics. The process itself adds to the sense of humiliation. A notice of the divorce filing is published in the newspaper for a given length of time. If the deserting party does not respond to contest it, the divorce is granted. There is no alimony or child support of course, only a divorce, and perhaps the further indignities of welfare.[13]

Poor families then are often female-headed. As a whole, nearly 50 percent of poor American families are characterized by father absence.[14] In a nation in which adult males are customarily the chief breadwinners, poor children are often robbed of models of how the ordinary American familial system works. In such homes there are no flesh-and-blood examples of employed adult males who are succeeding in the occupational and economic market. This deficit of males can have real implications for the urban church, for it makes many become decidedly female-dominated. Moreover, male children may be difficult to motivate along traditional educational lines as they see no real examples of successfully educated male adults living in their community.

Because many poor families are female-headed, and because even intact families are hassled with making ends meet, mothers seek employment outside the home. As a result, children lack adult supervision. Much of their socialization takes place in the street. For the poor child, there is an absence of constructive family conversation, family group activities, and even a sense of what an intact family unit is like. For many youth there simply is no adult to talk to, to listen to, or to learn from. The oldest daughter may raise her younger brothers and sisters while her mother is out working.

In some cases there is an extended family nearby, often consisting of grandparents, uncle, aunts, and cousins. Where the extended family is present, there can be real advantages. Aid in such practical matters as babysitting, changing residences, and even financial crises can be obtained at little or no cost.

For the poor, the only security in old age may be one's children, who will care for the parent until death. For most people old age is provided for by a pension, a savings account, and social security benefits. Poor families have few, if any, of these; so in the long run, children may actually aid the poor.

Education

Poverty is perhaps no more vividly reflected than in the institution of education. A survey was conducted several years ago at a large inner-city high school in Chicago to determine the reading level of the senior class. The results? The average reading score was at the third-grade level, with not a single student, of the hundreds of students involved, reading at a twelfth-grade level. This means that the valedictorian did not read at grade level.[15] I recall working with a sixth-grade youngster, while I was teaching in an inner-city middle school in the sixties, and discovering that the youth, by no means retarded, was unable to recite the alphabet. These are not exceptional cases.

There are many reasons for this educational outrage. One of them is a lack of models. In a poor urban community a youngster is likely to grow up without a single well-educated person with whom he can identify. Virtually every middle-class child is surrounded with literate models. In fact, it is largely to avoid the criticism and scorn of these models that many middle-class youth learn to read and write. Not so in the urban enclaves. The only well-educated inhabitants of the community are the social workers and teachers who labor in the community by day and then quickly exit to the suburbs by late afternoon. The role models of the poor are from the ranks of the unemployed, unskilled, alcoholic, disabled, and criminal. Ironically, the criminal group includes the most affluent of the lot: the three Ps—prostitutes, pimps, and pushers. In any case, time is spent on the street and watching television. Reading is obsolete.

A second reason for this educational outrage is the limited formal education of the parent(s), coupled with a lack of opportunity in general, so that the youth usually has little contact with books and newspapers. This limited involvement with print is a powerful factor in accounting for reading and writing difficulties among inner-city students. In short, there is a lack of preparedness in the form of experience and motivation for learning to read and write. Moreover, many children, because of large families and overcrowded surroundings, do not enjoy the common and delightful experience of millions of other children—having their parents read to them. It is widely known that reading to a youngster can be a powerful motivating factor in "turning him on" to reading by himself.

Yet another reason is lack of space. A child's room may be the room for four or five brothers and sisters. There is no solitude. Whereas most children have sufficient privacy and proper facilities for cogitation, the lower-class youngster must try to study in noise, heat, and overcrowdedness.

Overcrowdedness does not afflict home life only. Urban schools are almost universally characterized by high density. Bulging classes, filled to the brim with academically needy youngsters, are the rule rather than the exception. For a teacher to salvage even a paltry percentage of this teeming group is a considerable accomplishment, considering the magnitude of the task.[16]

A fourth reason is the condition of the schools and academic materials. Although some cities boast of their high per-pupil expenditure in the inner-city schools, they rarely mention the amount of this outlay that goes to the upkeep of ancient and collapsing buildings and the purchase of often sadly irrelevant textbooks.

Finally, poor education is the result of teacher transience and lack of accountability. Most urban school systems abide by the seniority rule, which means that any teaching vacancy in the district is open to application and granted to the teacher with the largest amount of seniority. Hence, as openings occur in the city's fringes, an exhausted urban warrior fills it, leaving almost all openings for first-year teachers in the most trying and needy schools.

This transience is particularly harmful at the administrative level. A key to inner-city education is the principal. However, functioning effectively in an inner-city position is energy sapping and not very overtly rewarding. Therefore, many administrators, like teachers, move up and out. The stability of models who are responsible and committed to educational growth—day in and day out, week in and week out, year in and year out—is removed. The only people of any permanence are the repeatedly truant students.

There is also the matter of accountability. Urban educational bureaucracies are infamous for their nonaccountability. Teachers come and go, administrators are shuffled like cards in the inner city, "downtown" policies are ever changing, funding is no more stable than the stock market, and programs seldom last for more than a year. As a result, no one is really in charge. The bureaucratic web is so intermeshed that it is difficult to determine personal or institutional responsibility. The result is that no one is accountable, and more importantly, with politics at the center, no one wants to be. All that is known is that the casualties of such a monstrous system are the children.

Out of all this emerges a rather ambivalent attitude toward education. As the children "progress" through the school system, they develop a vague awareness that the really good jobs necessitate a sound education. However, with no models and a biography of negative experiences with traditional forms of learning already built up, little of a concrete nature is done to actualize their academic potential.

The consequences these conditions have for the aspiring inner-city student are devastating. It is not uncommon for a diligent inner-city scholar, who has attained a near-perfect grade point average and ranked in the upper divisions of his class, barely to make a C average in college. This is because the quality of the education the youth received was so markedly different from that which is necessary to prepare a student adequately for a liberal arts college. With few of even the finest making it, it is only realistic that other students merely endure, rather than enjoy and profit from, the whole educational experience.

Recreation

Recreation is yet another institution that reflects poverty. In Cabrini-Green there is one swimming pool for ten thousand children and young people. Even that pool has limitations, however. It is only three feet deep at its deepest point, and it contains no water. Moreover, there are fewer than ten basketball courts. Certainly no coach need worry about players fouling out with so large a collection of potential participants. There are no tennis courts, golf courses, baseball diamonds, football fields, or handball courts in inner-city communities. The result? Idleness. Idleness breeds drug usage, vandalism, and petty crime. If there is anything from which inner-city residents in general and juveniles in particular suffer, it is the lack of life options. Nowhere is this more obvious than in the recreational dimension.[17]

It comes as no surprise that so many of the finest baseball, basketball, and football players in America come out of poverty environments, for these are sports which, with a bit of ingenuity, can be played in most inner cities. A hoop and a round ball provide countless hours of entertainment for thousands of urban youth, although even a hoop can be hard to come by. Baseball is often played with the building as the backstop and the street as the outfield, while football is squeezed into any noncement space. Dawn to dusk involvement in these sports, played under the most menial of conditions, creates excellence; and such excellence is a badge of status in these communities. Conversely, suburban youth dominate championships in swimming, golf, and tennis. In fact, it is not uncommon for the best of inner-city athletes to be unable to swim, hit a golf ball, or use a tennis racket at all.

All of this serves to reemphasize the fact that being poor means having less of everything, including the much-needed psychological relief that constructive leisure and recreation have to offer. Poor communities are blighted communities, and included in the blight is the lack of recreational facilities of all types—from big-league stadiums to city parks. The poor turn to destructive alternatives such as alcohol and drugs.

SUGGESTIONS AND GUIDELINES FOR MINISTRY

What can be done in terms of service, and especially stewardship, in the institutional arena? Below are suggestions in each of the six areas, or major institutions. Following that are some overall guidelines for developing programs or ministries.

Politics

In the area of politics, it is well for an urban pastor to gain a comprehensive understanding in order to see the political situation as a full system with all its attendant interconnections. He can learn from the community residents and local neighborhood organizations. In addition, he should become acquainted with political representatives and government workers. His understanding and knowledge will then enable him to give more effective counsel to various people in the community who have difficulties with the political forces. His advice may often be sought because he may be one of the few figures in the community who is both well educated and caring.

One important aspect of the urban pastor's political education is to determine the reputation of the various political officials working in the community in order to find which ones are sensitive to the needs of the area. Because a great deal of activity is accomplished at the grassroots level, a pastor can convey certain concerns to local caring officials and see that they are acted on.

A note of caution is in order regarding political involvement. As mentioned previously, it is vitally important that neither the church nor the pastor be aligned with any particular party or candidate. Parties, regimes, and candidates come and go, but the church's mission lives on. If the church should tie itself to any organization, it will be acquiring short-term gain at the expense of potential long-term loss. For if the political entity loses its base, the church will lose a great deal of its leverage and, worse, if the political candidate or organization turns corrupt, the church will be in the embarrassing position of either having to renege on the political tie or be found furthering the cause of exploitation. The optimal position is what Art Gish termed cobelligerence—aligning with issues rather than organizations or candidates. Opening the church for political discussions and debates can be beneficial, for its makes public the church's concern for justice and the New Testament call for faithful citizenship. However, an open forum for interaction and debate should not degenerate into endorsement and support.

One specific idea for the church's involvement in the political arena on behalf of the poor is the formation of a church justice committee. This group can examine community problems and seek solutions. Such a group can assess everything from the quality of merchandise in the neighborhood stores to the accountability of political candidates.

Finally, contact with other churches and pastors in the community can be of great value both in learning about the political scene and in garnering advice concerning what posture to take when faced with dilemmas.

Religion

There are a number of avenues open for bolstering the religion-as-an-institution aspect of the ministry. If the church is a part of a mainline denomination, it is helpful to make contact with pastors from some of the more affluent churches in the metropolitan area and make specific requests for help. A receptive pastor might be willing to identify several couples in his congregation who would be willing to make a one-year commitment to an inner-city church. This would include regular attendance at least in the morning, as well as tithing and voluntary involvement in at least one church ministry. The enlistment of a number of such couples can do wonders for budget, moral support, and leadership, in addition to spreading the word about the inner-city church more widely.

The urban pastor might also request opportunities to educate Christians as to what poverty is, how it is perpetuated, and what its consequences are. This can be done by speaking in other churches, writing articles for denominational publications, working with seminary interns, meeting with students on field trips, and so on.

No matter how the pastor develops an audience, it is of considerable import that the myths of poverty be exploded. For unless they are dissolved, urban churches will continue to operate on an economic shoestring as the second-class citizens of large, wealthy denominations. That crucial second chapter of James will be violated at every annual denominational meeting, as rank and file church members will continue to believe that poverty is the result of personal inadequacy and, therefore, does not merit much in the way of action and concern.

Christians usually can be divided into three categories with reference to urban concern: those who do not care and must be "written off"; those who are open but lack knowledge and confidence; and those who have a genuine interest in and knowledge of urban dynamics. The second group is not small in number and is salvageable if the pastor can get the message to them in their suburban, or at least suburbanlike, ecclesiastical enclaves.

Reeducation is a difficult task. Yet reeducation efforts can lead to greater interest and extended opportunities to proselytize middle-class parishioners into a passion for urban ministry. Opportunities to speak to adult education groups, college clubs, and home missionary committees are valuable. Joint worship services held both in the inner city and in the outlying areas can also serve to recruit support for the inner-city effort. The point of all this is rather obvious: If a network of churches can become involved in even the most ancillary fashion in the inner city, the isolation of such a pastorate is reduced and aid can be obtained in efforts ranging from food drives to prayer chains.

Opportunities to address seminary classes and students are also valuable. The urban location of the church is likely to place the pastor near such educational institutions. Seminaries are aware of their urban ministry deficits. Many realize they are short on street experience. The result is often an openness for an articulate urban pastor; and he can both spread the call for greater concern for urban ministry and recruit interns and volunteers for his particular parish.

As mentioned previously, forming alliances with other churches in the community is also expedient. Even where there are deep theological differences, there can still be common ground on temporal concerns. Coalitions formed on an issue-by-issue basis is a good way to make progress in the community.

Alliances with other pastors in the community can serve the dual function of presenting a united front when dealing with unaccountable secular institutions and being a base of fellowship and support to buttress the urban pastor against the forces of loneliness, isolation, and pessimism.

Economics

In the economic realm, much can be done without handing out any money. A critical economic front is always employment. There are several avenues the church can take.

If the pastor has some effective suburban and fringe connections, he could determine what potential job opportunities exist there. Then, consulting with pastoral colleagues, he can get the names of business people in these areas, requesting, say, one job a year for an able-bodied, energetic member in the inner city.

In the immediate neighborhood, job openings can be posted on the church bulletin board. The church bulletin board, by the way, can be of inestimable value and is often underused or nonexistent. These boards convey vital information and bring area residents into the church.

A survey of the industries and businesses in the community should reveal any discriminative employment practices extant there. Where they exist, the justice task force, an alliance with other neighborhood pastors, or some other entity can bring pressure to bear on their perpetrators.

At every opportunity the church would do well to employ neighborhood residents in paid positions. Often there will be less than top-quality labor because of limited education and underpreparation in handling institutional responsibilities. However, it is a prime example of practicing what is preached. If community residents are employed, they should be carefully selected and have clearly defined job descriptions, so that if they do not work out, they will realize it even before the church has to inform them.

Finally, a benevolence fund, coupled with a well-stocked and sharply supervised "pantry" can be very positive. Some churches more aptly call such a fund a sharing fund. This and the other ministries witness to the church's concern over hunger and poverty.

Family

To deal with the family the church may have to take an indirect tack. Sermonettes regarding fidelity, intact marriages, and responsible child rearing are usually not very well received. They tend to have a judgmental ring as they are based on some naïve assumptions. This is not to say that fidelity and family concern is only a middle-class ethic, but rather that it is too easy to treat such concerns without proper awareness of the pressures attendant to inner-city life.

If the church succeeds in attracting community members, there can be church educational programs on family enrichment, child rearing, hygiene, and other family-related issues. If such programs are offered, every attempt should be made to insure that the leadership includes community residents—whether formally connected with the church or not. This will avoid investing such programs with a heavy paternalistic quality.

Day-care programs can also be valuable. They can be pay-for-themselves efforts by employing neighborhood mothers and paying them with monies garnered from working mothers who need good baby-sitting services. Such a ministry can have far-reaching effects. It brings the community residents into the church, demonstrates the church's concern for temporal needs, provides more adequate community child care (freeing older children from the responsibility of being part-time mothers), and is a breakthrough in the area of family concerns.

Church events that have a family focus, ranging from potluck suppers to retreats, also witness to the church's commitment to family life.

Beyond this, the pastor may find it helpful to consult with neighborhood social workers and family agencies. These people can provide valuable insight into major family needs in the area as well as suggest realistic ministries that can address these needs.

Education

It is difficult to change educational institutions; however, there are a number of educational options available. One is to start a church ministry that addresses the peculiar problems afflicting community students, primarily illiteracy. A good start may be a well-planned, seriously aimed tutoring program.

A tutoring program will require good tutors. These may be obtained from among educated members of the congregation, concerned citizens in the community, nearby seminaries, other churches, and students from local Christian and public colleges and universities.

Colleges and universities are often extremely valuable but untapped talent resources. A few well-placed calls to departments of sociology, psychology, and education may yield a number of people who can aid in urban ministry. Many colleges have internship programs, independent studies, or community-field experiences designed to allow interested students to grapple firsthand with the realities of the city. Often these experiential programs lack strategic placement options and would welcome an urban church opportunity in tutoring, provided the experience is well planned and the student is effectively supervised. In addition, individual professors may grant classroom credit to a student who is willing to immerse himself in the life of the inner city.

Good, serious students in the tutoring program should be recognized early and, in turn, "promoted" to become teaching assistants. This gives the tutoring effort a healthy indigenous quality and facilitates peer learning, a method that seems always to outstrip traditional methods in effectiveness. It also develops models for other learners.

To motivate students in the tutoring program, commercial enterprises such as department stores and banks can be asked to contribute. Many large organizations pride themselves on any and all civic improvement activities. I recall requesting assistance in motivating youngsters to read in a program in Michigan. A department store chain sent a large quantity of coupons redeemable at their stores for merchandise, such as records, pop, ice cream, and candy.

If an effective tutoring program can be designed, it is helpful to inform the local schools of its existence. The purpose is not to suggest deficiencies on their part, but rather to alert them to the church's interest in assisting their academic efforts and to invite their suggestions. This is both honorable and good politics.

The political aspect is noteworthy, because it is important that the school not become the church's adversary. If the schools see the church as an ally, they are more likely to be responsive to those issues raised by the church that fall into the schools' sphere of responsibility. One church has done so well at both tutoring and school relations that some of the tutoring now takes place right in the school. Ultimately, the goal is better education and greater accountability.

A church task force on education may also bring fruitful results. Such a group could oversee the tutoring program and develop relations with the neighborhood schools. A primary objective of the task force would be to develop skill and motivation in students.

Educational concern can carry far beyond tutoring and church-school relations. Students who show particular academic skill and motivation can be steered toward Christian colleges or state universities that will give them maximal educational benefit.

Recreation

There are a plethora of possibilities in the recreational area. One is to develop church softball, basketball, and even touch-football teams and enter them in leagues. Such teams should be well supervised with clearly articulated expectations for team members. Lacking these guidelines, members can become careless participants who may "grandstand," fail to attend, quit during the season, or engage in other counterproductive activities. If playing is a privilege, with certain, easy-to-abide-by expectations, these teams can be wonderful vehicles for ministry.

In addition to the teams, there can be group outings to professional events. A call to the office of a professional baseball or basketball team, explaining the community's needs and the church's interest in meeting them, may bring reduced prices or even free tickets.

Another possibility is to develop a recreation center in the church itself or a nearby building. A pool and ping pong table makes a good start. The specter of making the church building vulnerable to the wear and tear of city youth is repugnant to many beginning pastors. However, if any ground is to be gained in urban ministry, people's needs must always supersede consideration for buildings. Beyond this immediate step, it might be wise to check out various youth organizations, such as Young Life or Youth for Christ, to determine whether they have a ministry nearby. If they do not, it may be possible to invite them in to work spiritually and recreationally with the neighborhood teens. A number of such organizations have become increasingly sophisticated in urban concerns over the past years.

If talent and interest exist, a church youth program that zeroes in on developing relationships with neighborhood kids can be inaugurated. The "relationship first" concept is critical, for any attempt to evangelize or change attitudes will be met with incredible resistance if the youth feel they are simply scalps for the kingdom rather than persons who are cared about. Again, national youth organizations can be helpful in developing such a program.

Guidelines

These suggestions are only a beginning. The larger and more energetic the church, the more that can be done. However, it may be helpful for the urban pastor in the storefront church simply to begin by getting to know the community and then developing manageable ministries one at a time. Inaugurating a melange of uncoordinated ministries will bring nothing but frustration.

Assessment. At the outset, the turf and its needs must be defined; then a sober assessment of the church's resources, actual and potential, must be made. After this step, the development of ministries is in order.

Goals and Procedures. Ministries should have clearly defined goals and procedures. Inner-city communities are often characterized by minimal organization. With morbidity (illness) and mortality rates high, constant fear of fire and police brutality, the ever-present threat of urban renewal and hence forced removal, the inability to meet next month's rent, and so on, the focus is so heavily on getting by and surviving that there is little time to develop community roots and unity. Residential mobility, chief among the producers of community disorganization, can be a consequence of death, illness, financial catastrophes, fire, or urban renewal. The Michigan school in which I taught saw fully 1,100 of its 1,200 students change residences within a calendar year.[18] Disorganized ministries play into this chaos.

Moreover, if goals and procedures are clearly laid out, certain expectations can be made of those to whom the ministry will be directed. There need be nothing high-handed about this, for to require certain very basic things of the community participants is to convey respect for their autonomy and independence.

Regular Evaluation. Defined ministries can and should be regularly evaluated. Inner-city neighborhoods are unceasing targets of governmental programs of every sort. However, these programs are almost invariably long on money and short on hard-nosed accountability and self-evaluation. The result is that they fail and the people become accustomed to their failure. Simply to replicate governmental failures is to waste God's time. Ministries that work should be continued, and those that do not should be scrapped or renovated. Failures will occur and are not to be mourned over; what is unforgivable is to give up trying when failures do happen. Evaluations should be periodic so that ministries run long enough to take effect, but not so long that they do not receive proper attention. Finally, and most importantly, evaluation processes should include assessments on the part of those served by them.

Knowledge of Resources. There is no substitute for simple knowledge of the community and its resources. The Chicago Social Services

Directory contains more than two thousand agencies. If the urban pastor simply gained an intimate knowledge of such services in the community and took the time to make phone calls to the appropriate ones for confused and needy community residents or, even better, taught community residents how to help each other, he could perform a major ministry and quickly be defined as a friend of the community. Though such a service lacks a spiritual emphasis, until the church can develop its own more tightly focused ministries, knowing where people can go for help and assisting them in getting there can be a major ministry.

For larger and highly motivated urban churches, it can be helpful to assess what federal monies may be available for ministry. The notion of receiving government funding is anathema to many orthodox Christians who feel the mission of the church has to be totally separate from governmental interference. Nonetheless, when earmarked for social ministries and requested in the context of very clearly presented, open-faced statements of goals, seed money from federal or state sources can be a real boon.

Closely allied with this is money from various foundations. There are many potential sources in this area. However, it is important to realize that foundations tend to contribute almost exclusively to new ministries and programs, and rarely to support and maintain existing efforts. Hence, if foundation money is sought, it is wise to think of ways in which the newly inaugurated program, once off the ground, can generate its own revenue to keep it afloat.

Conclusion. Whatever ministries are begun, every ministry should make the safeguarding of the dignity of those served a high priority. Any ministry that smacks of white liberal do-goodism, in the form of "Here, let me show you how to live better, like me," however well-intentioned, is utterly doomed and has no place in the church. There is level ground at the cross of Christ; status differences do not exist. Every effort should be extended to remove them in church ministry as well. James 2:1–13 emphasizes the doing away with preferential regard. The key is servanthood and concern. Those who minister can learn much from those to whom they minister. Optimally, the ministry will be two-way, with the inner-city residents teaching the church representatives much.

Finally, if not a single program is ever begun, successful urban ministry must begin on the street. The church building is only a resource, and often a rather minor one. The church is wherever the people representing it are ministering to others. In that respect, the pastor must be prepared to wear out shoe leather. The pastor's study will have to include the streets of the community, taking the gospel of eternal and temporal love to the people right where they are. The number of worshipers in the sanctuary on Sunday may well be inversely proportional to the time spent there by the pastor during the week. It is ironic that some of the largest inner-city sanctuaries are the emptiest on Sunday morning, while storefronts are bulging.

* * *

With this institutional perspective in mind, we turn now to a closer examination of psychological aspects of poverty.

5 | Insecurity as a Way of Life

Perhaps the most pervasive psychological quality of life in the inner city is insecurity. Most sociological analyses of poverty life omit this characteristic; however, living in insecurity is a realistic fact of life in the inner city.

Jesse Jackson is reported to have said that any black person who is not at least a little paranoid is indeed crazy. He, of course, was alluding to the three centuries of racism blacks have experienced on American soil. For inner-city residents, regardless of ethnic affiliation, paranoia is hardly a sign of pathology.

This paranoia or insecurity can be expressed as a lack of what is called "fate control." The poor simply are not in control of what happens to them. They are respondents rather than initiators, reactors rather than actors, passive recipients rather than active participants. It could be no other way because they are powerless in the educational, economic, and occupational realms of this capitalistic nation.

Whenever social programs are constructed, they almost never have adequate representation from the ranks of the indigent they are supposed to serve. The poor are simply on the receiving end of these often well-intentioned government efforts. However, while the economic quality of the recipients' lives may occasionally be affected positively, such programs underscore the lack of fate control; for the poor had nothing to do with developing the program and have no recourse if it is suddenly taken from them.

This issue of representation from among those served deserves repeated emphasis in urban ministry. For many church social programs have failed simply because the poor were "turned off" by the fact that they were not even consulted by those who designed the programs. The efforts had a paternalistic "we know what's best for you" quality.

A plethora of programs for the poor—ranging from welfare to model cities, from Head Start to the Great Society—have suffered, at least in part, from this lack of representation and consultation. Again and again, compensatory programs are developed as a substitute for changing the distribution of power and opportunity in America.[1] Often these programs are not optional but are foisted on the target population. That is, the programs are not done *for,* but *to,* the poor. Powerlessness and insecurity are reaffirmed.

SOURCES OF INSECURITY

Inner-city residents are dependent, in the most literal sense of the term, on the political establishment. As a result, any change in municipal policy is extremely threatening. This is especially true because city services are in greater demand in slum communities than anywhere else. Such services include protection of property and life by the fire and police departments, legal aid, housing assistance, education, welfare, health care, and sanitation.

Fire Epidemics

One of the city services on which inner-city residents are dependent is the fire department. There is a tremendous fear of fire in the inner city. Poorly constructed project buildings, nonmaintained slum housing, and overcrowdedness, along with carelessness, a top-heavy youth population, and delinquency, contribute to the fire epidemic. If city officials become disenchanted with the community, they can retaliate by reducing the responsiveness of the fire fighters. The people are never able to control their own destiny with regard to fire safety.

Property Over Life

This issue of safety and protection leads directly to one of the greatest sources of insecurity for the poor: the American tendency to value property over life. Dating back to the genocide of the American

Indians, one can find striking examples of property superseding life in importance. People will firebomb homes into which minorities have moved if members of the resident population feel land values are in jeopardy. During the riot-torn sixties, mayors in major cities sent out a shoot-to-kill edict with regard to looters. One Chicago policeman tells the story of a squad car racing to the scene of a discount shoe store during a riot. The shoe store was one of those two-for-five-dollars establishments. As the car screeched to a stop, one of the officers observed a very small child inside, reaching for a probably much-needed pair of shoes. Quickly, in obedience to the shoot-to-kill order, he drew his gun, aimed it at the unsuspecting child, and pulled the trigger. The speeding bullet tore into the head of the child, killing her instantly. Only one example, to be sure. But when one considers all such edicts, and other examples of property protection such as the well-armed legions of security personnel who watch over condominiums and businesses and the quick response of the police to any burglary call in a more stable neighborhood, the property-over-life picture becomes rather clear.

Inner-city residents, however, have essentially no property, just life. Without property their lives are not worth much in the American economy. The result is a less-than-vigorous response by the police and other protective agencies to their needs. What is more likely to occur is that what little property they occupy will be taken from them.

Urban Renewal

There is always the ever-present fear of urban renewal, even where housing is adequate. Urban renewal is a euphemism for poor-people removal. What occurs is that a city marks off an area (much the way a bank redlines) and decides to refurbish the neighborhood. However, this refurbishment does not benefit the present inhabitants of the community, as many people believe; rather, the area is "cleaned out," meaning that the existing buildings are leveled and new construction occurs. This new construction is often in the form of structures that cater to the residential and economic interests of upper-middle-class entrepreneurs. Housing developments, shopping malls, and other commercial entities are erected, signaling radical change.

It is no accident that urban renewal almost invariably is embarked upon in highly desirable locations. As affluence moves closer to the border of an inner-city community, insecurity increases, because it reminds the residents that they are sitting on coveted property, property that may soon become urban-renewal land as a justification to seize it. The federal government, though not always in the absence of political pressure from local land barons and business tycoons, becomes more mindful of choice property on which the poverty community rests.

Sometimes these urban-renewal–type programs are called, curiously, "land reclamation." This is a most interesting term. When broken down, it simply states that the land is being reclaimed—of course without any consultation with those who presently have squatter's claim to it. It amounts to much the same as a one-time property owner, who has long since sold his house, coming back to the former dwelling, walking in, and "reclaiming" the dwelling. A seemingly outrageous analogy perhaps, but not so outrageous when one considers how cities, under political pressure from land barons, simply move in and take residential property from those who desperately need it.

Once underway, urban renewal simply means the mass exodus of poor people, who are given minimal help in finding housing elsewhere. Never mind that they may be further separated from their families, neighbors, churches, and perhaps even jobs; because they are renters, they simply have to move—without recourse, without any say or control in the matter.

School Desegregation

Almost the entire school desegregation problem is actually a real-estate issue. The life chances of inner-city children are being swapped for continued residential segregation in the city. Parents from a variety of ethnic backgrounds hold some very justifiable objections to busing, but there remain citizens who cling to rationales based on illusory "neighborhood school doctrine" (illusory because no legal provision anywhere affirms this notion) in order to keep nonwhites in particular and the poor in general from invading "their" turf. If desegregation occurs in education, according to the domino-theory reasoning of many, it will soon become a residential and perhaps even a marital reality.

Realizing that their children are unwelcome pawns in the desegregation tug-of-war increases the sense of lack of fate control among the poor. It is interesting that those most victimized by segregated education are rarely consulted or made a part of any official desegregation power front. They simply wait to see if the powers-that-be will act in accordance with the now-three-decades-old Supreme Court doctrine of equal and desegregated education for all.

In the seventies, much of the educational desegregation that did occur involved busing; more often than not, it was largely one-way busing. The children of the inner city got up an hour or so early to get on what they derisively referred to as the "cattle wagon" and be bused across the city into an alien community, knowing all along that they were not welcome there. Tension and defensiveness ran high in forcibly desegregated schools. There was a constant fear of disorder. The resident community feared angry outbursts by the minority students, while minority students, ever aware they were on alien ground, were in continuous fear of arbitrary discrimination in the form of low grades, unwarranted suspensions, or violence.

Sanitation and Health Care

City inspection and code enforcement is another arm inner-city residents must lean on. There are usually more rats than people in poverty areas.[2] Rat-bite fever, illnesses resulting from bites by rabies-infected dogs, and disease emanating from unsanitary living conditions are daily occurrences among the city poor. The best way to combat these illnesses is with improved sanitation, rather than with more health clinics. In fact, in Chicago, CAM (Christian Action Ministry) Academy demonstrated this when it embarked on a preventive program on Chicago's poor west side, aiming at rounding up stray dogs and other clean-up activities instead of inaugurating additional treatment centers.

The poor, however, do not have authority over the vigor of city inspectors and other officials who can make certain that living conditions are sanitary. They can only hope that people who occupy these important posts are people of good will.

Nothing seems to produce instant anxiety among Americans more than a threat to their health. Yet, in the inner city, where living conditions are optimally ripe for disease, health care is the poorest, both quantitatively and qualitatively. The poor do not have nearby hospitals, "family doctors," or health insurance to prevent financial devastation when facing a serious illness. Rather, they join the lines at the neighborhood health clinic to see the overworked and under-scheduled physician who is on duty; or if the crisis is particularly severe, they enter the hospital emergency room, where they are likely to receive quick and less-than-comprehensive diagnoses and treatments.[3]

In the mental health care field millions of Americans spend large sums of money receiving psychiatric treatment for sometimes even the mildest of behavior disorders. But in the inner city, where basic day-to-day living conditions assault the psyche, competent mental health care practitioners are in short supply. So, again, where problems in living are the most severe and help the most necessary, it is the least available.[4]

Welfare

The welfare system is among the most insidious of the insecurity bacteria. Lewis Coser provides a poignant description of the entire process, illustrating the indignity and humiliation to which the recipients are subjected.[5] A trip to any public aid office will quickly underscore this. Long lines of gloomy, pessimistic, and depressed poor wait like sheep as harried and overworked middle-class personnel cryptically dictate to them the rules of the system and what aid, if any, they qualify for.

Once on public aid, there are the visits of the case worker, visits that amount to thinly disguised attempts at "checking up" on the recipients to insure that they do not spend their money foolishly or violate the public aid code in some fashion. Personal autonomy and fate control are again destroyed as the poor take on a dependent and childlike status before the all-powerful social welfare system. The entire process, from application to reception, is seemingly designed to remind the recipients that they are unilaterally dependent on the welfare system because they are noncontributors to the society on whose dollars they depend. The upshot of this methodical degradation is to drain out of them what little optimism and positive self-feeling they may have had. It is little wonder that the poor shuffle along aimlessly from office to office of social service bureaucracies, with a look of desperation and defeat etched on their faces.

Moreover, any change in the nature of public aid—whether in the form of disability benefits, welfare, or unemployment compensation—is totally outside the control of those who are most dependent on it.

Inflation

Whether one is on welfare or not, there is insecurity with every increase in inflation. One of the main afflictions of the poor today, as opposed to those of decades past, is that in earlier days, the price structure was geared to the poor, since few Americans were affluent. Now prices are standardized at middle-class incomes. The result is that a bargain is a bargain only if one can afford it. If one is poor, there are no bargains. If even the middle class is revolting over sudden jumps in the cost of living, how much more are the urban poor affected. They fear sudden price jumps in food, rent, energy costs, and other essentials. There is no protection against such increases, because the jobs the poor hold do not carry with them wage increases commensurate with the rising costs of living.

Employment Problems

Employment problems, named as a top-level, inner-city concern by the National Advisory Commission on Civil Disorders, are also a source of insecurity. If a poor person has work, his job is most certainly one that is devoid of power, authority, and security. That means there is no pension, seniority, or protection against capricious dismissal or lay-off. Once a job is lost, things get worse. Rising unemployment and inflation rates make getting another job more and more difficult. If a job is obtained, it will be an unskilled job that will also be subject to the vagaries of the national economic cycle. If inflation thickens, the minimum wage rises, but if the company experiences a fiscal downturn, the job will be among the very first to dry up.

Police Brutality

Another city service on which residents depend is the police department. And yet police brutality is a routine occurrence in American cities.[6] This practice is not only written about by sociologists but is acknowledged by the police themselves. The report of the National

Advisory Commission on Civil Disorders placed this, along with housing deficiencies and employment problems, among the top three factors involved in bringing about riotous behavior.[7] Moreover, almost every major urban riot of the sixties was set off by an incident with the police.

Legal aid clinics are besieged with complaints about police harrassment. The Cabrini-Green Legal Aid Clinic in Chicago actually grew out of problems the community was having with the police. Some of the cases handled there illustrate sharply why the residents often quake in fear at the sight of the big blue police car. In one case, documented by court records, an angry group of police officers were dead set to hang a murder rap on Roy Harris. They needed witnesses to sign statements that Harris had done the killing. They found a very effective method. A neighborhood youth, who had witnessed the killing and who knew Harris was not involved, was confronted with a typed statement fingering Harris to which the police wanted him to sign his name. After he steadfastly refused to sign, an officer went to the closet in the already intimidating Interrogation Room and pulled out a shotgun. The shotgun was then held immediately about the youth's head while the shells were ejected, caroming off the skull of the already traumatized youth. He screamed, became hysterical, and signed the statement. Fortunately for Harris, the shakedown came out in a dramatic court scene. This contributed to his being exonerated.[8]

In another incident, a man named Arthur Scott was riding with a friend through the community. The driver was pulled over by the police for a minor traffic violation. The police did not, however, stop with the motorist, but did something they never do in middle-class communities. They demanded to know who the passenger was. Hearing his name, one of the officers exclaimed: "Arthur Scott! We have several warrants at the station instructing us to find and arrest Arthur Scott!" Scott was then unceremoniously carted away to jail. Being indigent, he was unable to get a lawyer and was simply left to vegetate in jail for weeks, awaiting the disposition of his case. It was very apparent, once his case was investigated, that he was not the Arthur Scott in question. He did not even remotely resemble the description of Scott in the station files. This was of no consequence to the police, who could have easily checked this matter at the time of arrest. Why? Because Arthur Scott was poor and powerless and apparently did not merit first-class justice.[9]

The principal reason why inner-city residents are so often victims of police brutality and insensitivity is that they have little status or importance in the prevailing social structure. And, what's more, they have no real power to redress their grievances. They pose absolutely no legal threat to the police. It is little wonder that so often poverty communities redress their grievances with an assassin's bullet. Unfortunately, that bullet may kill a caring policeman, one who genuinely sought to serve the community. The assassin, however, does not see the policeman as a person, because the police do not view him as a person either. He reacts to the uniform just as the insensitive officers react to him as a worthless slum dweller.

Bill Leslie, pastor of LaSalle Street Church, received a slum dweller's treatment firsthand. One evening, attired in a sweatshirt and old pants, Leslie was carrying some chairs out of the church. Suddenly a squad car pulled up, jackknifing his car in. The officers leaped out, grabbed Leslie, and flung him spreadeagle on the hood of his car. "Who are you and what are you doing?" they demanded angrily. "I am the pastor of that church," responded Leslie, pointing to the church sign. With immediate apologies, the police discontinued their rough-house tactics. "The altercation would never have occurred if I were wearing a suit and tie," explains the street-wise Leslie. "I could have carried anything out of that church I wanted."[10]

I have spent some time with police officers and have found among them those who are crude and bestial as well as those who are serious and sensitive members of society. No single stereotype accurately describes police personalities or behavior. One thing is certain, however. There is a bent toward aggressiveness and intimidation in low-income communities. Police will use verbal or physical strong-arm tactics to intimidate the inner-city resident. Many officers openly acknowledge this fact. Such intimidation breeds insecurity.

The police side of the picture is that inner-city communities are long on street crime and short on cooperation. Open disrespect for officers and even violence are key concerns. The cleavage or alienation between the police and the urban poor is deep. It becomes a chicken or egg dilemma: Are the police abusive, producing this lack of cooperation? Or are inner-city communities hostile, giving rise to police aggression? It is perhaps a bit of both. However, the police are enjoined to "serve and protect," and in poor communities, where there is the greatest need, there is the least service and protection given. Many sensitive officers abhor the overaggressive behavior of some of their colleagues, for brutality incites assassins and stimulates community bitterness. That bitterness is often not so much aimed at the police as at the entire society that has left the community powerless and insecure.[11]

Justice System Inequities

Contact with the police is only the beginning of the insecurity-producing American urban justice process. No matter how important or trivial the offense, the inner-city resident almost never has a legal defense. This almost certainly leaves him with the public defender system. Public defenders are usually hard-working, inexperienced, very competent, but hopelessly overworked lawyers. A public defender may handle as many as fifty cases in a single day. This allows absolutely no time for interviewing, research, investigation, and careful preparation of a defense. It usually results in plea bargaining.

Plea bargaining involves pleading guilty to a lesser crime contained within the one the individual was accused of. The American criminal justice system could not operate without it. It is a trade off. When the defendant plea bargains he gets a lesser sentence, while the prosecutor gets a conviction with minimum effort. Whether guilty of the initial charge or not, defendants will often eagerly accept a plea bargain, simply because it means that things will not go as badly for them as if they are found guilty. In addition, the public defender will often urge a plea bargain simply because going through the whole trial process is time consuming and it is very risky if one does not take time to investigate the case and prepare an adequate defense. What the inner-city resident is not always aware of, however, is that by plea bargaining, he has pleaded guilty to a crime of some sort and has acquired a record.

In the case of a felony charge, such as murder or armed robbery, for example, the situation is much more serious. Without an adequate defense, a person is likely to be found guilty. Public defenders do have some assistance to aid in the preparation of felony defenses, but again, plea bargaining often is the accepted route, as it is the safest. Even if the person is guilty, however, there still has been a denial of an adequate defense, something theoretically guaranteed all defendants in the American justice system. And if he is not guilty, he is still officially identified as a criminal.

The contrast between this procedure and justice for the rest of society is scandalous. First, middle-class crimes are often white-collar rather than street crime. White-collar crime is almost never aggressively investigated. Hence, the likelihood of a white-collar person being charged with an offense is remote.[12] However, when charged, the more well-to-do defendant immediately contacts "his" lawyer—just as he calls "his" physician when ill. That lawyer will most certainly be in private practice and will present a most formidable defense. No plea bargaining here, unless the client is obviously guilty and the conviction is sure.

In the cases of misdemeanors and drug charges, especially among teenagers, there is always the pay-off route. It is not at all uncommon for a poor woman, working as a domestic in a suburban home, to hear a father chuckle about how he beat a legal rap, or got his wild-oat-sowing teenager off, while she worries about what will happen to her son if he is apprehended for a curfew violation. More affluent juveniles may be objects of tremendous concern to their parents, but they are almost invariably protected from legal proceedings if only to guard the family name.[13]

The police are occasionally involved at this level too. Many an aware urban pastor knows of the ghastly practice of policemen demanding sex with welfare mothers in exchange for not pursuing the prosecution of an arrested teenager.[14]

If a defendant is found guilty, the socioeconomic background of the individual is again critical in determining the severity of the sentence. Called discretionary justice, there is the tendency for the judge to sentence on a case-by-case basis. Often it means that a middle-class person will be allowed to return to his community with a probationary sentence, while the inner-city convict is incarcerated because, in the judge's opinion, the domestic environment is not conducive to rehabilitation. Whether this assessment of recidivism is accurate or not, it means preferential treatment based on social status.[15]

This is not even an adequate introduction to the inequities endemic in the American justice system. The problems are so severe that a President's Commission Report very nearly condemned the entire system for its extreme bias in favor of the rich.[16] Recently, with a cutback of funding for the Legal Services Corporation—a very helpful program instituted in the sixties to aid the poor particularly in civil matters—things appear to be getting worse. In any case, it is a brief glimpse into one of the greatest sources of insecurity in inner-city life.

Add to these the powerlessness of the poor in education, government, institutionalized religion, recreation, and the other spheres discussed in the previous chapter, and the insecurities and paranoias experienced by the urban poor are easily understood. In short, they emanate from the fact that "the system" was not designed for them and does not work for them.

RESPONSES AND ATTITUDES

The poor respond to this insecurity in a variety of ways. That response is seen both in lifestyle and in overall attitudes. Lee Rainwater suggests, in a somewhat oversimplified way, three lifestyle strategies common among the urban poor.[17] The first is an expressive lifestyle. This is a flashy style, which externally denies poverty. It may include gaudy dress, a financed car, and other material props to support the joking, impulsivity, and spontaneity at the core of this mode. Often, this expressiveness gives rise to drunkenness, drug addiction, and sexual promiscuity in an effort to appear "cool" and stylish.

Second, failure of this mode can bring on a strategy of violence. This unpopular, fear-producing activity in which others are forced to meet the needs of the poor person, is adopted out of desperation and out of rage with the hopelessness and degradation of poverty. The inhabitants of the inner city, though not pleased about it, accept violence as an inevitable ingredient in urban poverty existence. Murder, muggings, teacher and student assault, and gang conflicts are regular occurrences. For urban church workers, coping with violence is often the most difficult psychological adjustment.

Finally, there is the depressive strategy, which involves scaling down one's goals to the level of necessities and adopting a live-and-let-live, don't-bother-me-and-I-won't-bother-you attitude. Essentially a defeatist strategy, it insures against further disappointment and heartache. This strategy is common among older poor, whose spirit has been pretty well broken under the yoke of poverty.

As Rainwater suggests, some adjust passively to the messages of inferiority emanating out of poverty, low educational attainment, and joblessness, while others will challenge any bearer of the putdown.

Regardless of response or lifestyle strategy, coping in order to survive is the main issue. Survival may be achieved creatively.

Youngsters learn how to survive summer heat by cracking open fire hydrants, and winter cold by starting small fires. They use every conceivable method to "get over" in school. They are ingenious in petty theft of candy and material things. They try to dupe the police at every opportunity and they verbally put down authority with smart remarks as a necessary weapon in their arsenal for psychological survival.

Responses to insecurity are found not only in a lifestyle strategy and creative coping but also in attitudes. Poverty conditions and personality and, hence, certain attitudes are likely to be particularly common among the poor.

Localism. There is often a sense of localism—an apprehensiveness concerning the unfamiliar. Many urban youth have never been more than twenty-five blocks from their homes by the time they are in the sixth grade. Adults do not take vacations or go on business trips. Hence, the urban turf is the only familiar element. Suggestions for change and new experiences are often rejected, partly because of this localism. From a pastoral standpoint, it is important that ministries be rooted in the urban enclave to minimize responses issuing out of uncertainty.

Little Respect for Authority. There is often little respect for authority figures. Societal authority is peculiarly heavy-handed in low-income areas and almost never works to benefit the poor. In essence, middle-class authority tends to hold the poor "in their place" to insure that the status quo—favorable to the middle class—is protected. Experiences with the police are commonly so bad that the alienation emanating from police-public interaction permeates relationships with virtually every other authority figure.[18]

It is almost impossible to overestimate the degree of hostility that issues out of the experience of the urban poor with the police. In short, they view the police as a militia commissioned to patrol their areas to keep them under surveillance—and under control. While cases of police brutality are legion and well documented, the police realize that the highest rates of street crime occur in low-income communities and so they are "under the gun" to maintain order. This mandate to maintain order—as opposed simply to enforce the law—generates rather aggressive activities on the part of the police.[19] The psychology of fear and force predominate.[20] Fear and force produce insecurity and therefore hostility and retaliation—as the number of policemen murdered in poor neighborhoods testifies. The result is often more intimidation and an even greater devotion to maintaining control.

The bottom line is alienation, and this alienation and distrust soon invade attitudes toward any authority figures, whether they are policemen, firemen, teachers, social workers, or pastors.

Hatred. There is often a heavy dose of hate in the hearts of many poor. Martin Luther King is said to have spent the first few hours each of the many times he was imprisoned praying for deliverance from the bitterness he felt. If a man of King's character required divine intervention to overcome resentment, it is little wonder that many of those who live at society's bottom are filled with vengefulness. With every shred of American institutional life reminding them of what they do not have, it cannot be any different.

Moreover, this hate is fed by fear. It is often a defensive hatred, growing out of the fear of not surviving, of receiving the ultimate putdown in the form of academic failure, unemployment, psychological devastation, or a policeman's bullet. Because it is invariably an authority figure who delivers this knockout punch, there is a great potential for hatred.

Pessimism. Above and beyond everything else, the poor bear a heavy strain of hopelessness and pessimism. This is to be expected, for nothing in their lives has worked. The American Dream has been just that—a dream. Politicians give out promises but rarely deliver on them; and the community has remained poor as long as any of its inhabitants can remember. As a result, even when opportunities do present themselves, the people may be held back by pessimism. There is every desire to avoid yet another disappointment—an additional letdown.

Urban workers quickly discover these fundamental psychological responses and have to develop a great deal of patience and empathy if these barriers are ever to be penetrated and the people ministered to.

SENSITIVE MINISTRY

Ministering in the midst of this insecurity is a delicate task. It requires, above all, *awareness.* Any change must be presented with the people's background, both social and psychological, in mind. Tragically, so many well-intended programs and ministries have failed for lack of this awareness. They are presented from an alien world-and-life-view.

A theoretical example might be helpful. Suppose you were a reading expert and were able to teach anyone of reasonable intelligence how to read in the space of four weeks. Because you realize that literacy is closely tied to occupational success, you decide to open a reading clinic in a nearby poverty area. You rent out a room and offer reading instruction each Monday night for an hour, assuring the populace through your advertising that within four weeks they will be able to read. The first Monday night finally arrives and you are poised to deliver on your promise. No one shows up. Not a single soul comes to this free reading clinic, put together entirely at your expense to teach this absolutely necessary literacy skill. You have two alternatives: Either you can go home angry and embittered, or you can analyze why there were no takers. A bit of thought should reveal quite easily a variety of reasons why no one has come.

If your advertising was in print, it was probably useless, since the people cannot read the signs anyway. For those who are aware of your clinic, a number of deterrents confront them. At night some may fear walking the streets to your location. For those who work full-time during the day there is inevitable evening fatigue. Those with children are held back either because there are no babysitters or simply because they feel they should spend this time with their children.

But what of those not encumbered by any of these problems? For many of them, there is skepticism. How can anyone teach them to read in four weeks when they did not learn after ten or twelve years of formal education? The idea seems even more preposterous than many undelivered political promises. There is also the embarrassment and self-consciousness many feel of going into a clinic like this and admitting to a strange middle-class person that they are ignorant and need to be taught something so basic as the ability to read. This process of self-abasement is for some the most difficult barrier of all.

In addition, the whole literacy issue is an abstraction for many in the inner city. What these unemployed, would-be students need is a job, not reading skills. Although reading and employment are closely related, knowledge of this relationship is middle-class knowledge; the inhabitants of the poverty community lack any firsthand examples or models of people who were able to parlay reading skills into occupational success. If the reading expert could guarantee a job for every graduate, the rented room would likely be too small to accommodate the throng. However, simply offering the skill of reading is not enough—people see themselves struggling with bread-and-butter rather than reading-and-writing issues.

The foregoing example is not intended to discourage ministry creation or program development. Its purpose is to underscore the importance of serious reflection and careful planning in offering innovations.

An urban pastor will likely confront less than an accepting response from many poor parishioners. The skepticism of the poor, who have been promised to, preached at, and experimented on without significant improvement in their quality of life, is very understandable. Many will view a new urban pastor as a temporary prop who will soon be gone. Few urban workers—ministers, social workers, school teachers, or whoever—last long. After spending a frustrating year or two, they pack their bags and head for less stressful environments, taking their ideals with them. All that is left behind is the suffering population they attempted to serve. After witnessing untold numbers of well-intentioned middle-class professionals come and go, the poor are not likely to get very excited at the outset over new programs or goals.

Knowledge of the sources of insecurity and awareness of the attitudes of his poor parishioners will provide a basis for the urban pastor's ministry. What other ingredients are necessary for a sensitive, effective ministry?

Listening. It is important that each individual be accepted as a person. Operationally, this means that instead of stereotyping an individual as poor or handling him bureaucratically, the urban worker will care about the individual's feelings and will listen attentively to his needs. Listening and caring of any genuine sort is in short supply in an urban poverty community. All too many urban workers, besieged with seemingly endless multitudes of problem-ridden clients, feel forced to find quick solutions for any one individual's problems. A pastor has a calling to minister to whole persons, and therefore listening and resonating with the feelings of groups and individuals becomes a vital aspect of urban ministry. It is the difference between dealing with clients and ministering to persons.

Identifying and Suffering. Listening and caring develops the ability to identify with the people's needs and experiences. Empathy in the form of putting oneself mentally in the shoes of those he serves is vital; for once the worker identifies, he knows how to care, how to act, and even how to avoid being manipulated. Identification entails the ability to see the situation through the eyes of the other. This requires reading, reflecting, and listening. Identifying is a process rather than an event and so it will not come quickly. Almost any urban worker who has been reared in the middle class will find this difficult at first. But it is a necessary skill. Moreover, once the worker can identify, the poor quickly notice it, and he becomes one of them—a person they trust.

What is often the bottom line of effective ministry is the willingness not only to identify with but to suffer with a victimized community. This suffering is also a process rather than an event. Simply rushing in with the gospel of Christ, where other pastors have feared to tread, often leaves the impression that the pastor is more interested in proselytizing than serving, in winning followers than ministering.

Active Caring. Care must be active. In their epistles both James and John point to the ludicrousness of inactive caring, upbraiding those Christians who do not shelter those who are cold but simply wish them God's blessing (James 2:14–17; 1 John 3:17–18). Doing something is of the utmost importance. Therefore, when the urban pastor is confronted with a need, the desire to act on it should become an almost reflexive response.

Facilitating. Active caring does not necessarily mean *doing* for the person; rather, it usually means *thinking* of problem-solving ways that can be effective for the person in need. In many cases, the individual can enact these by himself, but he has not done so, simply because he is not aware of his options.

This engages the issue of facilitation. Wherever possible, it is helpful to devise strategies that enable people to be active in solving their own problems. It develops a sense of fate control and self-responsibility on the part of those who can. If a pastor only *does* for others, he risks both burning himself out and also creating unhealthy dependencies on the part of his parishioners. Realistic expectations for parishioner action are always appropriate. It is important, however, that they be realistic in the context of the inner city, rather than the middle-class milieu from which the pastor may have come.

It is also wise to develop participatory programs, that is, ministries in which the parishioners have a direct stake and responsibility.

This should not be overdone, such that unrealistic expectations are made, or genuine expertise sacrificed; but whenever reasonable, it is valuable to have people gain self-determination.

It is important, in this regard, that any and all church programs take into account the reactions and feelings likely to be elicited in the community by them. This can be done preferably by bringing inner-city residents in at the planning stage.

Reciprocity. In addition to helping his parishioners, it is important that a pastor ask his parishioners to help him as well, even in such practical ways as babysitting or repairing his car. Openness to being helped is often every bit as much a ministry in the inner city as openness to helping others. Mutuality builds relationships, trust, and respect. Kindness, openness, and appropriate vulnerability can go a long way in developing a sound relationship with the community. Being open and vulnerable humanizes the pastor, removes him from an ecclesiastical pedestal, and makes him part of the community. Praying for others is important, but asking for their prayers is equally important. A major enemy of pastors everywhere is social and psychological isolation. A major deterrent to such isolation is to open with discretion one's personhood to the persons one is serving.

Community Involvement. Showing respect for and encouraging involvement in neighborhood and community organizations is a way of combating the sense of victimization felt in inner-city communities. Often there are organizations that lack only a large, active membership to be effective. Attending meetings and encouraging others to attend may eventually bring about greater organizational stability and, ultimately, effectiveness.[21]

Although the use of the church facilities for civic meetings, discussions, and other public activities may cause some to see the church as endorsing a given point of view, it is important to model involvement and response in the community. The church does not have to compromise its spiritual mission to do this. Rather, it witnesses to the church's belief that organizing and planning strategies in a community are constructive ways to confront institutional problems. However, if the pastor in the church does not show *active* concern for the obvious afflictions of the community and the need for addressing them, it will be extraordinarily difficult for him to minister to people's souls with the gospel.

Again, there need be no compromising with ministering to spiritual needs and bringing lives to Christ by opening up on the other fronts. If the church's objectives and priorities are clear, other activities need not interfere with spiritual ministry. Instead, they are examples of a whole-person ministry which, of course, can augment receptiveness to spiritual concerns.

Showing Respect. Of greatest import of all in dealing with this reality-based insecurity is to evince respect for the human worth of each person. It is important that the dignity of each parishioner be carefully guarded. At the root of most oppression of the poor is a form of psychological assault and degradation—the insensitive, who-cares-because-you-are-nothing-anyway treatment they receive from bureaucrats. Even the sensitive and caring pastor may convey a patronizing notion that superior education and experience make him and his perceptions most valuable. If his perceptions are better, they should be so by their very own worth rather than on the basis of whose they are.

The reader may notice the absence of concrete examples of ministries to deal with the insecurity syndrome. That ought not to be surprising, for insecurity is a psychological, rather than a concrete or structural, phenomenon. It does, however, arise from institutional injustices. Therefore, on the surface, insecurity may be best dealt with through respectful and affirmative human relations. But, at a deeper level, modeling involvement and organizational activity, in addition to confronting the real problems of powerlessness discussed in earlier chapters, must occur in fighting the battle on larger turf.

6 | Youth

By percentage, youth constitute a major sector of almost any inner-city community because of the plethora of single-parent families with large numbers of children. Because youth are in such great numbers in the inner city, the topic merits special attention.

Almost every church has some sort of youth program. An awareness of the dynamics of the youth subculture in the inner city can be of value in developing effective programs.

ATTITUDES AND BEHAVIORS

At least partly because of limited parental supervision and an absence of constructive recreational alternatives, the youth in most poverty areas take on certain common attitudes and behaviors. These include a limited amount of time spent in the home; lack of appreciation for time-oriented routines; involvement in gangs, drugs, and sex; and lack of future orientation.

An instructive experience for the uninitiated is to drive through an inner-city neighborhood relatively late in the evening. What will amaze many is the number of children—even small children—playing out on the street well after dark. Some of this street-centeredness can be accounted for by a vacuum in parental attention, but much of it results from a lack of playthings and an overcrowded apartment.

When youngsters are not on the street, they may stay up late watching television and sleep well into the morning. This late-to-bed, late-to-rise syndrome desensitizes them to the notion of a time-oriented routine. Lacking adult work models (40 percent of Chicago public school children are from welfare families), youth find it difficult to develop an appreciation for dependability in work and time. This is not to suggest that their parents do not work in their domestic roles, but rather that this type of work is not congruent with the kind of demand expected in the employment market at large.

As a consequence of this limited contact with parents and other adults, along with the absence of success models, a peer culture develops. The peer group—greatly influenced by the usual youth-oriented appeals of thrills, excitement, and new experiences—develops its own code of conduct. Often this code places great emphasis on group loyalty and camaraderie; lone wolves become rather unpopular and even objects of harassment.

Gangs

In many urban neighborhoods, youth organize themselves into gangs. Gangs provide the adolescents with a sense of identity and belonging as well as a network through which opportunities and excitement can be shared. Many of these gangs are not violent to any appreciable extent, but they will become so if a member of a rival gang "picks on" one of their own members.

One feature of gangs is the establishing of turf boundaries. This turf boundary phenomenon is fascinating. Some years ago in a Chicago poverty community in which gang-consciousness was heavy, one of the neighborhood high school students was developing a very peculiar academic record. In all but one of his courses he excelled and received superior grades. However, in the remaining course he was obviously failing partly through excessive absences. There seemed to be no academic accounting for this anomaly. However, on closer examination it was determined that he was a member of one of several gangs in the high school and that gang awareness and competition were so acute that different areas within the high school were considered the property or turf of certain gangs. Unfortunately, one of the student's classes happened to meet on the turf of a rival gang, and rather than incur violence, he felt it wiser to accept academic failure.[1]

Admittedly, this is an extreme example, and in many cities aggressive gang activity has lessened. However, in any inner-city community, these alliances in the form of gangs and their structures, whether violent or not, do keep the allegiance of their members. Thus, this gang orientation is extremely important for church workers to understand, for it explains why one youth simply will not cooperate with another in a recreational activity or why some youth avoid "trespassing" on other areas in the community.

A second feature of gang involvement is the tendency to elevate collective gang values and depress the more individual, competitive values. For many youngsters, the gang or clique is the primary source of acceptance, attention, and identity, so a youth's stature in the group and integration into its activities and interests are vital. The notion of the non-conformist or "individual" is not very prevalent in the inner city.

Third, the gang structure itself militates against educational excellence. Whenever adolescents run up against a challenge too formidable for them, they tend to reject and belittle that challenge as not meaningful for them. In that vein, school in general and academics in particular are disparaged in the streets. The compensatory behavior often takes the form of gang activity, in which turf is ruled and others are manipulated. School can be a frightening experience for many youngsters, as often school gangs extract "protection money" from those who are not members of a gang in exchange for not being attacked or harassed on the way to school.

There is power in knowledge. However, if one does not possess book knowledge—the type that can be translated into success in occupational pursuits—gaining power on the streets through fear and intimidation is an appealing alternative. Power and influence are very attractive to inner-city youth. Thus the fourth feature of the gang is that it provides a mode through which to obtain power and influence.

Among the most cherished forms of power is gang leadership. In some gangs this is still determined through physical prowess, aggressiveness, combativeness, and toughness; in others the leader is simply the most persuasive or perhaps the oldest or most affluent member. In any case, with leaderhip come power and a sense of autonomy. Although there can be only one leader in the gang, all the members feel his power and admire his influence. Other members will frequently seek power in other ways, for example, by excelling in activities approved by the gang.

As the leader gains power through fear and intimidation, he

nonetheless shows a careful awareness of how the judicial system operates. In many gangs the fifteen- and sixteen-year-olds do the shakedowns because the gang leaders realize that seventeen-year-olds can be tried as adults if apprehended by the police. The victims of these shakedowns can be anyone, from children going to school, to shopkeepers who are ordered to come up with cash to ward off arson and vandalism, to senior citizens whose money may be taken as they leave a currency exchange after cashing their social security checks.

This careful awareness of the operation of the judicial system illustrates once more the highly developed survival orientation operating among urban youth. For a middle-class youngster, survivial consists of succeeding in school, going to college, and then landing an economically rewarding job. In fact, if a middle-class youth does not do well in school and at least go to college, he is often regarded as a failure. This can be very oppressive; a student once pointed out that whereas the poor are often denied opportunity for success, the more affluent youth do not have the right to fail. In any case, survival is equated in the suburbs with educational and occupational success, but in the inner city survival has a much different, close-to-the-bone quality.

Drugs

In the absence of other recreational outlets, there is a tendency among inner-city adolescents to become involved with drugs. Marijuana is as common as cigarettes in many inner cities, and, of course, a large number of adolescents look for something more powerful. The inner city is a haven for drug pushers, many of whom get their supply from someone outside the area and then sell to youth ranging in age from thirteen to twenty-five. Addiction rates are high as the power of the peer culture and its favorable view of drug involvement provides an optimum psychological setting for "getting hooked." Younger students are occasionally started by a pusher who simply laces candy with a powerful drug and gives it to the youngsters in the washrooms of the schools.[2]

The whole process can be seen as a cycle of victimization. The pusher is often someone who is himself an addict and is unable to get or hold a job. He rationalizes his pushing with the belief that if he weren't doing it, someone else would. The intense desire of the restless, excitement-starved youth draws other community youngsters into drug experimentation. At first the drug experience provides an exciting, boredom-breaking alternative to the usual forms of entertainment. Often beginning with mild drugs, youth are pressured by the peer group for higher-level experimentation and some become addicted to the "biggie"—heroin—while others top off on drugs of lesser potency. Drugs are expensive, and their costliness makes them all the more attractive. As a result, mugging, stealing, prostitution, lower-level drug pushing, and various forms of petty crime are engaged in to raise the necessary funds.

The police, with a mandate from both within and outside the community, become the chief adversaries as they work to break up the drug rings and kill the drug supply. Whenever there is a giant drug bust, non–drug-using veterans of inner-city life are ambivalent. On one hand, they rejoice over the cleansing effect such a bust might have; on the other, they realize street crime is likely to escalate because the bust will place drugs in short supply and raise the price necessary for purchase.[3]

This is not to say that all inner-city adolescents are drug involved. Nor is drug involvement limited to the inner city—it is a national trend. What is important is that drug activity is apparent, and whether a youth or his gang is involved or not, inner-city youngsters are products of an environment in which the devastating effects of drug addiction and pushing are a significant part.

Sex

As it is elsewhere in the society, sex is free and cheap in the inner city. Ever aware of adult street realities, urban young people thirst for adult pleasures, especially in the absence of the usual middle-class recreational outlets. For males, sexual conquests are measures of achievement and fathering a child is a sign of manhood. For females, sex and especially giving birth—in or out of wedlock—affirms desirability and maturity in an atmosphere in which there is little positive reinforcement. For females, who do not have the gang opportunities available to males, there is particular pressure. They tend to be regarded as sex objects to be used for physical pleasures. Although they long for more genuine forms of love, sexual attention provides some compensatory value.

Despite high levels of sexual activity, there is often an appalling lack of knowledge about biological and reproductive systems. It is not uncommon for a poor teenager to believe that pregnancy occurs only when one is in love with one's sexual partner.[4]

The illegitimacy rate among teenage girls has been rising. This stems not only from a lack of knowledge about reproduction but also in part from the absence of birth-control information and practice. Because of the high value placed on children among many poor, abortion is not a popular alternative. (This is an important point, for abortion is common among youth elsewhere in the society. The higher rate of illegitimate births creates the illusion that premarital sexual activity is much more prevalent among the poor than among other classes. Though there may be a difference, the difference is probably not as great as it appears.)[5]

The high rate of illegitimacy is also related to a desire for companionship, love, and a feeling of importance. For many poor girls, having a child is a sign of womanhood, and a child may provide needed intimacy as well as relief from the loneliness and isolation that poverty brings.

Lack of Future Orientation

One effect of having children is limiting future life options, especially for the unwed mother. However, poor youth place no greater value on future orientation than their elders do. The reasons for this are obvious. If the past is any indicator, the future holds little promise. The intense focus on present-day survival makes looking to the future a luxury only the more affluent can afford. And, again, inner-city youth just do not have contact with adults who have successfully practiced deferred gratification. Some inner-city residents have used future-focusing for advancement; the problem, however, is that their success has taken them out of the community and removed them as a model for the next generation. For many, the issue is nitty-gritty physical survival—today, not tomorrow or next year.

This lack of future orientation is illustrated in the case of a fifteen-year-old girl who was truant on a regular basis. On examination it was determined that she was making a very lucrative living as a prostitute, bringing in about five hundred dollars per week. When confronted with her truancy by the high school principal, the girl pointed out that school didn't pay; after all, she was making money comparable to that of the principal who was administrating the school. The principal's response was in the form of a question: "What will happen in ten years, when your flesh will no longer be fresh and salable?" The young prostitute had never projected ahead that far.[6]

Ministry to inner-city youth must take into account these attitudes and behaviors when planning programs—limited contact with parents or any successful adult models; absence of constructive recreational alternatives to gang involvement, drugs, and sex; and lack of time-oriented routines and of future orientation. Underlying all these traits the urban worker will be sensitive to the youths' needs for positive reinforcement and genuine caring and love.

GUIDELINES FOR MINISTRY

For those developing urban youth ministries there are a number of guidelines. These include focusing on groups, developing attractive programs, establishing expectations and accountability, and showing personal care for the individual.

Group and Family Focus

Formally educated people tend to prefer working with individuals— one-on-one. Counseling and many evangelistic efforts take that form. Although this may be effective with many youth, it is less effective with lower-income blacks, Appalachian whites, and Hispanics. Youth in these ethnic groups live in a clan culture and hence do not respond favorably to isolation. Thus, working with a group, preferably in a family context, is much more fruitful. There is scriptural precedent for this group approach. In John 4, Christ offered a spiritual decision for the woman at the well along with her family.

It is important to emphasize that all phases of a youth-ministry program should be conducted within the context of the family situation. This is consistent with the clan culture of the inner city. The vast majority of parents at least verbally subscribe to the goals and Christian values of the program; so their aid in encouraging their children, working with them, and/or assisting in the program is invaluable. If the mother is opposed, the effort will be quickly harpooned. The mother is one of the few constants, one of the few sources of care and love to the urban adolescent, and so she becomes central to the carrying out of the ministry. When adherence to a program's goals and roles is supported by the parent(s) and other family members present, there is a powerful added impetus toward opening the mind and heart of the youth to the ministry.

Young Life programs in various cities focus on working with entire gangs. In addition, a child who shows interest in the Young Life programs is often interviewed with his parent(s) so that the home can reinforce what the Young Life program is seeking to develop. Where individual attention is desirable, it is offered. But because the program has a group focus, the youth is not surrounded by outsiders attempting to change him. He is instead given acceptance and affirmation as a base from which to explore other spiritual and social realities.

Attractive Programs

Whether the program is as individualized as tutoring or becomes as broad-based as Young Life, it is important that it be attractive. Without attractive aspects of the program, there is absolutely no point in going any further. There is no inner-city tradition of going to church for abstract ventures into catechism and church doctrine. As important as this type of learning is, it has to be packaged in ways that appeal to the youngsters. Therefore, the urban youth worker must ask: What do I have to offer that will attract and appeal to youth at their level? Such programs may need to include tickets to major (especially sporting) events, campouts, and other excursions.

Reasonable Expectations

After an attractive program has been designed, the next step concerns the price the youth is willing to pay to be a part of it. This is a vital step, for if there is no responsibility incurred in involvement, the program loses its appeal. Moreover, a clear expectation for the youth not only enhances the look of the ministry, but also builds in a sense of accountability and reinforces a sense of "I can" self-concept— matters of significant import to inner-city youth. It is especially helpful if this expectation is in the form of a contract signed by the youth and his parent(s), for this gives it a sense of seriousness and dignity and will reduce the likelihood of "conning" and reneging on a verbal agreement.

The contract must have reasonable provisions that can be lived up to. In addition, it must be adhered to by each party. This again supports a fate-control orientation and makes the youth a responsible participant in the program. Dave Mack and Steve Pedigo, two veteran Chicago Young Life leaders, use the contract method with inner-city youth. One example from their experience involves an out-of-state camping trip. In order to be a part of the expedition, all Young Life members were required to attend a Monday night meeting. At the meeting they were told they must have a physical along with a permission form signed by their parent(s). Failure to comply with any of the foregoing automatically removed the youth from being eligible to participate in the camping trip. To be sure, some youngsters tested the limits by failing to comply. The rules, much to their surprise and chagrin, were enforced. The youth were not tossed out of the Young Life program as a whole, nor were they scolded, harassed, or preached at for not complying; they were simply and courteously informed that they could not go along with the rest of the group on the camping trip—maybe next year.

The expectations must be attainable so that no one has to fail. The youth can choose to drop out by not complying, but the program itself drops no one. It simply adheres to its "constitution." If the youth feel the program fails them rather than that they have opted to fail by not discharging their responsibilities, they will sense a strain of arbitrariness about it and become skeptical or even rebel against it. Nevertheless, this gentle, no-nonsense approach is highly effective for use in any attractive program.

Personal Care and Communication

Although the larger focus is on the group, there must be room for quality time with individuals. Listening to, conversing with, and caring for individual youngsters who respond to the ministry is essential. This can be done on an informal basis or in a very flexibly scheduled format. Important focal points in dealing on the individual level include finding out what a youth's life is like; how he feels about school; what his family life is like; how he resonates with the youth program; what, if any, life goals he may have; what recreational interests he has; who his friends are; and so forth. It must be remembered that inner-city adolescents often have few, if any, adults who show a genuine interest in their life as they live and experience it. A serious, nonpatronizing approach to them, by a concerned adult, is potentially very effective.

It is likely that many will attempt to con the adult who evinces such interest in order to test his sincerity. An urban church worker's character and commitment will most surely be tested. There is a tremendous desire to determine whether a person "is for real." The tests may be frequent and repetitious. But, once the test is passed, there is real potential for growth and relationship.

If there has been an effective demonstration of individual dealing and interest, a relationship of some quality and permanence is likely to result. It is through this communication and relationship that everything from evangelism to educational aid can be carried out. Without total, personal care and involvement, evangelism smacks of notches on a gunbelt. However, once a youth feels he is genuinely associated with an adult he respects and who cares about him, all facets of his being are open. When openness occurs, it is critical that no exploitation take place. Such abuse will be quickly spotted and cut off further ministry. At all points the youth's dignity must be protected. He must respond to the church's love just as the individual Christian responds to God's love.

In this atmosphere of personal care and communication, a youth's values can be challenged. In the earlier example of the high school principal's dealing with a young prostitute, the principal opted against lecturing the girl but instead used questions to challenge her values. Questions are almost invariably more successful with inner-city youth than declarative statements, for they carry a sense of respect for the dignity and worth of the other whereas sermons tend to make objects out of their intended audience. It is often the difference between an expression of authoritarianism and a genuine demonstration of interest in the youth's perceptions.

The key to inner-city youth ministry is unconditional love. This no-strings-attached love, however, must be both gentle and tough. If it is not gentle, it is not loving and caring in an environment devoid of much love and care. If it has no tough side, it becomes patronizing and can easily be undercut by con artists who will only scorn their gullible targets. Too soft an approach may also create unhealthy dependency and a lack of growth. Quality, caring love and involvement is time-consuming but enormously effective, for any real self-giving, agape love exists only in the abstract for many inner-city youth.

MODELS OF MINISTRY

This final section illustrates the kinds of attractive programs that have been effectively used in urban youth ministries. Two national groups have been active in various cities—the Youth Guidance program of Youth for Christ and Young Life. The final example is drawn from a successful youth ministry developed by an individual church—the LaSalle Street Church in Chicago—in conjunction with Young Life.

Youth Guidance

The Youth for Christ Youth Guidance program provides an excellent model of urban youth ministry.[7] The objective of the program is to offer hope to troubled youth and their families by developing personal relationships and engaging in whole-person ministry.

One of the focal points of the Youth Guidance ministry is neighborhood outreach. This involves a service ministry of helping to meet immediate needs as well as a stewardship effort of working with community organizations. One of the ministries is a self-employment program in which job skills are taught. In some cases youth are employed in a Youth Guidance business such as landscaping or repair work to develop a positive work record that will enable them to enter the outside labor market.

Another emphasis is juvenile institutional ministry. Here staff and volunteers work with juvenile institutions in developing relationships with youngsters who have delinquency problems. Youth Guidance also offers pregnancy counseling to unwed teenagers. In addition, Youth Guidance has a big brother–big sister type of program in which workers develop in-depth relationships with troubled teens. This program also includes a foster home referral service that places urban youth in Christian foster settings after they have been ministered to by staff and volunteers.

Youth Guidance is a large, national program, involving two hundred full-time staff and a thousand volunteers annually. Youth

Guidance works with sixteen thousand youth each year in seventy cities, including Houston, Los Angeles, Philadelphia, Detroit, Atlanta, and Miami.

Young Life

Successful urban ministries have also been carried on by Young Life in various cities. As mentioned earlier, the focus is on working with groups. The Young Life ministry offers interesting recreational opportunities for youngsters, such as winter ski retreats, trips to summer resorts, basketball leagues in the communities, appealing social functions, and a host of other attractive options. There is also evangelistic activity, but it is of a very low-key variety. It seeks values clarification and confrontation with certain spiritual realities that point to the meaning of Christ in an individual's life. [8]

In order for a teenager to be accepted into the Young Life program, he signs a contract with the leader that binds him to certain low-level, basic, and eminently reasonable demands. In addition, the parent(s) agrees to the contract as well. In this way, certain basic expectations are communicated, such as regular attendance and abiding by the stated rules for each activity. The parent(s) is usually overjoyed about the Young Life option, as it is a constructive antidote to delinquent activity on the street. This gives the Young Life leadership a bit of leverage with the youth for bringing about constructive behavior.

LaSalle Street Church

On an individual church level, LaSalle Street Church in Chicago has a rather successful youth-ministry program. Its effectiveness is the result of much experience in Cabrini-Green, a great deal of work, much trial-and-error effort, and plenty of failure. Associated with the Young Life program in Chicago, it has a staff of paid workers as well as volunteers. Some of the staff are graduates of the program and live in Cabrini-Green. Indigenous leadership is extraordinarily valuable, for these people not only develop powerful lines of communication with youngsters in the program but also function as models for them right in the neighborhood.

The LaSalle program has four major goals: to develop disciples of Christ who can function as Christians in any environment, to help youth develop a positive and accurate self-image, to cultivate skills and abilities, and to enlarge the vision of the youth and supply motivation. It is important to note that the ministry does not simply seek quick, shallow Christian commitments in the absence of growth. Rather, it looks to disciple the new Christians—to build a whole-person relationship with the youth that will enable them to live out Christian values in a vital Christian relationship no matter what their immediate life context.

Discipling inner-city youth is a very challenging task and must be undertaken with tremendous patience. At LaSalle the youth do not have to make a Christian commitment to be a part of the "club." They merely have to abide by the contract and attend regularly.

Club consists of recreational activity and personal and group involvement. One night a week there is an evangelistic activity. It takes the form of values clarification, Bible study, and sharing who Christ is in the lives of the leaders and how Christ is a motivation for the entire program. Augmented by frequent trips, basketball leagues, and camping opportunities, this low-key evangelistic approach has brought about a large number of Christian commitments from the youth.

Not all the youth make a genuine Christian commitment, but those who do are carefully and caringly discipled in the Bible studies and by personal contact, so that they can grow to spiritual maturity. The Bible studies emphasize application to daily life. They are practical and life-focused. Urban youth live from crisis to crisis and are best equipped spiritually when the Scriptures help them evaluate and act on each crisis.

The discipling process is carried on through dialogue and interaction. Preaching and other didactic techniques are discarded in favor of relating and discussing. The aim is to aid the youth in seeing alternatives to the street values—to open minds and enlarge perspectives. This is best accomplished by encouraging open expression of thoughts and ideas orally or in writing. Every effort is made at establishing candid exchanges and overt reflecting in order to bring about the greatest interpersonal impact. This relational method is a mutually beneficial activity, one that enhances the leaders' ministry as they learn more fully what is going on in the minds and hearts of those with whom they minister. The gospel must have credibility, and such credibility is best attained if the methods of communicating it are honorable and open—and above all, nonmanipulative.[9]

The second major goal is to help youth develop a positive and accurate self-image. Despite the bravado and rebellion so common among inner-city youth, there is often a sense of inferiority underneath. They live in a society in which they are disliked and degraded and they know it. They can attempt to reject that society's values but it is very difficult to do when that society controls everything from the labor market to the media, and ultimately controls one's economic and social destiny. As Malcolm Muggeridge says, we meet very few rich people who are happy, but we never meet a poor person who does not wish to be rich.[10] This is true largely because wealth translates as significance. Hence, any inner-city child, regardless of ethnic background, has a high risk of developing a less than positive self-concept. And without a positive self-concept, a cornerstone of motivation and drive is absent.

A part of developing a stable and positive self-image involves the third goal: cultivating skills and abilities. Some of these skills are physical. Each year at Young Life summer camps, the recreational deficits experienced by inner city youth are apparent. Many of the urban youngsters are unable to swim, play tennis, or even play basketball and baseball as well as their more recreation-saturated suburban counterparts can. Although many great professional athletes have emerged from the concrete playgrounds of the cities, there remain thousands who are left out of playground competition because of the lack of space on which to play. As one inner-city veteran stated, "You can mouth unceasingly that black is beautiful, but if you can't do anything of a skilled nature, it is not internalized." There must be a sense of achievement and accomplishment, and that requires appropriate skill development.

The youth program does offer opportunities to develop recreational skills by conducting basketball leagues as well as other sporting ventures. Achieving a bit of success in an amateur basketball tournament can go a long way in building self-confidence and a feeling of significance. However, excellence is not easy to come by in the academic domain. As discussed earlier, inner-city youth come from a nonacademic tradition and lack contact in the home and community with people who are accomplished educationally.

A fourth goal, then, is to enlarge the vision of the youth and supply motivation. The Young Life people discovered the need for this very early. At the outset of one of their programs, they inquired of the youth what they would like to be when they were adults. A sizable percentage of the youth openly expressed a desire to be a pimp, prostitute, or drug pusher. This is really not surprising, as these types are often the only community residents who do well economically and have a bit of social influence as well. The pimp drives the shiny new automobile, sits around and drinks wine all day, has attractive women at his beck and call, and above all, has a rather lucrative income. This is very appealing when set off against the dirt-poor unemployed or the overworked but underpaid laborers. For girls, the prostitute lives a rather charmed life. She has an attractive apartment, makes very good money, is protected by a pimp, and has men constantly desiring her favors. There is a sort of celebrity status in all this. The pusher, of course, is really into the big bucks. He has great power on the streets and carries a rather awesome profile. It is interesting that each of these is a type of self-employed businessperson. The note of free enterprise takes a delinquent turn, because of the lack of legitimate opportunities.

As a counter to this kind of world view, the Young Life program has developed what is called "Black Achievers" in Cabrini-Green. They realized that matching the achiever ethnically with the youth is very important. The youth are taken around various offices, factories, and other establishments to meet black adults well respected for their work. Some are executives; some are professionals in medicine, publishing, and teaching, others work in industrial plants. What they all have in common is success at what they do. These models tell the youngsters about their lives, how they got into their present occupation, and what it requires to succeed in it. The experience astounds many of the kids. Most have never seen anyone like themselves, from their own roots, who hold these kinds of jobs. The result at the end of the several months, when the youth are asked about their future goals, almost all have abandoned their desires to be a pimp, prostitute, or pusher and have set their sights on a more conventional occupational pursuit.

It is right at this point that the program objectives—self-concept, skill development, and motivation—could be approached by the youth leaders. The altered outlook indicated an elevated "I can" self-concept. Reminded of what the various models had said is necessary to succeed, some of the kids approached their school work with renewed vigor, attended the church tutoring program with a more serious outlook, and in general began making constructive progress toward what they now viewed as attainable goals. In short, enlarged vision and improved motivation paved the way for skills to be developed.

Worthy of note is the role of accountability and contracts here. The Young Life program, once a youngster has made a commitment to some achievement goal, has the student and parent sign a waiver allowing the staff to go into the youngster's school to check his attendance and academic record. The purpose of this is to impress on the youth the importance of making commitments and keeping them, while not being able to con anyone along the way. Again, this school checking is not done in any punitive or manipulative fashion. It is only appropriate in aiding the youth in becoming accountable to himself and the program, once he has decided to embark on something that will require that sort of diligence.

Commitment to self is a key. Youth are not asked to commit themselves to the Young Life leader or program. They are told that they are really making a commitment to themselves and their goals and desires; and making good on that commitment requires a certain accountability, which the Young Life leader will help the youngster to achieve.

* * *

In this chapter guidelines for and examples of ministry have been presented in the light of the attitudes and behaviors of urban youth. But a fuller understanding of urban youth necessitates studying minority experiences. Not only are our cities becoming more and more nonwhite, but those nonwhite populations are, on the average, much younger than the Caucasian groups. For example, 63 percent of Hispanic-Americans are under age twenty-five. Higher birth rates among minorities, coupled with the large number of children among some immigrant groups, mean increasingly that the face of an urban youth is likely a minority face. We turn now from our focus on youth to an investigation of racial and ethnic minorities.

7 | Minorities

Any white urban worker who underestimates the virulence and all-pervasiveness of prejudice and racism in American society and, hence, in his own experience is setting himself up for a tremendous amount of frustration and failure. The white pastor who works with minorities is working in a sociological tension, for any society with a number of distinguishable cultural or ethnic groups is a society in tension. Its members, especially the minority members, are constantly aware, at least subliminally, of that tension. They live, as Peter Rose points out, in a "We-They" society in which they are the "They."[1] If the pastor is white, he represents the "We" and has to demonstrate very clearly that he does not want to be aligned with the "We."

Gunnar Myrdal, the famous Swedish social scientist, pointed to a two-horn dilemma operative in America.[2] On one hand, the public ideology holds that each person is equal in worth before God and in the eyes of the law. This public ideology is celebrated, alluded to, and very nearly worshiped as part of the American democratic dogma. On the other hand, the private norm of prejudice and discrimination very clearly accords differential degrees of respect and deference to individuals based on group affiliation. This private norm is an operational or practiced norm, while the public norm is the doctrine that assuages the troubled collective conscience.

White urban workers have grown up in a society that daily socializes its members according to the private norm. In fact, it can be argued that any white urban worker or pastor is to some extent affected by prejudice or racism simply because he lives in a heavily racist society. This is not meant to be an indictment, for to be white and somewhat racist is normal. For just as a person who regularly breathes polluted city air should not be the least bit defensive about having some pollution in his lungs, so a person who is regularly exposed to a racist and prejudice-laden society could hardly be expected not to be somewhat prejudiced. The point is that one begins as a racist and then must make an active and ongoing effort to eradicate this racism.

If white racism is defined as having notions of white supremacy, it becomes rather easy to see how these tendencies become subconsciously internalized at a very early age. If a small child is taken to visit a number of major institutions such as a hospital, university, bank, or large corporation, that child would not have to be very astute to notice that the group in positions of power and respect is overwhelmingly white, while people of color are concentrated in such menial positions as dietary and cafeteria work and scrubbing and janitoring. Unless someone sits down with that child and explains the nature and history of prejudice and inequality of opportunity, he is certainly going to assume that there is something supreme about whites. As that child grows up he will probably live in an all-white neighborhood, go to a largely or exclusively white school, and attend an all-white church. Thus these racist notions calcify. All the well-meaning, patronizing statements he may hear about prejudice and disadvantage in society are counterbalanced by the epithets, racial slurs, and attitudes he encounters even among Christians.

Then as that child reaches adulthood and plans, perhaps, to go into Christian ministry, he attends a Christian college with a largely white faculty, staff, and student body, finally to finish in a white middle-class seminary that tries to prepare him for working with all kinds of people. If by then he is not to some extent a purveyor of racism and prejudice, it would be rather surprising, for all agree that a person's environment is a major influence on his attitudes, values, beliefs, and behaviors.

Thus a white pastor or urban worker is by conditioning and environment at least partly racist. One step in eradicating this racism in himself so that he can have an effective urban ministry is to understand the history of American prejudice and discrimination. His knowledge should encompass the historical and sociological factors in racism and majority-minority relations as well as the present-day issues affecting minority groups in America.

HISTORICAL AND SOCIOLOGICAL FACTORS

Academically speaking, prejudice or racism can be accounted for in terms of four related and interacting historical and sociological factors.[3] The first is *historical conditioning*. This refers to majoritarianism (or majority rights, discussed below) as well as the sheer inertia of history. From the near extermination of the American Indian to the enslavement of blacks, the heritage of the United States is heavy with prejudice and oppression.

A closely related factor is *cultural conditioning*. Prejudice, once it has endured over decades and even centuries, becomes institutionalized—sewn into the very life of the culture. A good example can be found in language. Such expressions as "eenie, meenie, minie, mo . . . ," and "shinier than a nigger's heel," "Indian giver," and "Jewing him down" illustrate this. Interestingly, no one ever "Catholics" anyone down or "Lutherans" others into economic submission. People become so accustomed to subtle forms of Caucasian supremacy that they go unnoticed and are simply accepted as the natural course of things. That blacks are more often arrested, constitute the majority of prison inmates, and receive humiliating treatment in stores and other public settings not only goes unquestioned but is hardly noticed. Even minorities eventually become habituated to such shabby treatment, viewing it as the American way of life.

A third factor concerns the *social structure*. The earlier example of the small child making his way through major institutions illustrates how the social structure communicates prejudice. Americans become conditioned to seeing whites giving orders and nonwhites carrying them out; whites coolly directing and nonwhites sweating in toil; whites in business suits and nonwhites in overalls. Although there is a growing number of exceptions to this rule, they remain exceptions and suggest a sense of white supremacy.

The fourth factor is *psychological*. Prejudice can be explained by a desire to feel superior to or significant in comparison with someone else. In a culture driven by strivings for status and prestige, it is only natural that scapegoats are created. "Free, white, and twenty-one,"

"Well, at least I am not black," and other verbal toss-offs are pregnant with this psychological factor. Lust for power and advantage gives rise to competition. When victory cannot be gained within the system economically, educationally, or occupationally, it will often be seized through forms of prejudice and oppression. To have advantage, even on illicit and immoral grounds, is preferred to risking a possible setback in status. While whites cringe at notions of black power, they have casually accepted white power as a way of American life.

Two of these factors—historical conditioning and cultural, or institutional, racism—will be looked at more closely.

Historical Conditioning

Historically, there are two major trends that have been factors in forming the American brand of prejudice. These include, first, the discrepancy between public ideology and private practice in administering rights. This discrepancy can be traced to the difference between European group rights and American individual rights. And second is the rapid urbanization of America, which brought a conflict between urbanism and ruralism.

European Group Rights vs. American Individual Rights. Not surprisingly, the American brand of prejudice can be traced back to Europe where the Peace of Westphalia in 1648 divided the continent in such a way that Protestants held dominance in the northern and eastern regions and the Roman Catholics in the southern and western areas.[4] As a result of this settlement, the religious group in the minority incurred rather distinct political, economic, and social disadvantages. For a Catholic living in the Protestant sector it was very difficult to succeed in business, any hopes of political power were completely unrealistic, and social acceptance was provisional at best. The same was true for a Protestant residing in a Catholic region. The notion was very simple: If you were unhappy with the disadvantages you incurred, you had only to move to a sector in which your religion held sway. In short, this majoritarianism was accepted as unquestioned reality.

The writers of the U.S. Constitution, realizing this rather oppressive state of affairs, decided to insure that America would not have this majoritarian flavor, especially since those coming to America were among the losers in Europe. For that reason it was made clear that religion would not be a test for political office or legal acceptance in the new land.

Despite their noble intentions, however, this constitutional safeguard was not adequate to prevent the activation of prejudice and discrimination. As certainly as the Europeans who came to America were Americanized, so also America was Europeanized by their presence. The immigrants took more than their physical necessities on the ship to America; they also took their political notions, prejudices, and other distorted attitudes. Hence, on the issue of human rights there can be seen a European and American dichotomy.

The European concept of rights was group-based; that is, rights were related to religious affiliation. A member of the "right" religious group could expect greater and more advantageous rights than one who was not. Rights were viewed as deferrable in that a minority person had to earn his rights—showing by diligence and dependability that he could rightfully be treated with human dignity and respect. Finally, there was obvious inequality in the possession of rights.

The constitutional notion of rights suggests that they are individual. Each citizen has his own individual rights. Before the law there is no group affiliation test that delineates differences in rights. Rights are not earned—they are present at birth. Rights are just that— rightful guarantees of proper treatment and human dignity. Lastly, all rights are equal. Not even a president should be treated in a different way from any other citizen.

On paper, the American concept is nearly ideal. It is what Myrdal would call the public ideology. However, at the private level there is still the application of a European approach. Such statements as "This is a white neighborhood; what are those people doing here anyway?" or "People should remain with their own kind; let them live over there and we'll stay here—that way there will be no trouble" are evidences of the group-based aspect.

The expression "They'll get their rights when they earn them" is a rather brazen example of the deferrable component. All forms of provisional social and occupational acceptance are also examples of this aspect.

Finally, any discrepancies in rights indicate the inequality component. Whenever groups are locked into depressed areas, have difficulty buying homes, are left with public defenders for a less-than-adequate legal defense, receive longer and more arbitrary prison sentences, are given lower-quality education, or are under undue disadvantage in seeking political office, inequality in rights is being observed.

In sum, America lives in a tension, straddling these two concepts of rights, and this straddling has lasted for three centuries.

Urbanism vs. Ruralism. The second major historical trend that has been a factor in American prejudice is rapid urbanization. Urbanization is not urbanism. The former refers simply to the physical movement of populations into urban regions. The latter means discarding or reducing a rural outlook and adopting a frame of mind, a social perspective, appropriate to urban life.[5]

Ruralism is characterized by smallness, simplism, homogeneity, independence, changelessness, and xenophobia (distrust of strangers). Ruralism can be found in tribal cultures and even in rural America where populations are small in number. In the rural outlook there is a lack of complexity and sophistication, the people are very much alike socially and ethnically, individuals are usually self-sufficient in that they hunt or farm and therefore do not have to rely much on others for their livelihood, life seems very static, and there is a clannishness that views outsiders with distrust and a sense of We-Theyness. This perspective, of course, works very well in rural settings. And since humankind has been rural in character throughout history world-wide, ruralism has been an effective mode of living.

However, when people reside in cities, this ruralism is counterproductive. It breeds distrust, prejudice, discrimination, bitterness, crime, and violence. What is needed to cope with urbanization is a healthy urbanism—a way of thinking that values (and is comfortable with) large numbers of people; is cosmopolitan, diverse and heterogeneous, complex and sophisticated, interdependent and reliant on others in all phases of social existence; accepts constant change and development; and is at ease in interacting with those who are culturally different.

What has happened is that humanity has, in the space of one century, been forced into urban living by the forces of urbanization, while doggedly retaining a ruralistic outlook. Prejudice and racism thrive on this problem. For not only does the ruralistic outlook feed clannishness and rejection on the basis of extrinsic factors such as skin color and national origin but also the diversity of the urban population provides millions of victims on which to visit this prejudice.

Institutional Racism

Even more devastating than individual forms of racism and prejudice bred by historical and social conditioning is institutional racism.[6] Whereas individual racism refers to a conscious or subconscious belief in white supremacy, institutional racism is prejudice and discrimination practiced in the day-to-day workings of large institutions.

There are a host of examples of institutional racism at hand. The need for affirmative action guidelines, set down by the federal government, is proof of the existence of institutionalized racism, for they would not be necessary if such racism were not being practiced. That no major political party in the United States has felt safe in nominating a black even for the vice-presidency is additional testimony to the existence of deep-seated individual and institutional racism. Standardized tests—whether for entrance to college or graduate school or for eligibility to serve as a policeman or fireman in a major city—have been demonstrated to be biased in favor of white, middle-class respondents and are also examples of institutional racism. Any and all unwritten but widely practiced quotas that limit the hiring of minorities, or limit the hiring of nonminorities because the quotas are not filled, are further illustrations of it. Redlining and blockbusting, discussed in chapter 2, are also examples. And on and on.

What is vital here is that once these institutional policies are put into force, they can be carried out by well-meaning, good citizens. In fact, often executors of institutional racism are wholly unaware of their deleterious actions. The urban pastor himself may be involved if he serves a denomination that has racist policies with regard to funding, location, and personnel. This subtle racism is practiced by many Christian colleges, institutions well-known for their Anglo outlook, unaggressive recruitment of minorities, white faculties, and, hence, lack of sensitivity to cultural differences among the student population.[7]

The matter of institutionalized racism is so critical and pervasive that it merits detailed attention.

Businesses. Businesses and corporations are tainted by institutional racism. The hiring record of major businesses on the fringe of a minority neighborhood may provide evidence. A disproportionate number of white faces is a symptom of institutional racism. In Philadelphia, a baking company refused to hire black drivers. An organized boycott of its products was begun in the black community, dropping consumption of its cake product by twenty-seven thousand per day. The company quickly changed its mind about the competence of black drivers.[8]

If minorities are visible in a business, a closer look may reveal a more common phenomenon: a swelling of the lower echelons with minorities, with the ranks getting whiter and whiter toward the top of the ladder. Moreover, the blacks who have moved up an organization's hierarchy, on merit, reach a certain level and then find themselves held there permanently, simply because the door to the executive suite has an invisible sign on it: whites only.

Labor Unions. Labor unions are notorious for discrimination.[9] Although many of the nationwide unions devoutly affirm openness, their local affiliates, who have the real power, are commonly operated by community hacks who have a vested interest in keeping minorities out in favor of the many blue-collar whites who are hungering for union work. Trade and craft unions are regularly taken to court where they lose civil rights cases.

Education. There is wholesale institutional racism in education.[10] This can be seen in the culturally biased IQ and achievement tests, the low priorities given the needs of inner-city schools, the biased textbooks—especially in history, and the tendency to place the least experienced and often least committed teachers in the most needy schools.

It is important to realize that much racism is carried on by very well-intentioned people, including politically liberal pastors. Overt feelings of prejudice or racism may well be absent; however, feelings of white supremacy linger on for all the reasons discussed. Unless a person stays consistently vigilant in dealing with such feelings through reading, discussing, and self-examination, he has no business dealing with nonwhites in an urban church.

Majority-Minority Relations

In addition to understanding the historical, cultural, social, and psychological factors underlying personal and institutional racism, it is helpful for an urban worker to have knowledge of the various ways majority and minority groups relate and the strategies each group uses to establish normalized relations.

The state of majority-minority relations in America can be seen quite vividly when one considers the various forms majority-minority interactions can take. As with any group encounter, whenever a majority and a minority come into frequent contact, they develop a regularized, normalized set of relations. Matters will not remain precarious for long. Sometimes relations will be marked by fairness and mutual respect, but more often by oppression.

There are essentially three major stages of majority-minority relations: accommodation, assimilation, and amalgamation.[11] These reflect a movement from rather strained, one-sided interactions to full equality.

Accommodation, the first major stage, suggests a minimal cultural exchange, sufficient to avoid open conflict and disruption. This accommodation usually necessitates that the minority divest itself of its most objectionable (in the eyes of the majority) traits in order to facilitate interaction. The minority is expected, primarily, to adopt the dominant language and economic system. Failure to do this will bring about serious conflict. Native Americans suffered genocide as a result of clinging to their own culture when they were confronted with white culture.

There are four subtypes of accommodation. The first of these is called *conquest.* This, as the term indicates, is the most brutal form. Here the majority simply conquers the minority and brings the minority under its control. There are a number of sorry examples of conquest in American history. Forcing American Indians onto reservations and making them learn Anglo culture in Bureau of Indian Affairs schools is one example. The institution of slavery is another grisly example.

A second subtype is called *toleration.* Less repulsive to the minority, toleration involves an acceptance (on the part of the majority) of a number of culturally different minority traits. Rather than forcibly moving the minority into the majority's cultural direction, the minority is allowed to adjust more at their own speed. In any case, the power differential remains, and this tolerance has very real limits. Almost every nonwhite minority has experienced this type of toleration during its American tenure—a condition in which they are aware that they can retain some of their own customs, provided these are neither offensive to the majority nor too overtly displayed.

Compromise, the third subtype, is the result of a bit more power equality. Although the majority still holds the edge, the minority is significant enough either in number or institutional position to necessitate less repressive treatment. Here a more peaceful relationship exists, one that is characterized by negotiation rather than coercion. Present-day America contains many examples of this. Such features as protection of minorities by law, increasing numbers of minorities, and the establishment of nonwhites in the United States labor market make it less advantageous for racist whites to discriminate openly. Hence, many grievances are bargained out, with minorities getting something (though perhaps less than an equal share) out of the bargain.

In *conversion,* the fourth subtype of accommodation, the minority willingly divests itself of its cultural distinctiveness in an effort to join in with and be accepted by the majority. What makes conversion different from conquest is that the minority converts voluntarily. This subtype is practiced more on an individual level than on a group level. That is, some minority persons will seek acceptance by whites and so blend in as much as possible with them. Many Orientals, light-skinned Puerto Ricans, and Mexican Americans have done this. However, conversion is only successful if the would-be convert is accepted by the majority. As a group, most minorities have been rejected regardless of any conversion strategy, and so conversion has its limits. Also of import here is that the price is high. Conversion means a denial of one's cultural identity, that is, what a person or a group really is, historically. Such a denial has psychological consequences, for it means turning one's back on one's heritage in quest of economic or social advancement—a form of selling out, repugnant to peoples of any ancestry.

The next major stage in majority-minority interaction is called *assimilation.* Much could be said about this stage, but in short, it suggests maximal cultural interchange. A relationship develops that is characterized by open, unselfconscious interaction between cultures. These cultures eventually become blended to the extent that they are fully united into one larger culture. The emerging culture will, in all likelihood, resemble the original majority culture more than the minority system; nonetheless, there is a unified mixture. Assimilation usually takes a long time if the minority culture is highly developed and quite diverse from that of the majority. What is especially important here is the sense of harmony and oneness in this stage. Clearly there is little white–nonwhite assimilation as yet in the United States.

The final stage is called *amalgamation,* and it comes on the heels of whole assimilation. Amalgamation refers to complete cultural and biological mixing. Here majority-minority differences disappear through cultural unity and intermarriage, such that there is ultimately no trace of the previously existing separate groups. There is amalgamation in Hawaii, where various civic organizations even boast of the new "Golden Man"—a mixture of a variety of different ancestries.

Both the majority and the minority have favored strategies for how they would prefer to establish normalized relations. Understanding these strategies can be very helpful at the parish level, for once an urban worker comes to grips with them in theory, it becomes easier to see how the minority and the majority are relating in the immediate community. These strategies are not openly enunciated, but are operationally demonstrated in majority-minority interactions.

Majority Strategies. For the majority, there are six strategies.[12] The first, by no means the most desirable in the eyes of the majority, is *pluralism.* Here there is unity with diversity; that is, the minority is allowed to retain its cultural identity provided it conforms to certain larger demands affecting the national interest. Such demands may include the payment of taxes and the observance of the laws. The advantage of this policy for the majority is that it minimizes open conflict. However, it means the minority can retain many of its aggravating (from the majority perspective) and threatening differences and thus demonstrate the divided nature of the society. Multiethnic churches that celebrate cultural diversity through carefully planned worship services, activities, and programs exemplify pluralism.

Assimilation is the second and more preferred strategy. This assimilation is not of the type described earlier, in which there is open and easy interchange. Rather, it has a coercive quality, expecting, perhaps even demanding, that the minority waive its cultural distinctiveness in exchange for at least provisional acceptance by the majority. It is unity with uniformity, with the bulk of the change being carried on by the minority. Many non-English-speaking European groups have willingly taken this option (a sort of conversion), while nonwhite groups have experienced more forceful treatment from the majority in bringing them into accordance with Anglo culture. Of import is that, especially in the case of nonwhites, this assimilation is often not full assimilation. For if they are brought into congruity with Anglo styles, they may still not be fully accepted into the Anglo world, although they will be treated much more humanely. Predominantly white churches that welcome nonwhites to join them but that make no real attempt to adapt to the cultures these minorities represent are advancing an assimilationist policy.

Legal protection involves the protection of the minorities from outside vicious attacks, while keeping them in subordination to the majority. American history is filled with examples of this policy. Keeping blacks safe from Ku Klux Klan attacks while stopping far short of insuring equal justice is one illustration. The protection of various Indian tribes from white violence and the holding of the Japanese in relocation centers are two other examples. Here the majority can congratulate itself for its paternalism, while making certain that the minority will not threaten them by being able to compete with them on a fully equal basis. Whenever a church takes minority children into its Sunday school program but, whether intentionally or not, shows little interest in bringing their parents into the fellowship, it is operating in a legal protection-like style.

Population transfer is self-explanatory. It simply refers to the movement of a minority from one region to another for its own or, more likely, the majority's good. The forced movement of the Cherokee Indians along the famous "Trail of Tears" is a prime example. The herding of the Japanese into the concentration-camp-like relocation centers is another. The placement of various Indian tribes on reservation land is probably the best-known illustration. In any case, this transfer may be done with or without the minority's approval.

Continued subjugation is a condition in which the minority is unceasingly oppressed and accorded less than equitable treatment. All cases in which discrimination and humiliation have endured are examples of this policy. Continued subjugation was the state of almost every nonwhite minority prior to the passage of the civil-rights legislation in the sixties. Any church that affirms segregation through intentional denial of minority membership is using segregationist tactics.

The final policy is called *extermination,* or *genocide.* American history texts have done a skillful job of disguising this policy, making it seem as if it never took place on this continent. Nothing could be further from the truth. The original, nonwhite minority—the American Indian—was the object of genocide. If indeed "the only good Indian is a dead Indian" as the cliché says, then there were many "good" Indians prior to the 1850s. It is estimated that there were about one million native Americans on the continent at the time of the arrival of the first whites. That number shrank to about 240,000 by 1900. Native Americans are the only ethnic group to decrease in absolute numbers in American history, and they decreased by three-fourths. Only recently have their numbers climbed above the original one million.

Minority Strategies. Minorities have four policies of their own.[13] One is *assimilation,* much like conversion. Interestingly, almost every nonwhite minority has at one time or another attempted this policy. Sadly, lack of acceptance by whites made it disadvantageous and forced these groups to opt for other strategies. As discussed earlier, assimilation is costly, meaning loss of identity. Nonetheless, even in the face of continuing disadvantage and possibly extinction, assimilation can appear very inviting. All-out attempts by minorities to join and blend in with a white church evince assimilationism.

The most favored of the minority policies is *pluralism,* also described earlier. This guarantees full societal participation along with the retention of favored cultural traits. This policy is often more ideal than real. Involvement in multiethnic churches that value their diversity reflects pluralism.

When attempts at pluralism and especially assimilation are thwarted by majority resistance and rejection, *secessionism* may result. Here the minority withdraws from the culture and even interaction with the majority, in an effort to develop its own culture in isolation from majority interference. The attempt to form a confederacy among the Southern states is the best-known example of this policy. However, black separatists in the late sixties also espoused a form of secessionism. Their argument was that after 350 years of kowtowing to white America, only to experience continued subjugation and oppression, it was time to separate, to develop their own cultural identity and strength, so that future encounters would take place on more equal footing. Totally black, Hispanic, and Asian churches suggest a secessionist policy, sometimes brought on by necessity rather than choice.

Militance, a word still much in use, is a strategy that means more than radical rhetoric, large Afros, or vivid Indian regalia. Militance refers to the minority's often violent attempt to overthrow a society's institutions to gain majority power and dominance. Militance can be a last-resort tactic when survival is threatened. Native Americans were forced to practice it when faced with the extermination efforts of white pioneers. In the church, majority-minority battles over power positions within major denominations can smack of militance.

If an urban worker is reasonably observant, he is likely to be able to observe one or more of these strategies as he analyzes almost any majority-minority encounter. As he comes to grips with this analysis, at the here-and-now parish level, he will find it much easier to predict majority and minority behavior and to know what action to take.

Overall, it is important to stress that knowledge of the majority's policy is usually the more valuable; because of its greater power, the majority is usually better able to carry out its policy vis-à-vis the minority. Also it is necessary to recognize that these policies are almost never entirely clear-cut. That is, they overlap to some extent. Finally, not all members of a majority or a minority will be in full accord on a given strategy. Nevertheless, the leaders of both groups need to be watched and their actions will indicate the direction the groups will go. Being able to discern this direction can be a valuable cue in knowing how to manage the role of peacemaker and minister of justice and reconciliation.

If an urban pastor is blessed with a multiracial ministry, special efforts need to be made to keep a balance of power. One example is found in Temple Baptist Church of Los Angeles. Because of a transition process in the community, Temple Baptist has separate English, Spanish, Chinese, and Korean congregations in its one facility. These disparate groups are part of one structure that is relational rather than hierarchical so as to avoid any one group dominating. The church-at-large also affirms this cultural pluralism and the dignity of each culture and is structured to provide for the addition of new groups or the phasing out of a declining population.[14]

Uptown Baptist Church in Chicago is another example. It has five different language-group congregations in one church. Like the Los Angeles model, no group is permitted to dominate, because church board representation is designed to prevent any power bloc from gaining an edge. While all are members of the larger congregation and meet occasionally in a mass worship service, each group has its separate worship and fellowship opportunities as well.

Knowledge of the historical and sociological factors, then, is vital. Although it is beyond the scope of this book to provide a comprehensive review of the American experience of every nonwhite minority group (because of the many Hispanic and Asian peoples), what follows is a more condensed presentation of life in the United States for five mainline minority groups. It is hoped that this will provide a basic perspective on minority experience for those who are interested in effective ministry with various nonwhite groups.

MAINLINE MINORITY GROUPS

Native Americans

Native Americans are the only ethnic group who have never really desired assimilation at any time in their American experience. Much of this hesitancy is traced to the multiplicity of tribes. In fact, it is incorrect to speak of an all-inclusive minority group called American Indians or native Americans.[15] It is more accurate to speak of Navaho, Sioux, Blackfoot, Hopi, and so forth, for each tribe has a unique culture of its own. Urban Indians are often separated from their tribes; hence an Indian area in a large city may consist of a conglomerate of tribal traditions. However, it is well not to assume this in ministering to them, as a neighborhood may very well be dominated by the ancestry of a particular tribe and so be resonate with that tribal tradition.

Anthropologically, native Americans are a mixture of many peoples. Some are from China and Southeast Asia, but most are from the inner recesses of the Asian mainland—from Siberia to points west. It is assumed that many entered the New World across what is now the Bering Straits and headed east, and then south, all the way to Mexico and even South America.

In contrast to television portrayals, many of the tribes had very highly developed cultures, reflected in the architecture of temples and religious centers as well as complex agricultural systems. In order to minister to and among Indians it is necessary to understand their religious and cultural heritage.

The religious culture of native Americans is permeated with respect for and even worship of nature in general and the earth in particular. The notions of private ownership and capitalism, with the accompanying land rape and air pollution, are repugnant to the very heart of native American culture and are considered sacrilegious. Today many Indians, especially those on reservations, still cling to native faiths, or at least aspects of them, while others embrace some form of Christianity. Effective Christian ministry obviously has to accommodate some of the essentials of native American religious culture—essentials that can be argued to be more in harmony with Christ's teaching and life than much of our contemporary industrial exploitation.

Indian culture is very nonconfrontive, very accepting of others' freedom and dignity. As such, native Americans have considerable difficulty understanding or certainly appreciating contemporary America's competitive and adversary notions—such as labor versus management, plaintiff versus defendant, and team versus team. In that sense, a patient, low-key, and respectful tone is most effective in dealing with Indians truly steeped in native American culture. The aggressive, intense way of the white man is brutish and discourteous to the native American. Developing sound relations, then, necessitates sensitivity, respect, and understanding.

In addition to understanding the culture, it is important that an urban minister have an accurate view of the history of the relations between the Indians and the white settlers. The history of white-native American interaction is best written in blood. The native American stood in the way of the white settlers' desire to push west. That the Indians did not immediately convert to European notions of Christianity was a primary enzyme in the justification whites felt to destroy them. Indians were regarded by the whites as the Philistines were by the Israelites. The result then was the massacre of 75 percent of their numbers.

To accomplish their move west, white settlers at times turned to treaties. Literally hundreds of treaties were made by various legislators with individual Indian tribes, often after attacking whites forced the Indians into having to bargain from weakness. Treaty after treaty was made in good faith by a tribe, only to have the treaty brazenly violated when such violation was in the white man's best interest. Almost none of the treaties were kept.

Moreover, during the late 1800s, when the federal government realized the necessity of protecting Indians from continuing extermination efforts, they made them wards of the government and developed the reservation system. This move brought on still more atrocities. Perhaps the main one involved land. The government, in the Dawes Act, determined that property should be individually owned by American Indians, with the proviso that it could not be sold. This provision was for the native Americans' benefit in that it prevented unscrupulous land sharks from preying on their lack of economic savvy. However, once it became apparent that this provision worked against the interests of many enterprising white land hustlers, the Act was amended three times, each time weakening the no-sale clause. The result was that land held by Indians dropped from 139 million acres in 1887 to about 47 million by 1933. And that remnant consisted of the worst, most infertile land available.

It is important that an urban pastor be aware of this tragic heritage if he is to minister to native Americans, for Indians today are aware of these travesties. A white pastor is a symbol of the white man—the native American's mortal enemy. Learning to trust and respect the white man is learning to trust and respect a killer of the Indian's ancestors, the robber of his land, and the destroyer of his culture. The barriers are high, but many native Americans are courteous and kind people, and many remain open to better relations.

As is the case among many minorities, contemporary American Indians are much more acculturated to American life than their forebears were. Older Indians tend to be more tied to the past and more docile, while their younger counterparts are hungry for pluralism and activism. Many younger Indians, excited by the bright lights and wonders of white society, leave the reservations on which they were raised and head for the city. Those who survive the transition occasionally melt in with the white urban society, even to the point of intermarriage. Others, however, find themselves in the most depressed areas of the metropolis and are lost amid poverty, unemployment, illiteracy, alcoholism, and hopelessness.

Whether on reservations or in urban centers, educationally, economically, and occupationally, American Indians are at the bottom of the heap among American minorities. There is simply no end to the needs of native Americans for relief and improvement in their social condition.

In ministering among native Americans, then, it is important to understand the culture, history, and current needs. It is also important not to stereotype American Indian culture, for there are differences by tribe, city, circumstance, generation, and family.

Japanese Americans

The Japanese have experienced almost every form of American discrimination and oppression. Yet today they are pretty much in the mainstream of American life.[16] Much of the acceptance accorded the Japanese owes to their rather stoic attitude toward hardship and injustice. This attitude stems in part from their previous experiences in Japan and the influence of Buddhism on Japanese culture. Japanese Americans come from a native tradition filled with governmental oppression, economic reverses, land droughts, and other catastrophes. Therefore little in America could be much worse than conditions in the homeland. As a result, the Japanese exhibit a willingness to persevere in the face of hardship, believing that things can only get better if they are faithful and persistent. The net effect of this outlook is to make the Japanese nonconfrontive and nonmilitant in the face of discrimination. Over the decades, whites began seeing Japanese as nonthreatening, decent people. That Japan now is more highly industrialized than the United States is yet another force that has prepared the Japanese to blend in with the American social system.

Acceptance by whites, however, has not always been present. Most Japanese immigrants to the United States came from the agricultural class. Having suffered from agricultural disadvantage in their homeland, these farmers prospered when they settled in the San Francisco area. Around the turn of the century, the success of this group so angered and threatened white agriculturalists, however, that severe anti-Japanese rioting took place.

Jealousy over agricultural success of the Japanese gave rise to legal attempts at disenfranchising them. In 1894, 1913, and 1920, laws were passed in California that were designed to prevent the Japanese from purchasing land. In addition, an immigration law passed by the federal government was intended in part to limit Japanese migration to the United States. These laws greatly disadvantaged the Japanese in America. The worst, however, was yet to come.

On December 7, 1941, Japan bombed Pearl Harbor, setting off

American involvement in World War II. By the middle of 1942, all persons of Japanese ancestry were moved into what were euphemistically termed relocation centers, scattered about the Rocky Mountain region. This forced evacuation was done partly to protect the Japanese from white attack in response to the Pearl Harbor bombing and partly because there was some suspicion that the Japanese might sabotage the American war effort. The latter rationale is a curious example of prejudice, for even though Germany was the main adversary of America in both world wars, those of German ancestry were not quarantined.

In any case, the relocation experience was devastating for the Japanese. Life in the centers was more reflective of concentration-camp living than political shelter. In addition, the Japanese lost all their holdings. After the war, when the Japanese were released, they had to start all over, devoid of everything from land to occupations. That Japanese now live in every state in the union rather than exclusively on the west coast is in a large measure a result of their World War II nightmare.

As with native Americans, Japanese have little reason to trust whites. They remain, however, very kind and genial people; by reason of the industrialization of their native country, their strong family unit, and their stoic persistence in the face of tremendous obstacles, they have overcome the disabilities placed on them twice over in America, surpassing whites in median family income and educational attainment.

Chinese Americans

The Chinese have endured almost unparalleled amounts of discrimination in international migrations.[17] Like the Japanese, they seem to have been able to press forward nonetheless.

Chinese immigration first became significant in the middle 1800s, with the California gold rush. Men worked principally in the mines and on the railroads. The Chinese were subjected to harassment, attack, and even murder during this era, largely because of four cultural characteristics that irritated white males who worked with them. First, Chinese men wore their hair in braids down their backs—a style Anglo laborers regarded as feminine. Second, they wore skirt-like apparel, further feminizing them. Third, many were especially adept at cooking, washing, and laundering, traditionally viewed as women's work by whites. Lastly, they spoke in a sing-song fashion, because in Chinese the pitch of a word contributes to its meaning. These four factors taken together caused the Chinese males to be regarded as half-men and half-feminized freaks. Hence, many received the type of treatment homosexuals have frequently received.

Additional problems were caused for Chinese men because immigration restrictions caused the sex ratio to be overwhelmingly male. Interracial marriage was strictly forbidden, so some Chinese men were drawn into homosexuality and liaisons with white women. This led to further oppression.

Growing hatred for the Chinese brought about a series of legal attempts to disenfranchise them. In California, special discriminatory statutes were enacted. One statute imposed on laundries that did not use horse-drawn vehicles a laundry license fee nearly four times higher than usual. Another law taxed those who wore their hair in a queue, the braided style. Perhaps the most outrageous of all was the cubic air ordinance in San Francisco. Realizing that the Chinese were forced to live in the most overcrowded of quarters, the white legislators advanced several statutes that outlawed high density on the grounds that it violated cubic air space.

In addition, the Chinese were affected by discriminatory immigration laws designed to limit their growing numbers. Matters became so extreme that between 1882 and the end of World War II, more Chinese left for their native land than entered the United States.

The Chinese have little reason to be trusting of whites, who have offered only grudging acceptance of them over the last century, and that not without a sizable amount of oppression. Not dissimilar to both the Japanese and American Indians, the rather genteel and low-keyed Chinese culture clashes with white America's much more confrontive and competitive way of life.

As with the Japanese and American Indians, younger-generation Chinese are more Americanized than their elders. Many are doing so well economically, occupationally, and educationally that, like the Japanese, they are ahead of their Anglo peers. Some of this success stems from the fact that most of the recent immigrants have come from the professional class.

As the Chinese continue to become urbanized, urban pastors are increasingly likely to come into contact with them. There is no way to generalize about urban Chinese, for some will live in various types of "Chinatowns," while others will, like the Japanese, be scattered throughout the metropolitan area. Regardless, the Chinese are friendly and courteous, though very private and somewhat resentful of white investigations of them and their culture—this is especially so in predominantly Chinese communities.

Religiously, the Chinese have been slow to accept Christianity. The urban pastor will find that Buddhism dominates the Chinese-American religious life, with religiosity being an intensely personal matter, not necessarily given to practice outside the home.

Mexican Americans

Mexican Americans are a mixture of Spanish and Indian ancestry, having their origins in the Spanish overrun of the Indian cultures in what is now called Mexico.[18] Because the Spanish were almost exclusively Roman Catholic, most of the area was quickly Catholicized, a fact that accounts for the strong Roman Catholic imprint on Mexican-American culture. The strain of imagery in Catholicism appealed to the Mexicans, whose native Indian religions were also full of imagery and ritual. Hence, what resulted from the proselytizing of Mexico was, in many cases, a hybrid religion—a mixture of Catholicism and native American faiths.

Mexican migration to the States became especially heavy during the Mexican Revolution in the early twentieth century. Numbering in excess of five million, Mexican Americans (or Chicanos) are the second largest ethnic minority in the United States. Nearly 90 percent of the Mexican-American population resides in the Southwest (Arizona, California, Colorado, New Mexico, and Texas). Much of the Chicano population in California is urbanized. Often Mexican Americans who reside in cities live in what are called *barrios*, enclaves rich in Mexican-American and occasionally Puerto Rican culture.

One of the cultural traits of the Mexican immigrants was a sense of fatalism—an acceptance of life as it is without a sense of mastery of personal destiny. This outlook was similar to the stoicism of Orientals, but without the optimism and conviction that an individual can effect change. This fatalism goes back into the Mexican religious past and clashes rather dramatically with the Anglo emphasis on conquering and subordinating nature through technology.

Mexican culture also favors the notion that work is to be done for its own sake rather than for economic gain. It is honorable to work, regardless of trade, and dishonorable not to. The shrewd and calculating approach to labor taken by whites is alien to this orientation.

There is a high value placed on courtesy and charm. Although conflict is not uncommon and may be resolved with confrontation, daily casual interaction is nonconfrontive and marked by respect and deference.

Easily one of the most powerful Mexican-American cultural traits is *machismo*. There is a strong, traditional male-dominated pattern to sex-role interaction. Men are the authority figures and are obeyed. Men demonstrate *machismo* by pursuing women for seductive purposes, drinking heavily without losing control, and being willing to fight to defend their honor or respect. Women are expected to stand by, being both subordinate and supportive. In an era of radically changing notions pertaining to the female sex role and social identity, this male chauvinistic orientation does not facilitate communication with Anglos.

Since the sixties there has been such an upsurge in Chicano identity that Mexican Americans define themselves as a group, pointing with pride to their heritage. Cultural pluralism is usually the favored strategy in relating to the majority, with some effort at assimilation. There is a rather sharp cleavage between generations here, as the younger Chicanos opt for a more activistic approach to the disadvantages placed on them by Anglo prejudice, while their elders are more passive and philosophic about such matters.

A major problem among Mexican Americans is the status of the illegal immigrant. A large number of Chicanos mask their identities because they are illegally in the States. Illegal entrance is tempting because there is almost always a job waiting. Many American businessmen welcome illegals, offering them employment below the minimum wage and without fringe benefits. For many Mexicans, coming into a new country with work waiting is a pleasant alternative to the near-starvation conditions experienced in such places as Mexico City. Moreover, illegal entrance is very easy, as the United States and Mexico have a common border stretching 1,600 miles, devoid of natural obstacles. In addition, many have entered the United States by swimming across the Rio Grande to avoid detection by the border patrol. It is from this practice that the term *wetback* was formed.

Those in urban ministry will need to deal with the cultural traits of Mexican Americans as well as with their many needs and problems. The urban worker may well encounter avoidance and resistance from Mexican Americans because of their fear of having themselves, a family member, or a friend detected as an illegal immigrant. Protestants will confront the rather strong Catholic tradition operative among Mexican Americans. Although many are Roman Catholic only in the most nominal sense, the influence of Catholicism so dominates the art, architecture, and symbolism of Mexican-American culture that, for many, not to be Catholic is not to be truly Mexican American. Understanding and appreciating the people's culture is the most important first step toward effective ministry.

Seeing needs and meeting them is the second step. The temporal needs of the Mexican Americans are many. They are disproportionately represented among the ranks of the poor and the unemployed. Educationally, there is the problem of bilingualism: Spanish-speaking children enter English-speaking schools, only to fail there. Inability to speak English also accounts for much unemployment and underemployment. The possibilities for effective social ministry are myriad. Employment, education, and English language skills for all ages are crisis areas where timely aid can open lines of communication.

As is the case with any crosscultural ministry, patience and service should characterize the effort. Establishing solid bonds of communication is not an uncomplicated process, and patience will maximize the likelihood of developing solid relationships.

Black Americans

Black-American experience can be divided into three major epochs: slavery (1619–1865), segregation (1865–1967), and ghettoization (1967 to the present).[19] To understand black-American life necessitates a sensitivity to these eras, for the present social and economic condition of black America is largely the outgrowth of slavery and segregation.

What makes black Americans unique among American minorities is that they did not come here by choice. They were rounded up in Africa and placed on galley ships designed to bring them to America. The shipment of the slaves was particularly devastating. Most ships were three-decked vessels, with the slaves packed like human cargo.

They were placed in a prone position with legs askew so a fellow slave could be seated in front of them. Greed hurt the shipping merchants. Overcrowding the ships made disease rampant, with frequently 30 percent or more of the slaves dying during the trip to America.

Once in America blacks were to confront one of the most savage institutions in human history. A full treatment of slavery is beyond the scope of this book; however, a review of some of its major characteristics is in order.

There was, first of all, denial of family. Slaves were not allowed to marry. Hence, every black child born prior to 1865 was illegitimate in the official sense. Slaves were forced to cohabit and were bred, in a manner similar to the breeding of cattle, in hopes that sexual unions would spawn strong male offspring suitable for field work. In short, black propagation was designed and controlled by the white man.

Along with this there was sexual violation of black women by white men. Because slaves had no legal standing, black women had no alternative but to succumb to the advances of the white slave owner. Between two-thirds and four-fifths of all American blacks have some white biological ancestry. Much of this interracial ancestry is a result of this sexual practice. Moreover, the offspring of an owner-slave union was always a slave, for any black ancestry made one black. (This incidentally is still true today. The child of, say, a black man and a white woman is invariably classified as Negroid when, in fact, the child is most likely primarily Caucasian because of the mixed ancestry of the black parent.)

While the offspring of a black-white union was considered a slave, the lighter-skinned slaves often became house slaves rather than field slaves and had less arduous working conditions. Thus, sewn into the slave system was the principle that the lighter (or whiter) one was, the better.

A second characteristic of slavery was denial of human, legal, and political rights. The slaves were totally without legal protection. They could be abused, sexually molested, attacked, beaten, or even killed at the whim of the master, who had to account to no one for his treatment of slave property.

And the slaves definitely were considered subhuman property. When the Constitution was being written, the South wanted the slaves to be counted in the population because the larger the population count, the larger would be the representation in the House of Representatives. The North objected to this, believing that if slaves were not to be considered citizens, they should not be counted in the population. After much discussion and wrangling, a compromise was reached. For every five slaves the South would be credited with three persons in the population. In other words, a slave was three-fifths a human being. Although little noted in American history textbooks, this measure underscored the truly dehumanizing nature of the slave system.

Third, slaves were denied both education and communication. In some states it was a capital crime to teach a slave to read or write. To educate the slaves was to make them dangerous. Knowledge was power, and ignorance guaranteed an absence of communication and potential revolt. In addition, once off the galley ship, slaves were often tribally separated so that all possibilities of communication between slaves would be eliminated.[20] Many language patterns of blacks today derive from the clever adaptation of slaves to this vicious communication-denying practice.[21]

Fourth, slaves had no residential mobility options. Once one was bought by a slave master, he served on that owner's plantation until he died or was sold. All power of movement was beyond his own control.

There was, fifth, massive economic exploitation. The South was built by black slaves, for the Southern economy was based on what was called King Cotton. Slaves worked for nothing day-in and day-out, week after week, year after year. Yet the capitalist South today does not acknowledge its debt to blacks, who made it what it is.

Finally, slavery was characterized by widespread violence. Because of the absence of rights and the belief by whites that slaves were subhuman, slaves were regularly the objects of white violence. There are numerous records of lynchings, beatings, rapes, and other atrocities that occurred during the seemingly endless 250 years of American slavery. Any paranoia blacks have developed toward whites has a solid basis in their American heritage.

In 1865 slavery ended, but subjugation continued. Although blacks were officially regarded as human beings and as citizens, it was still legal to deny political process, educational opportunities, employment, land ownership, recreational options, or public service in restaurants and hotels simply and arbitrarily on the basis of race. One example is that although major league baseball is over a hundred years old, it was not until 1947, fully eighty-two years after the legal termination of slavery, that the first black player entered the big leagues. And blacks are still underrepresented as coaches and managers.

Segregation was an era in which blacks were legally depressed in every facet of their American existence—perhaps most importantly in the area of human dignity. To be black was to be socially inferior and to be accorded humiliating treatment. This was a century during which black parents had to explain to their children that the reason they were unable to go to school with whites and the family could not go to the museum, movie theater, recreational center, or nearby church was simply that they were black.

Often people wonder aloud why blacks have not succeeded in the same fashion as white immigrant groups.[22] Reciting the tenets of the bootstrap theory, they forget that minority groups were locked in the segregationist era while whites were moving upward. White groups came in droves during the nineteenth and early twentieth centuries when they heard of the unskilled labor opportunities in the new land. Land itself could be obtained at no cost or at a pittance. For the factory workers, unions were formed as early as 1902 to increase pay and shorten hours. Income taxes were not levied to any appreciable extent until World War II. Moreover, the standard of living was not particularly high, so the entire price structure was geared to the poor. Finally, white groups never suffered segregation and no group other than blacks spent 250 years in slavery. It is easy to talk of legal equality now, but the methods for progress available to white immigrant groups are now long gone. Unskilled labor opportunities do not exist, land is gone, income taxes are high, and the cost of living is exorbitant.

The passage of the civil rights legislation in the middle sixties spelled the end of segregation. However, the ghettoized circumstances in which a large percentage of the 25 million black Americans live today are the result of 350 years of disadvantage. To expect any group to endure 350 years of assault and be anywhere but at the lower end of the social and economic structure is unrealistic. That blacks have even survived is testimony to their fortitude and character strength. They have not only survived, but have developed a culture in language, food, drama, sports, and music that is abundant in diversity and impact.

The black church has a particularly rich heritage. Constituting over 40 percent of the urban congregations of some cities, the black church has a myriad of strengths. Worship is filled with expression, intensity, and meaning. Members are imbued with a profound sense of peoplehood and celebration of their Afro-American identity. Relationships within the body are celebrated and affirmed. Activities such as traveling choirs and joint worship services provide contact with sister churches in other parts of the city and across the country.

The service ministry of the black church has over the years addressed virtually every human need of black America. It was among the first institutions to do effective social work. And out of its service orientation much evangelism has been generated.

Black urban churches have also set the pace in stewardship ministry. As the focal point of the black community, the church is the hub of social and political as well as spiritual activity. Because of its holistic approach to life and ministry, the black church has provided a host of opportunities for its members to develop leadership skills effective in large organizations. It should surprise no one that so many national black figures, among them Dr. Martin Luther King, Jr., and Rev. Jesse Jackson, have their roots in the church.

It is imperative that an urban minister view current black-white relations against this historical backdrop. Blacks, for the most part, are acutely aware of their American origins; and, of course, they are reminded of them daily in their encounters with personal and institutional racism. Disadvantage and lack of respect live on for black America.

Knowledge of the history and culture of minorities is increasingly important, for, according to a government study, within a hundred years whites will be in the minority in the United States. The numbers of Hispanics—Mexican Americans, Puerto Ricans, Cubans, and South Americans; Asians—Japanese, Chinese, Vietnamese, Filipinos, Koreans, and Pacific Islanders; and blacks are on the rise as a result of immigration trends and birth rates.[23] In fact, the 1980 census indicated that Anglo birth rates are below replacement, while blacks average 2.3 children per couple, and Hispanics 3 children per family.[24]

Moreover, Hispanics and Asians are no longer assimilating quickly. The issue for these groups is how to retain their cultural identity in the new country. They are proud of their heritages, taking particular satisfaction in their long histories and different values. As such, these groups are tied more closely to their sending than receiving culture. Contact with the culture of origin, particularly for immigrant groups, provides a greater sense of security and continuity. Ironically, however, crosscultural studies indicate that a sense of security is necessary in order for people to assimilate.[25] Urban ministers will need to take these changes into account.

MINISTRY AMONG MINORITIES

It would be very easy to see an aspiring urban pastor being overwhelmed by all this. The problem of racism—prejudice and oppression—is indeed severe. Nonetheless, all too many pastors are simply unaware of its magnitude, and as a result they cannot relate effectively to its victims in the neighborhood. The first step in ministry, then, is to become aware of the devastating effects of individual and institutional racism and the problems faced by minorities. Many urbanites would be comforted if they only had a pastor who would listen to, understand, and care about their frustration.

Awareness

For any urban pastor who needs greater awareness and motivation to deal with minorities and the oppressed, there are probably two main steps to take.[26] The first is to study the Scriptures on this issue. The Bible is filled with passages (some were pointed out in chapter 1), that indicate God's care for those waylaid by the system. In addition, Christ's life stands as a living witness to divine concern for society's rejected victims.

Christ not only took the side of the oppressed, He spent most of His time with "publicans and sinners." In fact, in the social sense He was certainly civilly disobedient. He associated with the undesirables (the minorities) throughout His earthly ministry: His friends were the poor; He took the revolutionary step of caring about and ministering to the Samaritans (the "nonwhites" of His era, in that they were Jews of mixed ancestry); and He was perhaps the only man of His time who treated women with the respect and dignity accorded only men in that thoroughly chauvinistic society.

The second step to create greater awareness is to listen to those who claim to be oppressed. Once an urban pastor has logged a sizable amount of time listening, the injustices perpetrated by the daily grind of the institutional system will become readily apparent. No one can really listen to those who profess to be oppressed without returning with a new awareness of the pervasiveness of institutionalized evil.

Attitudes

Once the urban pastor has become aware of the problems facing the oppressed and of God's viewpoint, his next task is to examine his own attitudes and to eradicate any personal prejudice.

Minorities are peculiarly sensitive to the varied forms of paternalism, patronizing treatment, and a host of other subtly debasing forms of insincerity. Any shred of white supremacy an urban pastor carries into dealings with them is not only immoral but self-defeating. Ministry in a minority community, as anywhere else, is finally a matter of sharing, not arbitrarily distributing. Hence, the single most important principle for effective ministry with minorities is an absence of white-supremacist notions. There is no reason for any white to feel superior to nonwhites on the basis of ethnicity. Once this prejudice is controlled (and because most of it is unconscious, the control of it must be an everyday exercise), there is room to develop an identification with minorities. This eradication of personal prejudice and a growth of identification are the foundations for the development of healthy relations and effective ministry.

Identification

Identification with the oppressed, however, will have its costs. Any urban worker, regardless of ethnic affiliation, must be aware that no matter how hard he pushes for change, there will be those on one hand who feel he is going too slow, selling out to the system, or, in the case of blacks, "uncle Tomming" (playing into the hands of white interests at the expense of black people). Charges of paternalism, patronizing treatment, and insensitivity are to be expected. They come with the task of identification. The white pastor may be the only available white symbol in the community. As such, he can fully expect to be a lightning rod for much of the pain and anger of minorities. Enduring the onslaught with Christlike patience and dignity is the surest route to effective ministry.

On the other hand, middle-class parishioners and certainly middle-class operators and owners of institutions will regularly accuse the pastor of pushing too hard, expecting too much too soon. Any pastor who wishes to get involved in the matter of minority issues, and it cannot be avoided if that pastor seeks to serve effectively, must take the role of peacemaker.

James White helps explain this problem when he discusses multiracial churches.[27] He feels that the barrier to white and black parishioners being one people in word, deed, and spirit lies in the differences between their American histories. Common roots and historical experiences build peoplehood, and, lacking this commonality, it is difficult for one group to affirm and communicate with another.

One way of dealing with this problem is to be reminded that, as James Conklin reminds us, we are all immigrants.[28] Even American Indians came from other countries. We are all in various stages of acculturation, or inculturation (holding on to old, more familiar customs and perspectives).

Communication

In addition to developing keener awareness and eradicating personal prejudice and learning to identify with minorities, the urban pastor must develop skills in crosscultural communication. Leonard Rascher gives sage counsel.[29] He urges, first of all, that the urban worker be informed. It is important to be a student of the people at all times. Second, Rascher says, be yourself. Being genuine, forthright, and above all honest is essential. Third, be flexible. There is too often an unwillingness to do anything in a new way, a tendency that smacks of arrogance and authoritarianism. Rascher further advises the pastor to be sensitive. Learning to be alert to other groups' feelings and cultural customs is imperative.

Crosscultural communication can be enhanced if the urban pastor learns the group's language (this can be slang as well as a recognized dialect)[30] and its values. With this knowledge the pastor is less likely to violate a group's culture. It also enables him to communicate according to the group's thought patterns and life perspective. The ability to use illustrations and anecdotes in the context of the people he serves is invaluable.

In communicating the gospel through crosscultural evangelism, Rascher feels it is important to emphasize the universality of Christ's atonement. It must be made supracultural and stripped of its ethno-centricity. If properly done, Christianity will not be seen as just another religious option among many others.

Ministry

While it is important that the pastor develop the characteristics mentioned above, it is also important that the ministry itself be characterized by affirming the dignity and value of the person ministered to. Respecting minorities as worthy human beings who have survived the ravages of American prejudice should be foremost. There needs to be openness and respect.

Unless minority cultures are affirmed and respected, the church risks losing its members. Studies by Father Joseph Fitzpatrick of New York Puerto Ricans indicates a strong relationship between loss of cultural and personal identity and entrance into cult groups. In Miami there have been similar experiences with other Hispanics. The anonymity of the large urban church must be replaced by building bridges and increasing communication.[31]

The ministry should also be characterized by placing minority persons in positions of leadership. The more committed minority persons available for ministry, the better. However, employing people, either gainfully or voluntarily, solely on the basis of ethnic background will simply aggravate the situation. It is imperative that any church worker who ministers in the name of that church be dedicated to the church's objectives, and that the individual's behavior reflect that dedication. There are enough potentials for misunderstanding as it is without getting into a divided-loyalty problem.

If whites are the only ones available, then it may be better to employ a somewhat naïve but eager-to-learn person than a smooth but arrogant individual. When misunderstandings arise and confrontation occurs, the latter may prove stubborn in order to save face. A person with a genuine servant orientation will grow and will be respected by the community he is willing to become a part of.

The South Bronx Pastoral Center developed a very effective

program for developing discipleship and leadership among Hispanics. The church embarked on a sixteen-week program aimed at deepening faith and fellowship. Continuing ventures such as these brought about effective lay leadership in the parish. In 1979, a Pastoral Center was formed that included a four-year leadership training program emphasizing religious studies and communications skills. Although leadership development is a slow process, carrying it through has been found to be a major force in church renewal.[32]

Ministry to nonwhites by white urban workers should be characterized by four additional elements. These four will serve as a summary and conclusion. First is *credibility*—trust is the watershed. No nonwhite groups really have a good reason to trust whites, given their experience with white America. It is crucial that minorities know that the pastor and church want to minister effectively, and that fact must be communicated with the utmost sincerity. Without credibility there is no ministry.

A second and related element is *servanthood*. Christ's life was characterized by a "What can I do for you?" approach. This must characterize the urban worker as well. Of course, it is vital that the worker be discerning so that his desire to serve does not carry a naïve strain, which can easily be exploited by people of any ethnic group. However, servanthood is primary. People respond to the love of God through the service of His agents. That response cannot occur if it is not preceded by the kind of service that does not demand a response of any type. No-strings-attached service, unconditional love, is God's way of dealing with humans and must characterize much of the urban ministry. This servanthood orientation is perhaps the one feature that most strikingly distinguishes urban ministry from secular programming carried on by well-paid, middle-class personnel.

A third element must be a *desire to learn*. Interacting with and being immersed in literature pertaining to the minority group are critical to effective ministry. There is no counting the number of ministries that have died simply because of ignorance on the part of those carrying them on. There must be no excuse for cultural insensitivity or ignorance. An urban worker must receive advance training in the culture and lifestyle of the minority group, along with ongoing education, identification, and involvement.

A seemingly less critical but important fourth element is *support of worthy minority causes*. Whether it means patronizing minority establishments, backing political candidates, contributing to fund-raising efforts, or visiting cultural displays, it is important that the urban minister be involved actively in advancing the best of minority life in the city. To do so is not only right and honorable, it also sharpens the minister's sensitivities and demonstrates the sincerity of his concern.[33]

Effective ministry among minorities must be characterized, then, by credibility, servanthood, desire to learn, and active support of minority causes.

8 | Socialization Into Victim-Blaming

Socialization is a process by which an individual learns his culture and internalizes it. The term *culture* refers to the socially standardized ways of acting, feeling, and thinking characteristic of the community or society in which the person lives.

Culture makes an impact on each of these three dimensions. There is little difficulty in seeing how cultures differ in *acting* or behavior, for it is these variances in behavior or customs to which most people point when differentiating among cultures. However, cultures also have a powerful effect on patterns of *thinking* and *feeling*. In an industrialized country such as the United States, people are tuned to think in terms of free enterprise, money, luxuries, power, and status. They are also conditioned from childhood to have certain feelings or emotional reactions to them. Americans will scheme, steal, and kill in an effort to gain power and status. Adults order their entire lives to attain power and dominance through leadership positions. Yet there are other societies where individuals do not venerate leaders, but rather are suspicious of them.[1] As a consequence, few members of such societies are inspired to be leaders of their fellows in any situations.

Culture is also analyzed in terms of norms, beliefs, symbols, and values. There is some overlap with the foregoing categories of acting, thinking, feeling.

Norms are usually divided into folkways, mores, and laws. *Folkways* are essentially minor norms that govern day-to-day conduct. Brushing one's teeth, combing one's hair, bathing regularly, responding in a civil fashion to one's peers, and other conventional expectations held by members of a society are examples of folkways. They are not to be underestimated in terms of the degree to which they shape behavior. In fact, the majority of the things most people consider "normal" behavior is not so much normal or natural as it is a matter of learning and internalizing folkways. They are internalized early in life because they are the key to social acceptance. Failure to abide by existing folkways—such as neglecting to mow one's lawn regularly, missing appointments, dressing grossly out of style—is likely to bring on gossip, ridicule, and even rejection. Because folkways are not of a heavy moral nature, this gossip and rejection is often not exhibited openly by one's peers, but is carried on rather quietly behind the individual's back.[2]

Mores are norms that carry considerable moral weight. These norms are devoutly held to by a society's members. They often involve the cardinal taboos pertaining to family, community, and civic matters. Violation of these almost certainly results in expulsion from the community. Mores are especially important in small towns. It would be easier for the proverbial camel to pass through the eye of a needle than to attempt to survive in a rural community after publicly violating, for example, one of its sexual mores.

Laws may be either folkways or mores. Some laws, such as those governing parking and street crossing, carry no great moral significance. Others, for example, those that outlaw murder, rape, and armed robbery, are deemed necessary for moral order. In either case, they are norms brought into existence by a recognized, organized, civil body empowered by the state.[3]

Beliefs in a culture are very similar to thinking patterns discussed above. Each culture teaches certain doctrines formally and informally. Certainly one of the most powerful teachers of cultural beliefs is the school. Concepts of citizenship, democracy, free enterprise, cooperation, and authority are riveted in the student's mind. These beliefs underlie and justify the norms and values that people espouse and abide by.

The primary system of *symbols* of a culture is its language. Language is absolutely critical to any culture. It is the key to it. Embodied in the language of the culture are history, values, ideologies, and norms. An analysis of a culture's vocabulary reveals almost everything of the culture.[4]

Values are a bit more difficult to define. One definition might term them a culture's cherished entities. The values taught in the culture and internalized by its members are its life blood. "Where your treasure is, there will your heart be also" is both a spiritual and a sociological truism.[5]

What makes awareness of culture vital in urban ministry is that each social class constitutes a culture of its own. That is to say, each social class has its own peculiar ways of feeling, thinking, and acting; its own set of norms, beliefs, symbols, and in some cases even values. Stratum subcultures, as described in chapter 3, illustrate this fact.

Socialization of a Middle-Class Pastor

Most urban pastors have been socialized to live most comfortably in the middle class. They are largely from upper- to lower-middle income families and have lived all or most of their lives in middle-class communities.

The model white urban pastor has usually been reared in an intact, God-fearing family. The family was most probably of ordinary size (certainly not containing ten or twelve children) and well controlled, with father as the authority figure. It is probable that this pastor was introduced to cultural values and mores in middle-class schools. Research indicates that the middle class tends to emphasize good grades in traditional academic bodies of knowledge —reading, writing, spelling, and computation—and self-controlled, self-directed conduct. His leisure time was spent playing with siblings and other children in the neighborhood.

For many, their life included going to church, Sunday school, and perhaps Bible class or catechism. These programs were customarily operated by people who valued order, respect, and conscientious attention to duty. Even those wayward youngsters who "cut up" in these sessions realized they were defying the established order. If this future pastor became a full member of his church before completing high school, his decision entailed taking responsibility for his own spiritual state.

Although all this socialization is carried on in a larger urban, suburban, or rural environment, the community that really counted, meaning those with whom the family regularly associated, was most likely quite similar to the youth's own family. That community was most probably short on violence, divorce, poverty, and rebellion, and long on order, conformity, respect, and cooperation.

Once leaving the community, the future pastor headed for college. If the college was a private Christian one, then middle-class socialization was probably intensified. For there is no greater bastion of American middle-class culture than the small Christian college.[6] The charges at such private institutions, without public funding require that the student have at least a middle-income status. The seminary this future pastor then moved on to was probably quite similar. Heavy on theory, abstraction, and polite conversation, seminaries can be heart-warming oases from the real world. The high value placed on quietness, reflection, and grade-currying is extremely middle class. Colleges and seminaries are sometimes so openly middle class that they institute special programs to expose their students to non–middle-class life. These are commonly given euphemistic, academic titles, but they amount to little more than a look at "how the other half lives."

Though there is nothing inherently wrong with being middle class or appreciating middle-class institutions, what is important is that the urban pastor will probably not serve a middle-class congregation or work in a middle-class neighborhood. And so, despite the growing tendency of television to homogenize the outlook of the various social classes, he is probably in for a good bit of culture shock when he encounters the urban milieu. This may be an understatement, for it is possible that almost none of the urban pastor's socialization has prepared him for the lifestyle of the congregation he is about to serve. In fact, that socialization is probably in direct contradiction to his parishioners' culture. That is to say, it may often have used the way of life of lower-class people as an example of the kind of living that contrasts to what is viewed as virtuous Christian living.

If an inexperienced pastor is to swim in the urban ocean, he will have to be resocialized. He will have to understand, appreciate, and identify with the way of life of the urban poor. It will not be easy, for almost every behavioral precept taught in his family, school, and church is rooted in the unconscious and almost certainly unarticulated assumption that the individual comes from a background with a sufficient amount of money, education, status, and, most importantly, opportunity to find this precept meaningful and constructive.

Perhaps one of the first things an urban pastor will confront in dealing with lower-income people will be radically different responses to middle-class values. It bears repeating that inner-city residents do not necessarily reject, in principle, middle-class values. They simply find them irrelevant to lower-class life. What follows is a brief (in order to avoid unnecessary overlap) treatment of seven cardinal middle-class values. Although these matters have been touched on in the previous chapters, the purpose here is to demonstrate the perspectival variance of the middle-class pastor from those he will serve.

MIDDLE-CLASS VALUES

Education

Few matters receive as unanimous an acclaim from middle-class people as the importance of education. They may criticize the poor quality of the schools, but they heartily agree on the value of education. In fact, many believe that education is simply good in and of itself. "The answer to the problem of _____ [fill in the blank with almost any social dilemma] is education." Such a statement regularly concludes any lengthy analysis of a social problem. Few even bother to ponder whether education cannot also be insidious, making the avaricious and power-hungry more able to manipulate their victims; the criminally inclined more able to escape justice; and the deceitful more skilled at duping their victims.

Education is so highly valued among the middle class that many will uproot their families when the oldest child is six, saddling themselves with an enslaving mortgage and a greater commuting distance to work, in order to provide a "good education" for their children. In some suburbs, virtually every intellectually normal child is expected to go on to college.[7]

The lower class, contrary to the belief of many people, also places a high value on education. The 1966 Coleman Report and many other studies underscore this fact.[8] Lower-class adults, especially, are aware that one of the primary differences between their occupational niche and that of the middle-class professional is the amount of formal education they have had. The problem is not only that formal education of any quality is in short supply in inner cities, but that other priorities may intervene.

As discussed earlier, older children may be required to tend the younger children, placing the care of these children ahead of their own education. This means that if any of the younger children is ill, an older child, usually a daughter, must stay home with him. In addition, the simple awareness of this responsibility often can stand in the way of being able to devote one's energies solely to educational tasks.

There is also a lack of role models. Many poor children do not see their parents rise early every morning to go to work whether or not they feel well. Therefore, there is no model to emulate in getting up faithfully and going to school under virtually every condition. Easy middle-class assumptions about the role of education in family life will prove unworkable.

Property

The love of property is a middle-class epidemic. People will purchase it, insure it, beautify it, put up signs protecting it, and become almost insane with rage when it is somehow defaced. Homes, townhouses, condominiums, and forest acreage appeal to this middle-class thirst. The "condominium craze" is illustrative of this property worship, for with it comes only an apartment—no land—along with continuing rentlike joint responsibility for security, maintenance, and improvement.

Property also takes the form of material luxuries. People will neglect their families, sacrifice their health, and sell their soul to obtain more "things." However, equally as important is the jealousy with which the middle class will care for and protect their possessions.

Christians may call this stewardship, others simply call it common sense; but virtually everyone agrees (often at an emotional level) on the importance of taking good care of one's goods. Damage to a car, building, or item of clothing could spark a colossal outburst, one much larger than the sorrow over having damaged another's feelings or emotional well-being.

To the poor property is, of course, an abstraction. Hence, especially with housing, there is neither pride of ownership nor experience in maintaining one's own dwelling. Inner-city youth, therefore, are less than meticulous in caring for their possessions. This will be particularly true of the church building. It will be "used" in the fullest sense of the term when city youth are in the facility.

A postscript concerning an exception may be appropriate here. Occasionally middle-class people remark on seeing shiny cars and expensive clothes in otherwise blighted areas. One of the reasons for this is that, in an area surrounded by so much economic and material deprivation, these possessions become a symbol of affluence—something to be proud of. In a nation where one's worth is so strongly attached to the symbols of wealth he can display, owning a fancy suit or a new car has great meaning and does wonders for one's depressed self-concept. Nevertheless, this experience is often short-lived, for economic stringency often brings default and repossession.

Work Ethic

To the middle class, work is not only a means to an end, it is an end in itself. People speak of liking their work, finding fulfillment in their work, and growing in their work. Moreover, work is not only honorable, it is necessary. He who does not work (gainfully) has no right to eat. It is excruciatingly difficult to get middle-class workers to accept the fact that many poor cannot work. In some vague and abstract sense, they agree that some sort of welfare system is necessary. But certainly those who are healthy and able-bodied have no right to it. They should get a job.

There is a wholly different concept of work in the lower class. First of all, it is not an end in itself. The jobs the poor get are often demeaning exercises high in frustration and low in pay, jobs many of the middle class would flatly refuse to perform.[9] Notions of personal growth, occupational goals, and life fulfillment are met with sardonic humor. In addition, last to be hired and first to be fired or laid off makes employment unstable and unemployment less stigmatizing. Attending to and understanding the radically different significance of work to the lower class is necessary in dealing with employment issues in the inner city.

Economic Savvy

In a middle-class dominated, capitalistic society, thrift and money management are central themes. Children are raised on the notion that money is nearly as critical a part of the environment as air. This fiscal socialization, then, prepares them for an adult role that is organized around financial acumen, from dealing with mortgage interest rates to paying grocery bills.

There is a wholly different fiscal consciousness in the inner city. It is utterly fruitless to expect the poor (with little money and less experience in handling it) to understand fiscal management. Protracted periods of being broke make a bit of money such a welcome sight that it is something to be celebrated rather than scrupulously saved. For while the larger society has only to wait until the next paycheck to purchase luxuries as well as necessities, the poor view a luxury like a stalk of wheat in a field of stubble.

Appearance of Respectability

There is probably no value that better highlights middle-class hypocrisy than the appearance of respectability. Middle-class people are obsessed with appearing respectable. Reputation and community acceptance are necessary for maintaining their sanity. They will go to ludicrous extremes to preserve a respectable image, even lying, covering up, falsifying records, making payoffs, and putting on façades. Soap operas watched by millions of matinee addicts are built around a series of plots that involve individual attempts to save face by duping a curious community or group of acquaintances.

This insatiable desire for respectability even extends to the law. For decades, not a word was said while thousands of poor teenagers were placed in juvenile homes for possessing and using marijuana. Then in the seventies, when the forbidden herb began being widely used in suburbia, the cry for its legalization was heard nationwide. Why? At least partly because it is repugnant to the middle-class psyche to regard their children who use it as delinquent. If their children use marijuana, then, because they are good and decent people, marijuana use must not be wrong.

Much the same sentiment prevails with regard to abortion. With the growing concern about birth control and a rising number of middle-class women "disappearing" for several weeks of vacation after becoming secretly pregnant, the society began clamoring for a more liberalized set of abortion statutes. In a matter of a few short years, abortion ceased being murder and commenced being pregnancy termination. It is not my intent to take a political stance on an issue as sensitive and complex as abortion; what is central to the topic, however, is that the impetus for political and social change came when class interests were at stake.

Although almost no one is devoid of the desire for some social approval and respect, poor communities are refreshingly liberated from conventional concerns over positive social images. Therefore, although unemployment, alcoholism, and pregnancy of unwed women are unpleasant, they do not necessitate the victim's hiding from the community until "the problem" is taken care of. An arrest record is never welcome, but not something to hang one's head about either. In short, people present themselves for who they are without undue self-consciousness about how congruent their image is with the mores of the rest of society.

It is easy for a pastor to interpret this openness as brazenness or defiance of social standards. It rarely is that. More often, it is simply life in the raw, without all the attendant pretensions and stagings. What may appear to be a casual attitude toward certain sins may well be the acceptance of the flawed nature of humanity and a realistic outlook on behavior practices in this particular environment.

Future Orientation

Future orientation is so riveted into middle-class culture that not to have a five-to-ten year outlook is adjudged irresponsible. People purchase homes, save money, buy bonds, go to college, start a business, and change residences on the basis of present sacrifice in favor of future outcomes. Eighteen-year-old youths who enter college with a commitment to become physicians know full well that this goal is at least seven years away. College, medical school, internship, and residency are all required of the aspiring physician. Yet he is undeterred, for there is no foreseeable reason, such as poor health, lack of money, or heavy family responsibilities, to slow his pace. His goal, then, is very realistic. In fact, were the enterprising youth not zeroing in on a career objective, he might well be upbraided by a parent who fears he will never "make anything of himself."

The view from the bottom is starkly different. The future looks no more bright than the present, and the past is the basis for this judgment. Federal statistics regularly reveal growing unemployment figures and increasing poverty rates rather than the amelioration of these ills. Meanwhile, inflation steadily gnaws away at the overall economic structures. As the minimum wage goes up, the number of unemployed increases, for employers can afford proportionately fewer workers.

The result of this grim set of circumstances is that the poor protect themselves from the psychological pains of disappointment by not setting their sights too high. Not only do they not lay up treasures for the future, but there is simply nothing in the way of treasures to lay up. There is no saving for a "rainy day," because every day rains economic misfortunes. Whereas the middle class speaks of "getting ahead," the poor talk of "getting by" or "getting over," for survival is the chief concern.

Responsibility for Personal Fate

With the topic of personal fate control we come to perhaps the central doctrine of the civil religion of the larger American society. The ethic of individualism, and therefore responsibility for one's own fate, is woven into the fabric of American society. All achievements are considered individual achievements.

If a youth who comes from a well-to-do family with well-educated parents and a firm grounding in the basic academic skills receives high grades, he is rewarded as if the results were based solely on his own efforts. No note is taken of the influence social class has on his academic achievement. On the contrary, he is given honor-roll designation, faculty approval, and guarantees for a successful future.

The student who does poorly, by middle-class academic standards, is regarded as dead educational wood. He is eventually programmed for educational and perhaps occupational obsolescence by being routed through the lower track of the curriculum.[10] Only the most astute school officials will note the poverty of the family, the lack of formal education of the parents, the family stresses with which the youngster copes, or the lack of academic success models available to him. The student will be held totally responsible.

This is unfortunate, for some very ordinary people are lauded for simply reaching expected heights, while some very extraordinary people are condemned because of circumstances well beyond their own control.

But this doctrine goes further. For example, people are often led to feel that because delinquency rates are lower in the suburbs, somehow the youths who reside there are more moral. What is forgotten is that urban youth lack the space, recreational facilities, and such alternatives as travel, vacationing, golfing, and summer baseball that money brings.

This blindness to inequality of opportunity, or this adherence to total individual responsibility for one's own actions, comes to final expression in the American justice system where the poor are regularly sentenced to prison terms because of higher arrest rates, poor defense, and unjust sentencing procedures.

These seven value dimensions divide the poor from the dominant society. Each class adopts a realistic view of these values with respect to social and economic position in the American stratification system. Indeed, for a middle-class person to affirm middle-class values is prudent. However, for the poor, their applicability is, to put it mildly, limited. Education may be valuable, but only in the abstract, as its quality in the inner city is thin. Property is much to be valued as a tool of affluence and power, but the poor invariably live on someone else's property, making him rich by their rent payments. Working hard is virtuous, and indeed, as the Protestant work ethic affirms, it is the secret to wealth; however, if there are no jobs with genuine opportunity, hard work may only guarantee early death. Thriftiness is a central skill to economic coping for many, but one must have financial resources with which to be thrifty. Appearing respectable is not only psychologically constructive, it is perhaps necessary for the maintenance of career and social position in most communities. However, such a façade may only make an inner-city resident appear "uppity" and insensitive. Finally, the key to much success is deferring present gratification in favor of reaping a future harvest, but this assumes there is something to sow beyond the seeds of survival.

Nonetheless, what makes these values critical here is that they are burned into the psyche of the vast majority of candidates for the pastorate. These values and their attendant attitude systems are, as Henry Lindgren puts it, ways of perceiving reality.[11] And this perceptual stance leads to victim blaming.

VICTIM BLAMING

If there is one book every urban worker would be wise to read, it is probably *Blaming the Victim* by William Ryan.[12] In fact, most of the rest of this chapter is devoted to reviewing and discussing the issues raised in it. Ryan very methodically and spectacularly explodes a host of unconscious myths held by most well-meaning, well-educated, and well-intentioned members of the middle class who would seek to redress the devastating effects of what are conventionally termed "social problems." Although many millions of city dwellers are victims of poverty, poor education, prejudice, unemployment, and a host of other maladies, those who seek to help these victims are victims as well. They, in Ryan's judgment, are victims of an ideology, a social perspective, that renders them all but useless in their zealous attempts to heal the wounds of the obvious victims with whom they deal.

Ryan calls blaming the victim an "ideology, a mythology, a set of officially-certified non-facts and respected untruths, and this ideology—which has been infused into the very cells of his [the middle-class victim's] brain—prevents him from seeing the process of victimization as a total picture."[13]

What is victim blaming? According to Ryan, it is a four-step process that begins with the identification of a social problem, say poverty. Once identified, the problem is studied by focusing on its victims (the poor) in terms of how they differ from the rest of the society, that is, how they deviate from the norm. Then assuming, in the case of poverty, that the economic system is sufficiently equitable that any reasonable or average person can succeed in it, lifestyle differences are stipulated as the core of the problem. That is, the reason poor people are poor is that they do not live properly. Once this has been established, some humanitarian strategy or program is developed that is aimed at changing the victim by eliminating these differences and bringing him "up" to the level of the rest of the society.

A baseline assumption that runs through victim blaming at all levels is that it is normal to be decently educated, have a productive job, and earn a livable wage in America. Anything less than achieving this social status makes a person abnormal, even deviant. Failure to reach this plateau may be met with sympathy and compassion; nonetheless, it is dealt with by attempting to change the victim so that he can become "a productive member of society." Implicit is the belief that there is enough to go around, there need not be any losers. Institutional causes such as redlining, miseducation, economic downturns affecting employment opportunities, racism, and any other maladies that may be at the root of victimization are admitted into consciousness, but only in passing. America remains the land of opportunity for all, and seizing the opportunity through hard work and adjustment to the system is all that is needed. Why there are always so many millions of victims every year is rarely if ever explored, as the humanitarians zealously turn their attention to retreading the victims.

This focus on the victim is fundamental to the failure of a host of governmental and ecclesiastical social programs. Why is it, one wonders, that nothing, from the Great Society to the local church program for unwed mothers, ever seems to work? Many theological conservatives chalk it all up to sin. If only everyone were evangelized, then these problems would disappear. Would they? Many evangelicals work in institutions that, albeit often unintentionally, both create and perpetuate racism, economic exploitation, and unemployment as a matter of course. Liberals take the education-brings-enlightenment view. If only the victims were better educated, they might escape their plight. What is necessary *is* an education, but it is the middle class that should be educated to circumvent them from enlisting in institutional enterprises that victimize masses of people. However, the public is often rather godless, and even the most well-educated are woefully ignorant of the effects of the status quo.

What this victim-blaming perspective does is cause the would-be helper to shift his focus away from the institutional injustices at the heart of the problem in question and toward the victim, who is trapped by the problem. There are two approaches taken by such helpers, both based on this victim-blaming perspective. The first approach is to volunteer to help within the very system that is itself the problem. The second approach is to find ways to change the victims themselves. Examples of both follow.

One example of the first approach is found in school volunteer helpers. People often read of the miseducation of children in a ghetto school and respond with horror at the insensitivity of the school personnel about whom they read. They quickly set their sights on helping these victimized youth escape the carelessness of the school officials who neglect them. What they pass by is the stark reality that ghetto education is an accepted, ongoing practice, carried on in virtually every major city in the United States to the detriment of literally millions of children each year. Many of the most caring will decide to take action. So, what do they do? They volunteer to help as teacher aides or in related capacities within the schools. All the while they remain unaware of the school tracking system, which sorts out students on the basis of IQ and other standardized test measures, sending some into enriched classrooms, while others are doomed to sit out their educational experience until they are old enough to quit.[14] Tragically, the well-meaning teacher aide frequently gets caught up in assisting the testing program, unaware of how the tests are used. In short, the would-be helper becomes part of the problem he desires to eradicate.

Another example of the volunteer approach is seen in urban renewal. Appalled at the quality of slum life in major cities, some would-be helpers quickly get behind the local urban renewal, slum clearance effort. Again, however, the individual, while feeling good about taking action, simply exacerbates the institutional injustices at the heart of the problem: clearing space so that more affluent residents and entrepreneurs can move into a refurbished region while the poor are left to find another overly dense enclave in which to exist.

These two cases are examples of simply joining in with sweeping institutional programs that perpetuate problems by bypassing the interests of the victims and extending the power of the larger system. Often, however, the focus is directly on changing the victim. The victim, viewed with concern and sympathy if not genuine love, is seen as the cause of the problem. Poor health in slum areas is often attributed to faulty health practices. Ramshackle slum living is chalked up to a lack of adjustment to urban life. Poverty is accounted for by the inability of the poor to escape a living pattern marked by a culture of poverty. Once this focus on changing the victim has been clearly set, programs are designed to change, enrich, upgrade, or in some other fashion better the victim.

In education, these programs are called "compensatory education" or "enrichment" programs. In short, these are organized attempts at elevating the low achiever to the level of the average student in the school. Absolutely nothing is done to change the structures and processes that methodically grind out millions of victims yearly.

Rather than realize that much of the educational enterprise is humiliating to those who fail, that those who fail can be identified by prejudicial standardized tests in the primary grades, and that many teachers are deeply imbued with the belief that teaching the "disadvantaged" is really useless anyway, students are corralled, tutored, and cajoled in an effort to bring them up to standard.

In medicine, health-care information is scatter-gunned throughout low-income areas and hygienic practices are preached faithfully over radio and television. But the gross inequities involving the costs and availability of health care for the poor go unaddressed.

One of Ryan's prime examples involves lead-paint poisoning. A pharmaceutical company with social conscience and civic concern may, at its own expense, print thousands of signs warning against eating lead-paint chips, and make certain that these posters are distributed throughout a major city. As humanitarian as this action may be, it diverts attention away from the real problem: that lead-paint poisoning is an outgrowth of the institution of slum landlording in the United States. The real cause is that lead-paint use (in many locales illegal for residential buildings) and mass disrepair of buildings are tolerated by city inspectors. What is really going on is that slum landlords are clearly living in violation of the legal code, while contributing to the death of their victims. Yet the problem is addressed by informing the victim that he better beware to sidestep the effects of an illegal practice by members of the landowning class. The process begins with the use of lead paint, continues as repairs of buildings are not made, and ends with the grief-stricken urban mother looking with guilt at the body of her dead child, who she believes would be alive today if only she had warned him against eating the paint chips.

Virtually every social problem is dealt with in some victim-blaming form. Millions of dollars have been dumped into federal programming, all designed to change the victim. For that is the simplest thing to do. To change the status quo, to alter the system and make it equitable, would be to remove the advantage the dominant group has. If all the inequities were removed from the system, those in power would be in power no longer. The middle class would no longer be assured of their middle-class status, and being successful would no longer be a routine matter of effective socialization but rather a matter of greater effort.

In the church, this victim blaming has a double jeopardy. On the one hand, it undercuts so many energetic service ministries; on the other, the church simply becomes a supporter of the sins of institutional injustice that victimize its own parishioners. There is neither honor nor credibility in such an approach.

A key to escaping the subtle, octopuslike clutches of victim blaming is raised consciousness. There must be an ability to distinguish between victim-blaming and non–victim-blaming approaches. The figure and explanations that follow seek to provide examples of such distinctions.[15]

VICTIM-BLAMING VERSUS NON–VICTIM-BLAMING APPROACHES

INSTITUTION	PROBLEM	DOMINANT VIEW	ANALYSIS AND NEEDS
Education	Low Achieve-ment	Cultural deprivation Apathy Limited academic skills Enrichment needed	Decentralization Money Community control Teacher-attitude change
Economics	Poverty	Poverty culture Poverty-oriented values Child-rearing differences Educational apathy Immediate gratification Hopeless situation Acculturation needed	Jobs Income maintenance Power Access to opportunities Change in the system
Justice	Crime	Crime rate highest in slums Warped personalities produced by slum living Criminals a distinct subgroup Role of police to suppress these people	Emphasis on street crime rather than on organized crime or white-collar crime Crime unrelated to socio-economic status Differential enforcement of the law Emphasis on order rather than on law Comprehensive definition of crime, adequate legal defense, fair sentencing, and reha-bilitation needed

Figure 2.

Education

Looking at the institution of education, the major problem seems to be low achievement. As previously discussed, achievement has been found in repeated studies to be very closely associated with socioeconomic status. That is, the lower the student's socioeconomic status is, the poorer his academic achievement will be.

Dominant View. The conventional or dominant explanation for the association of low achievement and low socioeconomic status is fourfold. First, those who are poor economically and whose children do poorly in the nation's schools are living in a state of cultural deprivation. The culture out of which the children come is simply not adequate—not up to sufficient standard to assure success in the classroom.

Second, poor parents are thought to be apathetic about education. Their depressed aspirations for their children rub off on the youth and so, over time, no one in the community cares to exert himself enough to insure academic success.

Third, limited academic skills are also cited. The belief is that, because of a series of rather unspecified social and environmental factors, these children just don't have it anyway. Trying to make scholars out of these youngsters is viewed as akin to attempting to make a bulldog run like a greyhound.

Finally, *enrichment* is usually the byword for what is needed. Head Start and other types of compensatory programs are inaugurated in the hope of surrounding the children as early as possible with the proper environmental forces conducive to doing well in school. All stops have to be pulled out to compensate for the deficiencies of the students' environment and bring them into step with the middle class.

The dominant view places the blame squarely on the victim. The victim must do the changing; the school system is all right. Before turning to a non–victim-blaming perspective, it would be well to examine more closely the dominant viewpoints.

Cultural deprivation assumes a cultural superiority on the part of the larger society. It suggests not that the poor are culturally different, but also that they are culturally inferior and that the quicker that culture is undercut and replaced with a more enlightened way, the better. Such a supremacist notion is insulting and says more about the middle class than the poor who fail in the public school system.

As emphasized earlier, almost every scholarly study done on aspiration refutes the charge that lower-class people have a more apathetic view of education than the middle class. The difference is not in aspiration but in the ability to act strategically and effectively on these lofty educational goals.[16]

Limited academic skills exist when measured by middle-class standards. Indeed, at the first-grade level, middle-class children are much more prepared for the kinds of experiences afforded in the conventional school than their less affluent counterparts. Middle-class children often know the alphabet, can do simple computation, and are able to read with considerable proficiency before entering school. That poor children do not come to school with those skills does not mean that the capacity for their development does not exist. However, when the school curricula and the expectations of the middle-class teaching personnel carry the assumption that these rather cognitive skills are already or should already be developed, then anyone who is not at that stage of academic development is already behind and will likely remain behind.

The enrichment panacea really zeroes in on the victim. Instead of taking the student where he is, determining his abilities—latent and actual—and working from there, educators deluge the unsuspecting student with "enrichment," that is, experiences assumed superior to his deficient and inferior environment. The hope is that some of this enrichment will "take" and the student will survive in the conventional academic environment. If he doesn't survive, then he just doesn't have it.

Analysis and Needs. Moving from the dominant view's focus on the victim toward a non–victim-blaming analysis of the needs, the first need is for decentralization of the school system. Decentralization means more community control and, therefore, community involvement in the educational process. As it is now, a host of downtown bureaucrats control the purse strings and the procedures operative in the schools they rarely if ever visit. It is extraordinarily difficult for them to appreciate the problems and needs of the individual schools. With greater decentralization there is likely to be a greater commitment on the part of faculty and administrators, as well as parents, all making a more conscientious effort toward improving the education of the children.

The second need, money, is also important, especially in view of the fact that suburban per-pupil expenditures are greatly in excess of urban. That is, the individual suburban child has much more money allocated to his education than his urban peer. In addition, the money should be spent where it is needed most: where achievement is the lowest, buildings the oldest, people the poorest, teachers and administrators most given to turnover, and so on.

The third need, community control, has already been touched on; however, it is important to add here the importance of community pride. Where there is a sense of fate control, there tends to be more energy and enthusiasm as well as a sense of responsibility.

Finally, teacher attitude is especially vital. Rosenthal and Jacobson's classic, though much-criticized, study suggests that teachers tend to get out of their students what they believe they are able to get.[17] If, in other words, the teacher expects growth, he somehow seems to get it; if the teacher feels the child is hopeless, the child vegetates academically. Other studies, as well as my own observations and experiences, lend support to this notion.

This presentation of analysis and needs is not advanced as a panacea for the eradication of the problems associated with low academic achievement. It does suggest, however, that the starting point is to abandon the notion that the system itself is just and that if one is normal one should succeed, and instead examine the institutional process with an eye toward finding its inequities and injustices—faults that have the effect of systematically producing failure for millions of victims who, because of the system's biased assumptions and processes, are not able to compete on equal terms with their middle-class counterparts.

Economics

The major social problem in the institution of economics is, of course, poverty. Here again the public notion is that the poor develop a self-defeating culture of poverty, replete with values and behaviors that doom them to live at the bottom. This culture carries with it poor child-rearing patterns, educational apathy, and a tendency to look for immediate gratification rather than carefully storing up money and opportunity in order to succeed later.

Dominant View. The dominant view subtly suggests that the situation is really hopeless. Indeed, as Christ said, "The poor will be with you always" (Mark 7:14). If only the poor could be acculturated—socialized—into a different outlook that would enable them to lift themselves into a more productive life, the problem would be solved. As it is, however, they are going nowhere, trapped in the web of a culture of poverty. In short, America is the land of opportunity, but the poor, as a result of their own intellectual, social, and cultural deficiencies, are unable to seize the opportunity and so they live pathetically in the economic dungeon.

Harrington sees a particular prejudice toward the poor among businesspeople.[18] Federal efforts at eradicating poverty have met with intense opposition from the business community, including the editors of the *Wall Street Journal.* Most of the opposition issues from the belief that the poor must "pull themselves up by their bootstraps" as did other poor before them. There is no mention as to where these bootstraps can be found in a nation that has few land opportunities, needs little unskilled labor, and suffers from continuing inflation.

Prejudice toward the poor is found also among politicians, who are probably the group most responsible for spreading antipoverty propaganda. An article by Elizabeth Drew, entitled "Going Hungry in America: Government's Failure," gives several examples from recent decades.[19] Mississippi is the poorest state in the nation, yet one of its most powerful congressmen, Jamie Whitten, once opposed a plan developed by then Secretary of Agriculture Orville Freeman to distribute food equitably to the hungry in his state, because he believed that poverty is based on personal inadequacy. Even President Johnson, long seen as a champion of social causes, was reluctant to embark on some of his relief programs for the hungry, because he simply did not believe that hunger in America was as serious and widespread as it is. Nixon and Goldwater have been renowned for their lack of compassion for the poor, Goldwater particularly being adamant in his belief that poverty grows out of a lack of intelligence and ambition. These are just a few examples.

In short, the dominant view focuses directly on the victim. The system is fine. There need be no losers in the capitalistic economy. Any person of reasonable intelligence, ability, and drive is perfectly able to garner a solid job and make a decent living. People who do not survive at a middle-class level need to change—to be rid of the faults that make them unable to compete.

Analysis and Needs. From an institutional standpoint, the problems look radically different. One area of concern is jobs. It is very difficult to succeed in a capitalistic market if one cannot find a decent, well-paying job. With an unemployment rate frequently in excess of 10 percent nationwide, and three to four times that in low-income areas, it is hard to imagine how people are able to survive. There may have to be some sort of much-debated family income maintenance if no plan is implemented to "put America back to work." As it is presently, unemployment compensation, aid to dependent children, disability benefits, and all other types of public aid are scarcely sufficient to keep a family alive, much less to allow them to have a decent standard of living.

A primary area of need is greater social and political power and greater access to opportunities for the poor. As discussed in chapter 4, the poor remain politically unrepresented, and they live in areas in which educational opportunities are the poorest and where industries and other job sources do not exist. Unless there are real changes in the system, all the acculturation in the world is likely to do little good. Indeed, there may occasionally be a character out of a Horatio Alger novel that rises to the top, but such a figure is an exception and leaves millions of average people behind.

To be sure, many Americans chafe at welfare programs, grudgingly watching their tax dollars eaten by various forms of public-aid allotments. The only alternative to such a procedure is to change the whole institutional system by making it truly open, equal, and democratic in opportunity.

Justice

The major problem in this area is, of course, crime. There is no shortage of concern about crime in America. Americans are particularly frightened by the extent of crime in the major cities, most notably in the slums. Why is there such a high crime rate?

Dominant View. The dominant view suggests that slum living warps the personality of the slum dweller, desensitizing him to right and wrong, law and order. Moreover, criminals are viewed as a distinct subgroup in the society; society can be divided into criminals and straight people, the law-abiding and the evil-doing. The role of the police in such a society is to crack down on urban crime, holding it in check with methods ranging from detection to intimidation.

Although the dominant view allows that there are some environmental factors attendant to slum living that may pressure people toward lawlessness, there is little attention focused on what these factors are. As Ramsey Clark, author of *Crime in America,*[20] points out, if a circle were drawn on a city map around the spot where education is the poorest, and more circles where health care is the scarcest, unemployment the highest, political power the weakest, incomes the lowest, housing the most difficult to obtain, family life the most strained, recreational facilities the fewest, and street crime the highest, the same spot would be circled again and again and again. Street crime, then, is associated with a myriad of variables, quite unrelated to the skin color or personality makeup of the people who commit it.

Analysis and Needs. Americans suffer from a myopic view of crime. In reality, there are three types of crime: organized crime, white-collar crime, and street crime. Of these three, street crime is highlighted and focused on. Yet organized crime involves more money than the other two combined, and white-collar crime, especially as it is practiced in government and big business, has more far-reaching consequences for the society. Yet those involved in organized and white-collar crime are simply not regarded as criminals. The barons of organized crime are the subjects of novels, biographies, and movies, while those who commit white-collar offenses are viewed as law-abiding citizens who temporarily go astray. The prisons are built for the poor who offend on the streets.

Research attempts have indicated that crime is actually unrelated to socioeconomic status.[21] If every violation of the law (whether or not the perpetrator was apprehended) were defined as a crime, then almost everyone in the society would bear the label criminal. People who bilk the government out of vast sums of money with dishonest income-tax reporting; businesses that price fix, pollute, and defraud; consumers who shoplift for fun and profit; pleasure-seekers who illegally smoke marijuana and indulge themselves in the use of harder drugs; and that vast number of Americans who each week illegally bet on football games and other sporting events—all are criminals. It is not that there is a distinct group of criminals, but that there is a differential enforcement of the law.

But what of street crime? It is violent and disruptive of public order. Indeed it is, and its disruptiveness is why it is focused on. The fact is that American justice is much more concerned with order than with law. White-collar and even much organized crime is carried on within the normal workings of major institutions. In some cases, white-collar crime not only does not disrupt order, but actually cuts through bureaucratic red tape, hastening needed action. Crime of this sort is carried on by what are called productive members of society. Street crime is disorderly. It obstructs the smooth workings of the institutional system, and it is carried on by the least socially useful.

It is for this reason that an executive who is caught knowingly polluting the air and water by tolerating the use of equipment below pollution-control standards, and so jeopardizes the health and well-being of the millions of residents in a major metropolitan area, is granted 120 days to bring his plant up to standard, while a city youth who is apprehended for snatching a purse containing ten dollars will go to jail that very night. The former is on balance a law-abiding citizen who necessitates prompting. The latter is a young criminal.

What is really needed is a more comprehensive definition of crime, a much more adequate defense system, and fair sentencing procedures. As it is now, the rich are defended by high-power private attorneys who rarely lose a case even if their clients are guilty, while the poor are left with an overworked public defender who finds it most propitious to plea bargain. Overall, it is the system that needs to be rehabilitated, not just the street criminals. Without needed changes, the jails will continue to swell with the poor.

The solutions to problems in society, then, are not more programs that focus on the poor, not more victim blaming, but a reevaluation of the role of institutions in producing the problems and creating victims.

REFOCUSING URBAN MINISTRIES

Urban ministries tend to fail. Although success should not be the goal so much as faithfulness in service, it is important to examine why these failures occur. Often the ministries are based on the same victim-blaming foundations that premise so many failure-ridden governmental programs. This is not surprising, for those who structure urban ministries have few other models than the government and the public sector to emulate. However, as long as the victim remains the focus, what occurs is the rehabilitation of a few, the loss of many, and no change in the source that is creating the problem.

With this point in mind, it is easier to understand why a church needs to refocus its ministries to include not only service ministries but also stewardship ministries. Although it is helpful to have a tutoring program, it is also important to focus on the accountability of the local school in an effort to encourage more effective teaching/learning processes. Helping residents find housing is a necessary "cup of cold water" ministry, but actively working against malicious redlining practices is perhaps even more important. Counseling and befriending neighborhood youth is necessary in building healthy relationships and modeling what adult life can be, but having a youth program that both attempts to reform and redirect the energies of the gangs and also is vigilant about ways in which the city and its officials can provide a more equitable environment for the youngsters is just as important. Directing troubled residents toward legal aid clinics and even charitable private lawyers is a worthy enterprise, but no more so than working with community organizations and other groups toward guaranteeing more humane police treatment and fire service.

At LaSalle Street Church in Chicago, the Young Life program has developed such an effective track record that judges have granted youthful offenders probation, provided they will get involved in its program. Here is an example of urban workers approaching systems rather than working exclusively with individuals. Aiding an unemployed resident in his efforts to find work is an honorable as well as a difficult and often frustrating venture. But encouraging local businesses and corporations within or adjacent to the community to hire the poor and indigent may provide jobs for many. It may be necessary to help some citizen who has had an unhappy experience with the city political organization, but it can be even more effective to have various political candidates and figures speak at the church in hopes of extracting pledges from them for more equitable treatment of the entire community citizenry. It may be a significant act to help one of the senior high students get accepted into the church college of his choice, but if that youth is nonwhite, it might be more effective to examine why so few minorities are enrolled in these institutions. Finding companionship and entertainment for lonely youngsters is a humane thing, but so is approaching the local powers-that-be about opening more recreational space for the neighborhood youth.

It would be humanly impossible for a single pastor or even a team to address every problem at the institutional level with real effectiveness. That is not the point here. In fact, it is important that any urban worker assess his resources—including time—before taking action. Then he can determine priorities and set objectives based on community and church needs.

The point here is that those who do urban ministry should refocus their efforts to include stewardship ministries and not allow themselves to be limited by a victim-blaming perspective. The victim-focusing ministries tend to help usually one person or at most just a few people at a time. Such relief efforts are worthy and scriptural. However, an institutional-reform approach, which can turn the tide for many, perhaps thousands of people needing relief and justice, is also scriptural in view of the many calls for justice in the Bible. Moreover, every victory carries with it an enormous sense of satisfaction because a social problem has been attacked at its root. Such a satisfying experience can pump new energy into all ministries, regardless of focus.

If the urban minister keeps his eyes fixed on the real causes of the ills of the poor, he is likely to be more effective in working with them. All too often the poor are encountered by well-intentioned workers who are unwitting pawns of these larger systems. Such people are of limited value to them and receive provisional respect. Workers who openly acknowledge the victimizing tendencies of unjust institutional systems can help those victims survive in the system by offering them personal change options to their present way of living. Such workers are likely to develop much better rapport.

Although Ryan is singularly condemnatory toward individual-based, victim-focus programs of any sort, it is not being suggested here that all such programs be abandoned because they have a blaming-the-victim strain to them. These ministries, which work toward bringing about change in the victim such that he can adjust to and function within the system, are absolutely defensible in view of the fact that without them and without any change in larger institutional systems, these victims will remain hopeless victims. Ministries such as these at least provide opportunities to develop skills that enable those held under by the institutional system to avoid drowning.

However, knowing that such ministries are important ought not to divert urban workers' attentions away from the real causal factors at the institutional level. Any and every opportunity to address these causes should be taken advantage of. Here again, care is needed. Reckless confrontation of institutions is not only un-Christian, but foolish. Moreover, it will only brand the church as the enemy of the institutional community. Diplomacy is always in order. Nonetheless, diplomacy should not be a password for cowardice or passivity in the face of a need to call institutions to a higher awareness of their social and civic responsibility.

The bottom line here is awareness. The whole task of urban ministry, whether individually or institutionally focused, carries with it a plethora of problems and frustrations. However, when working in the social arena, if a pastor can avoid being duped by already duped well-meaning officials, who would shift the focus away from unjust systems and toward deficiencies in victims, he will at the very least have the confidence that he knows what he is doing. In addition, he will be able to analyze his current set of ministries in terms of their effectiveness and inaugurate new ones with realistic expectations of what they may accomplish. Without such an awareness, he is in jeopardy of blindly following the victim-blaming procedures of governmental programs, only to wonder openly and alone why nothing ever really seems to work.

9 | The Urban Church and the Urban Minister

This final chapter on urban ministry looks at the differences between inner-city churches and middle-class churches—differences in style, in expectations, in priorities, in general makeup. It is here that the sociological traits of residents of inner cities make their impact on the nature of the church. Social stratification, institutional oppression, poverty, insecurity, and victimization need to be addressed by stewardship and service ministries of the church. But the very nature of the church itself—its worship services and its programs—is affected by its urban locale. The urban pastor must know and appreciate these differences in order to minister effectively.

The chapter—and book—close with advice to the urban minister on the psychological attributes and survival techniques he will need to cultivate in order to avoid burnout and instead reap the rewards of urban ministry.

THE URBAN CHURCH

Differences Between Inner-City and Middle-Class Churches

There are a number of ways in which inner-city churches tend to differ from their more affluent counterparts. Some of these disparities are necessary and appropriate, given the differences between inner-city and middle-class life. Some, however, suggest deficits in one or the other's parish style. Although each of the following areas merits extensive research, here is a brief review, adapted from Anthony Campolo's work, of fourteen areas of difference.[1]

People vs. Buildings. Inner-city churches tend to put their money into people-oriented ministries, while an emphasis on building size, stability, beauty, and maintenance eats up a greater share of middle-class church budgets.

Basic vs. Dissertational Preaching. Inner-city pastors preach from the "gut," and in a more affective domain than their middle-class peers whose preaching often sounds more like a lecture or scholarly treatise.

Personal vs. Theological. Because of the great need for basic human care, inner-city churches have a more personal style. Middle-class churches often tend toward a more theological, catechetical strain. Both elements are important in church life, but the emphasis is different. Moreover, whereas middle-class churches are often able to apply neatly their theology to most congregational issues, the complexities of inner-city life make direct theological application well-nigh impossible in many cases. The issue of ambiguity is discussed more fully later.

Communication and Identification vs. Education and Sophistication. Inner-city pastors are judged much by their ability to communicate and identify. Academic degrees and a sophisticated style are much more highly valued in more affluent churches. This does not suggest that communication and personal warmth are not important in a middle-class congregation, but that they are all-important in the inner city.

Heterogeneous vs. Homogeneous. Inner-city churches often are more diverse economically, socially, occupationally, educationally, and in some cases ethnically than most other churches.

Community-Centered vs. Property-Centered. Inner-city parishes tend to see themselves in the context of their turf—the geographical community. Their ministries reflect this neighborhood quality. Middle-class churches tend to center their activities and ministries around the immediate building, taking a more isolationist position.

Community Service vs. Congregational Nurture. Inner-city churches emphasize serving the residents of the neighborhood—socially and spiritually—whether or not they are affiliated with the parish. Middle-class churches tend to look more toward nurturing and developing their own members and fellowship.

Present vs. Future. Owing to the crisis-interventionist nature of inner-city life, inner-city churches tend to respond to the immediate. Traditional, stable churches are more given to five- and ten-year plans.

Transience vs. Stability. Because of poverty and community disorganization, the congregation of an inner-city church will turn over much more often than those of other churches. This transience is particularly frustrating to urban pastors, as it means not only losing the pillars of their churches but constantly having to instruct and orient new people.

Changing vs. Defined. Inner-city churches are constantly experimenting and adapting. New ministries and programs are regularly being developed to keep pace with the volatile nature of the social environment. Middle-class churches usually have a more defined and routine operation.

Ambiguous vs. Clear. It is difficult to describe comprehensively and accurately what an inner-city church is really like—its ethos and operation. This is partly because of the changing nature of these entities. Middle class churches are less ambiguous institutions and, therefore, easier to get the pulse of.

Informal vs. Formal Hierarchy. Inner-city churches are much more *ad hoc* than traditional churches. The pecking order, with more frequent changes, is both looser and more given to change than the more tightly defined hierarchy of the more stable congregations.

Anti-Status Quo vs. Status Quo. This is a major area of difference. Inner-city churches view the prevailing sociocultural system as oppressive and laced with class interests. Middle-class congregations feel more comfortable with the capitalistic, economic, and social system. While inner-city churches cry out for justice amid oppression, other churches emphasize Pauline injunctions to obey the civil authorities.

Redemption vs. Avoidance of Guilt. Inner-city churches exist among so much sin and misery there tends to be a rather positive, redemptive emphasis about them. Wrongdoing, though often acknowledged, is less emphasized than forgiveness and fresh starts. In many middle-class churches, there may be a tendency either to avoid the matter of sin—dealing with it in generalities—or to emphasize its heinousness to such an extent that burdens of guilt are carried for a long time.

Awareness of these different emphases is important for new urban ministers as well as those people, from suburban or middle-class churches, who are considering urban work.

Review of Recent Scholarship on Urban Ministry

A number of authors have dealt with the problems facing inner-city churches and their pastors and people. The recommendations they make range from preaching style and program development to renewal and community ministry. Some have developed urban strategy models. Although there is of necessity some overlap in these recommendations, no attempt has been made to systematize or synthesize their remarks. They are presented here because they contain outstanding ideas and examples for effective urban ministry. Running throughout is my commentary or expansion on these ideas.

George Baybrook looked at six rather successful churches to discover their points of commonality. Four of these points are pertinent to this discussion.[2] One, surprisingly, is that *money is not emphasized*. There are few if any appeals for dollars and no heavy-handed tactics.

Second, *buildings are not stressed*. When facilities are outgrown, these churches consider creating "spin-off" churches rather than "pulling down their barns and building greater." It may be added here that with energy and environmental concerns high in the nation, how the church deals with expansion is important. With the United States constituting but 6 percent of the world's population and using 30 to 40 percent of the world's mineral and energy output, the church needs to model better stewardship of resources. Moreover, with a high incidence of cancer resulting from environmental factors, ecological concern might well be emphasized.[3]

Third, *spiritual gifts are focused on*. People are enjoined to assess their gifts and use them for the common good. Members are evaluated for positions on the basis of their gifts, and there is no stress laid on doing what one is not "called" or able to do.

Finally, *people are emphasized* more than publicity-oriented programs are. The stress is on relationships, affirmation, and growth rather than on grand-scale programs. The word *program* used in this sense is not to be confused with its use in the sense of ministry.

Willie Jemison looks at preaching and personal style and makes five recommendations for growth, particularly of black congregations.[4]

First, *the message must be relevant.* By this he means that the illustrations and points raised should be adapted to the experiences and lifestyles of the congregation.

Second, *the pulpit ministry must be strong.* The pastor must believe what he preaches and preach what he believes. The sermon is the solidifying element and must be powerful.

Third, *worship must be exciting.* There needs to be movement—singing, praising, and dynamic preaching—that leaves people lifted and inspired by the experience.

Fourth, *the message must be holistic*—aimed at the whole person. This means a ministry that acts to meet the day-to-day concerns of the parishioners. Jemison uses education as an example, encouraging black ministers to stand up and protest against high schools and colleges that have blacks matriculating without offering them anything to affirm or deepen their black identity; there must be models other than white. Too often white institutions are careful not to say anything bad about minorities, but at the same time make certain the presence of minorities does not in any way affect the routine operation of the school. In any case, Jemison feels addressing this rather practical area is an example of a holistic, and hence a rather personal, orientation.

Finally, Jemison emphasizes that *the pastor must be a caring person.* The pastor is central and he must be where the parishioners are, sharing their joys and sorrows, victories and defeats.

With this emphasis on people and personal involvement found in Baybrook and in Jemison, there is no discussion of program. Donald Benedict finds that at the denominational level, programs are helpful. Benedict suggests five major areas of program development to aid urban ministry.[5] The first urges denominations to design strategies that will enable churches in the inner city to survive. This means *financial aid.* Second, there must be theological attempts to filter out the *message of Christ* from the prevailing middle-class, materialistic culture. Where the gospel gets entangled with class interests, it becomes short-circuited and heretical. Third, attention needs to be drawn to the *issues of race and racism*. Benedict suggests that a denominational newsletter focusing on race and race relations be published. The *Chicago Reporter* is an example of such a consciousness-raising and maintaining effort. Fourth, the development of *alternative Christian schools* is encouraged. These schools can be located in the inner-city church and should include parental participation. Though costly, they would meet many critical youth needs. Finally, the *issue of unemployment* must be addressed. Denominations must be engaged in dialogue and research in an effort to remedy this problem.

Bill Leslie, feeling that if the church is to model Christ it must get outside itself and perform a ministry, makes a number of pertinent points.[6] He gives advice for developing programs but he continually stresses the fact that programs come alive through persons. First he points out that too much time is burned up arguing about theological issues while so much plain biblical truth has not yet been put into practice. Believers, he says, must be ready on all fronts to serve in the city. Urbanites have many more problems than just spiritual ones. They lack money, proper housing, adequate education, and legal protection. They are often plagued by relational or family problems, such as having a family member with a drug or alcohol problem.

Leslie also emphasizes the need for renewal. A hindrance to renewal is the spectator attitude prevalent in churches. Like the sports crowd, the congregation gathers weekly at the church to watch the performance, ready to cheer or critique. The parishioners come to be entertained rather than to be equipped for carrying out the church's ministry.

Leslie searched out some scriptural principles undergirding the ministering rather than the spectating church. First, the Bible indicates that the kingdom of God is present, even though its fulfillment lies in the future. This means that churches need to seek the *reign of Christ* presently in the lives of individuals, institutions, and whole societies. Second, throughout the Scriptures is the pervasive concept of *servanthood*. Christ's model, as expressed in Matthew 20:28, was one of ministering rather than being ministered to. People need to discover their gifts and put them to use. Third, servanthood stems from the principle that the church is the *body of Christ*. As Christ's body, it must do His ministry. When the church embodies the Spirit of Christ, results occur. Fourth, the members must be *equipped* to perform the ministry. Finally, like Christ, the church must not opt out of *difficult circumstances*. All these principles point to the pastor as a player/coach who tries to get his entire congregation on the field and into the ministry.

A renewed church will put programs into effect. But those programs need a personal touch. Bill Leslie and Keith Miller once led a meeting of about a thousand people asking them to list the actions of a church or person that had the greatest impact on them. Not one mentioned a program. All alluded to a caring person and a caring act.

Equipping parishioners for active ministry is not an easy task. Michael Roschke points out real impediments to lay ministry.[7] For one, seminaries train pastors to do rather than to equip or to enable. This tendency, coupled with a stratification structure that places the pastor at the top of the ecclesiastical flow chart, makes it difficult for parishioners to assess their gifts and put them to use.

Second, there is always a tendency for urban workers to see the poor as those with less education, less power, and less wealth, and therefore as lesser people. However subconscious this may be, it short-circuits effective urban ministry.

In spite of these impediments, it is Roschke's conviction that everyone has a gift with which to minister. He relates anecdotes in which a senile woman, a reformed alcoholic, a vagrant who lived in a parked car, a suburban woman on a kidney dialysis machine, and a depressed urban woman all provided a caring ministry.

Roschke sees this transformation from being a needy person to being one who is able to give as a three-step process. First, the needy person must be helped in a holistic fashion. This is followed by a developing relationship between the person who is being helped and those who are helping him. However, the helper-helpee labels should melt away quickly, giving rise to a mutually caring alliance. Finally, the person who initially needed help should be included in a close fellowship group. In such an intimate setting he can find his gift, be encouraged and strengthened in it, and so be prepared to use it.

James Conklin stresses the need for *unity and commitment*.[8] A church, much like an individual, has a self-concept. Its corporate self-view can range from positive, aggressive, and victorious to weak, despairing, and defeatist. In building a strong "we can" self-concept, it is important to develop unity. One church developed a prayer covenant and designed a little pin as a symbol of their mutual commitment. Such creative approaches can be helpful in reminding parishioners of their oneness. When there is unity, there is commitment and accountability to one another. Such mutual accountability energizes people in working at church programs and can insulate them against personal and relational breakdowns.

There are a number of examples of ministering churches that exhibit these many traits. Chicago's Broadview Baptist Church, sponsored by Northwest Baptist Church, has grown from 480 to over 1,200 members. This black church attributes its growth to an emphasis on Bible study and Sunday school opportunities. Christine Daniels, the director of the all-volunteer education program, feels that when church members feed others spiritually they remain involved.[9]

In Denver, the presbytery developed an urban strategy that was keyed on remaining in the city, making disciples, and then sending these disciples out to meet the needs of the community.[10]

In Detroit, the Church of the Messiah has extended-family households, a day-care center, and an alternative school. The church in Detroit is referred to as more than a program; it is a way of life. When the church is a verb rather than a noun, things start to happen.[11]

For all churches, evaluation is important. For churches involved in urban ministry it is particularly important. From a specifically urban perspective, Lyle Schaller poses twenty self-evaluation questions for downtown, though not necessarily inner-city, churches.[12] Following are the ones most relevant to this discussion.

1. What is the combined contribution of the top ten and top twenty giving units? To the extent that money is an issue, it is helpful to know whether the top givers are good models or whether they are so generous that the church depends too heavily on them.

2. What types of skills are formally and informally rewarded? Growing churches emphasize creativity, dedication, and outreach as opposed to verbal and social skills.

3. What items dominate the agenda of the church's governing body? While declining churches emphasize means to ends, focusing on survival questions, growing congregations look at effective ministering, caring, and nurturing as they observe community needs.

4. Is parking ample? Unless there is sufficient parking, non–Sunday-morning events will not be attended well, because of inconvenience and fear of street crime.

5. How effective is the communication network in the church? Do messages get to the members? Five of these seven communication modes should be used for important messages:
- Bulletin
- Newsletter
- Pulpit announcement
- Telephone
- Poster
- Personal visit
- Special mailing

Attention also needs to be given to the general communication level in the church and the community. Are there cliques? Is there smooth relaying of information? Good communication results from effective planning and much attention to detail.

6. What is the turnover rate? Is the church gaining or losing members? This is a good measure of how people feel about the church.

7. What is the church's image in the community? If outreach is to be at all effective, it is vital to get a good reading on this. The real image of the church may be a far cry from the intended one. It is important that the image be both positive and clear.

8. What is the attendance rate among confirmed resident members? Keeping tabs on this is valuable in evaluating the quality of corporate worship as well as the vitality of the church in general.

9. What is the age distribution of the church? Is it a young church? An old church? A changing church? Who is being ministered to and who is doing the ministering?

10. What is the attitude of members toward visitors and potential new members? Are the members service-oriented and responsive?

11. What is the nature of church leadership roles? Thriving churches place less emphasis on clergy leadership and more on lay involvement. Volunteer staff, temporary staff, and short-term specialists are common in growing churches.

12. Is the pastoral care to the members adequate? Members must be cared for in order to grow and minister themselves. Failure to perform this care gives rise to irritations, divisiveness, and stagnation.

The real goal for the urban parish is discipling whomever God sends it. This allows the pastor a tremendous sense of freedom from the usual clerical derby. Effective discipleship and personal development is the mark of the successful urban minister. In order to enjoy this success, he must strike a balance between piety and action (inward worshipful growth and active outward thrusts) as well as between evangelism and social action.

THE URBAN MINISTER

The stresses faced by an urban pastor are great. In order to live that balanced life personally, as well as model balance for his parishioners, the pastor should develop particular psychological attributes that will make his ministry effective. In addition, he needs to pay attention to the well-being of his personal life. The dangers of burnout are very real, but the rewards of a successful, enduring ministry in the city are very great.

Psychological Attributes

There are several psychological attributes in particular that mark an effective urban pastor or church worker. One is *respect for and appreciation of cultural diversity*. Urban communities are forever in transition and are filled with personal and cultural differences. For those who have been well socialized into the mainstream culture, this is psychologically unsettling. In fact, if they can even reach a level of toleration for this pluralism, a considerable personal victory has been won. The prospective urban pastor would do very well to immerse himself in as many different cultural experiences as possible, so that pluralism comes to mean beauty, and diversity to mean stimulation. It is only through this developed appreciation that the urban pastor can become truly a friend of the community. Friends appreciate, help, and serve others. To lack appreciation of the prevailing culture means to distance oneself from its practitioners and thus to be unable to serve without manipulation and conditional forms of love.

The pastor's appreciation of cultural diversity will lead him to find ways of dealing with the problem of developing a pluralistic atmosphere in the church. Several brief guidelines for this are worthy of mention. One is that a rather heterogeneous principle should dominate the Sunday-morning worship. Worship should be experience-centered every bit as much as content-centered. Music, meditation, and response by the congregation, in unison and individually, can facilitate the development of an experiential worship. In regard to music, everyone should hear his own kind occasionally. There should be soul music, rock, traditional hymnody, and classical sounds often enough so that the members of the congregation can feel their own preference is being presented.

Lay participation in the service is helpful. Members of the congregation can lead in prayer, Scripture reading, presentation of announcements, personal response to sermons, dramatic vignettes, testimonies, sharing of concerns, reporting on the progress of various ministries, etc. In short, the only thing the pastor need do is preach the sermon. Lay involvement not only encourages the congregation to feel a part of the worship experience, it also allows members of various cultures to be publicly a part of the church worship.

Preaching must necessarily be profound, but presented in basic terms. Urban churches contain people who have Ph.D.'s and those who hold welfare cards, and so the preaching needs to get at profound but practical and basic issues. Illustrations should be multicultural and plentiful so that application of the message is not lost. Lengthy forays into theologically abstract matters will hold little appeal. City people want and need inputs that are usable in urban day-to-day living. Theology can be worked into other types of activities, such as evening forums or discussion groups, postworship fellowship hours, and other events.

Besides respect for and appreciation of cultural diversity, the urban pastor needs the psychological characteristic of *servanthood*. This has to be kept uppermost, for it frees a person from feeling that there must always be a return on every investment, and prevents him from falling into the trap of cost-gain barter thinking. Knowing that his calling, like Christ's, is to serve regardless of the outcome is liberating. It removes the pressure of having to succeed and eliminates a tendency to indulge in self-pity when people do not respond.

Yet another psychological attribute involves the *tolerance of ambiguity*. A city and its people teem with diversity, complexity, and confusion. Working in the inner city, a pastor quickly realizes the depth of this ambiguity. Bureaucrats do not always return phone calls and they often change their minds; city governments lie or stall or change policies; streets are built and destroyed; urban renewal comes and goes; and businesses come into existence and then even burn down. Parishioners are unfaithful, late for appointments, dependent, and erratic. Their problems differ each day, requiring a crisis-interventionist approach. The whole environment is one of uncertainty and impermanence, and the residents incorporate a good deal of this feeling into their own lives and psyches. Being able to be calm and consistent and able to wait things out, is necessary. Needing clear-cut answers from everyone, from parishioners to city officials, is not healthy.

One correlate of this tolerance for ambiguity and change is *understanding and compassion* for the temptations faced by urban dwellers. Most urban pastors will have been socialized into a middle-class ranking of sin. Although many evangelicals attest that sin is sin, and there is really no difference in the gravity of one sin or another, they tend to be particularly disturbed by illicit sex, drug abuse, alcoholism, deviance, street crime, shoplifting, and other overt behavioral misdeeds. These sins are particularly common in low-income urban environments. It would be well to inquire from poor Christians what they consider to be the "Top Ten" sins. One might find that they place particular emphasis on the misuse of affluence, insensitivity toward poverty and oppression, lack of concern about justice, coldness and inhospitable behavior, arrogance of power and its manipulation, and an attitude of judgmentalism and self-righteousness. These are the sins most common among the privileged.

Thus it would be well to adopt an attitude of understanding and compassion toward the poor and the wrongs prevalent there, just as tolerance and patience are extended for the wrongs of the middle class. A pastor need not compromise his ethics of right and wrong nor preclude calls to repentance; he need only expand his consciousness so that he deals compassionately and sensitively with inner-city parishioners, knowing the full context of their lives. For example, he can empathize with the rejected pregnant teenager, rather than focus on how she should have been able to avoid creating this particular dilemma. He can try to understand the reasons why some youth busted on drugs became involved with narcotics, rather than peel off a sermon aimed at convicting him of sin. He can abhor the pressures and miseries of life in the crucible of poverty that drive a mother or father toward alcoholism, rather than simply condemn excessive drinking.

There used to be a special summer program in Chicago called UMPS—Urban Ministries Program for Seminarians. Enrollees began the UMPS experience by being given a few dollars and a ride to skid row. There they were dropped off and told to spend the weekend, not to return to the middle-class seminary until Monday. Once they had endured a weekend in the wilds of the inner city, it is amazing how empathetic they became with the poor and the dubious strategies they often use to cope in the city fifty-two weeks and weekends a year.

Another correlate of this tolerance of ambiguity involves *making decisions and taking action* on issues not yet resolved by theologians. The urban pastor will deal, not in a textbook but in real life, with violence, homosexuality, divorce, liberation movements, radical politics, and nonmarital sexuality. He will not have the convenience of confronting these matters ideologically over coffee and a textbook. They will stare him in the face. He will need patience and the ability to suspend his desire to be doctrinaire and dogmatic so that he can come to grips with the complexity of these matters. They are even more difficult because they are encountered in the form of persons—persons who need service and ministry. He will probably find himself coming out in much difference places on these matters than he did in seminary; often he will say, "I don't know," on issues to which he responded outspokenly in the past. Coping with this type of ambiguity, making decisions and taking actions about which he will never be entirely certain, necessitate a type of spiritual and psychological maturity of which he was previously unaware.

Another psychological trait is the *ability to deal with criticism and rejection.* Many urban pastors have thrown in the clerical towel because, instead of being supported by their denominations, they became objects of criticism. The urban church worker should expect to be branded a radical or an apostate by many of his denominational peers who hear of his work and style of ministry.

But this outside rejection may not be so bad, for a pastor can shut much of that out. What is more painful are the breaches and cleavages likely to develop within his own congregation and the community he serves. The pluralism of the population absolutely guarantees breakdowns of communication and the emergence of criticism and condemnation. Bill Leslie well remembers the controversy in his church over the inauguration of the tutoring program for the community children.[13] Many devout members felt that this nonevangelistic, nonspiritual ministry of a purely social nature was a way of compromising with the soul-saving mission of the church. When the matter came to a congregational vote, it passed by one ballot. Ordinarily, Leslie would never have proceeded on such a lack of consensus. However, he was so convinced of the necessity of this type of temporal ministry that he went forward anyway.

There will be people who will be critical of the pastor for not being more socially and politically radical. Others will feel he is not attending sufficiently to the spiritual needs of the church and its evangelistic thrust. Some in the community will view the church as self-righteous, while others will see it as not adequately prophetic and evangelical. With the congregation scattered ideologically, politically, socially, and even geographically, the pastor will necessarily become the lightning rod for much of this criticism. It will hurt and cause anger, but that is to be expected. In short, neither the church nor the pastor will ever be able to be all things to all people; and recognizing that is the first step to resolving much of the potential agony.

The *ability to live with compromise* is also imperative. There is a constant necessity of having to settle for second best in urban ministry. Often a pastor may wish something to go a certain way in the church, but because of the pluralism of the congregation, the lack of money for funding, the absence of sufficient workers, or any of a host of other reasons, he will have to settle for an inch instead of a foot. The previously mentioned tutoring program illustrates this point. Leslie saw many other ministries he would like to have incorporated at the same time. Nevertheless, he settled for tutoring as a start, realizing the congregation was simply not ready for additional ventures. Much intrachurch compromise arises from this problem of the pastor being ahead of the congregation in awareness and vision. It is frustrating to know what needs to be done, but to have to wait for the parishioners' awareness to be raised sufficiently to be supportive of it.

Compromise is everywhere in urban ministry. The needs are so pressing they cry for powerful activist ministries and solutions. However, the reason they are pressing is that economic, social, and political impediments prevent reaching a solution. Victories, then, are often limited. Tutoring programs are begun before legal-aid clinics, senior citizens' breakfasts precede counseling centers, and local youth activities come before summer camps. Vision is important to the pastor, for dreams sustain effort. But the visions need to be weighed against present realities, so that dreams for the future do not fuel frustration in the present.

One additional but often overlooked psychological trait is that of *a sense of humor*. There is an old adage that one should take his responsibilities, rather than himself, seriously. Humor is a guardian of sanity. If one cannot laugh, one will be left only to cry. Realizing that he is but a single servant in a giant vineyard can free a person to see failures and incongruities as opportunities to laugh and appreciate the delightful yet frustrating incomprehensibility of life. Laughter is a therapeutic gift, and finding as many ways as possible to exploit its use will be in the best interests of the urban pastor.

Personal Life

In addition to the foregoing psychological attributes, there are a number of behavioral guidelines that should mark the personal life of an effective urban minister. At the outset, the importance of *reading* needs to be stressed. There is a tremendous energy drain in urban ministry—reading has a refueling quality. Reading materials can be chosen to increase cultural awareness and sensitivity. Reading can fill the mental shelf with ideas and creative options for more effective ministry. In addition, reading is a very constructive way to use time alone, away from the endless demands made on a pastor's energies. A pastor who does not read goes stale.

Reading should be done in devotional, theological, and particularly social areas, for it needs to be used to develop the whole person. However, recreational reading—sports, novels, the arts, whatever—is not only defensible, but highly appropriate.

Part of the pastor's reading time should be devoted to research into local history. Ray Bakke, giving us the benefit of his rich experience ministering to Hispanics and Appalachian whites in Chicago, urges church workers to begin by studying the local community and the histories of the peoples who have settled there.[14] With many groups, the workers minister to families or clans rather than individuals. The clan concept is especially relevant, for problems plaguing an individual in St. Louis may stem from decisions made by a person in Kentucky. It is also helpful to study the role of the pastor in the ethnic tradition of the people he serves. These role definitions vary mightily from one group to another. Finally, a pastor should be familiar with the local church history. Doing new things is important, but one should not be too critical of the past, for it is a foundation of the present. Alluding to earlier precedents can make that foundation stronger and build a sense of affirmation and appreciation for the enduring nature of the particular church.

Another important guideline for the pastor's personal life concerns *budgeting time*. One effective way to do this is for him to keep a time log for a week or two, accounting for every fifteen or thirty minutes spent for the designated period. From there, one can assess how it can be spent more constructively and productively. Time is the urban pastor's most precious and limited resource. Ineffective use brings on guilt, depression, and despair. There is always more to do than he has time to accomplish anyway. Therefore, any inappropriate use of time will have a grating effect on his feelings. Time budgeting should be done realistically but with a certain amount of flexibility to account for the unforeseen.

However, the urban worker should zealously guard his free time. The tendency to feel responsible for all the ills and traumas in the community can predispose one to skip recreational time in order to crowd in some more service-oriented activity. Other than assuaging his conscience from false guilt, such a practice is of absolutely no value. That free time is every bit as important as any other, and without it the nerves wear thin, exhaustion emerges, and soon he will be looking for another pastorate.

A related guideline is *establishing family priorities*. If the pastor is married, and especially if he has children, family concerns are inevitable. It is important that the entire family have a very clear understanding of the nature of the work and its demands. There may need to be a considerable amount of negotiation involved so a pastor can meet his responsibilities to his family as well as perform in the ministry. Moreover, if family matters are not of sufficient priority, the stresses that may result could ultimately undercut effective ministry anyway. So it becomes a pragmatic matter as well.

Many a pastor has lost a marriage, either through divorce or because it has become vapid and lifeless, simply because his family was not a sufficient priority. It is not unreasonable to argue that if the wife does not feel resolved about moving into an urban pastorate, the husband should not feel called to such a post. It is vital to feel the support of the family in such a challenging work. If adversary relationships develop within the home, the ministry will likely soon be over.

The most critical family problem for those in urban ministry is time. Unless one zealously and defensively guards family time, it will soon evaporate. Budgeting appears imperative here. Almost any type of ministry, because of its spontaneous nature, seems to work against family life. But inner-city ministry, with its additional burdens, can destroy family life unless clear priorities are set.

Finally, the urban minister needs to see the importance of *giving recognition to others.* Urban ministry is often not filled with very many strokes. If such is true for the pastor, it is even more so for other willing workers and staff members. So it becomes important that staff members regularly be reinforced, praised, and encouraged in their work. One helpful way to do this is to recognize them and their ministries periodically in the morning service. Such featuring of different ministries and their workers gives these selfless servants a bit of attention and identity. It will elicit prayers and support from a better-informed and more appreciative congregation.

Survival

Considering the magnitude of the urban-ministry challenge, it is difficult to imagine how it can be endured. Among urban workers in general, whether they are teachers, pastors, social workers, or any other professionals who work regularly with problem-plagued people, the average length of service is not much more than four years. Many experience what is called *burnout.*

David Frenchak describes burnout as "the snowballing effect of physical, emotional, psychological, and spiritual fatigue."[15] It is fatigue on all fronts.

Symptoms of Burnout. Among the symptoms of burnout Frenchak mentions are increasing negative, cynical attitudes. This defeatism is followed by a detachment from people. This often involves categorizing individuals and dealing with categories in blocks rather than as persons. There is also a tendency to intellectualize problems rather than respond with passion and commitment to their solutions. Injustice is seen as inevitable, and tragedy as a part of city life.

Physical symptoms are legion, including psychosomatic illnesses, sleeplessness, ulcers, migraines, and back pains. There can also be personal symptoms in the form of marital problems, possibly alcoholism, and even suicide attempts.

Causes of Burnout. Frenchak sees burnout as caused by a number of factors. One of them is the constant confrontation with failure—treadmilling. There is a never-ending job to do—with every ten people helped, there are a hundred more who need help. This frustration gives way to repressed anger, which in turn can lead to hostility and bitterness.

There is also a feeling of guilt over a lack of success. We are, says Frenchak, in need of a theology of failure. It is difficult to draw much satisfaction from faithfulness in the absence of measurable success.

Perfectionism and inability to delegate authority and share the ministry with parishioners also leads to great fatigue. Frenchak calls for a realistic theology of sinfulness. Such a theology would acknowledge the imperfection and sinfulness of the pastor as well as those he serves, and equip ministers with the ability to accept themselves and their own inadequacies rather than let those shortcomings destroy the spirit.

The conflict emanating out of confrontation with power structures is another factor in burnout. Along with a theology of failure, Frenchak calls for a theology of power. Effective urban ministry means confronting institutions. It is important that one know how to deal with them.

The regular confrontation with and awareness of violence is also fatiguing. Violence, either potential or actual, against oneself or a friend, breeds anger and fear. It is quietly draining.

The irregularity of the work schedule also takes its toll, says Frenchak. There is no nine-to-five quality about urban ministry. Frenchak points out that few tasks are as brief as they are expected to be. What looks like it should take a half hour often stretches into a half day—especially when it includes confronting a bureaucratic system.

A major psychological factor Frenchak cites is loneliness and isolation. Lack of companionship makes the worker feel like an Old Testament prophet, scorned by his own people. Closely related to this is the feeling of alienation growing out of the lack of denominational support and even abandonment by parishioners. He is rejected on one hand because he owns the causes of the oppressed. Yet, urban ministers are not always seen as allies by the oppressed either. For, as Frenchak says, "everyone knows we fit better with the oppressors."[16]

Antidotes to Burnout. Among the antidotes to burnout suggested by Frenchak is an *alertness to symptoms* so that, because of early diagnosis, the fatigue is not irreversible. *Proper training* for the task is also vital. Much exhaustion could be prevented if workers simply made certain they were adequately prepared for the challenges they must undertake. One simply must be immersed in the culture of the community as a part of that preparation.

Bud Ipema, of the Chicago-Orleans Housing Corporation; Ray Bakke, a highly successful pastor of Fairfield Avenue Church; and Bill Leslie met together in Chicago to discuss ways to prevent burnout. Out of their discussion and interaction came four main points.[17]

The first emphasizes *having a theology that keeps one in the city.* During the sixties and especially after the publication of Harvey Cox's bestselling *The Secular City,*[18] there were a host of churches and church-undergirded programs in poverty areas of major cities. Many were radical and spectacular in style; others were more conventional. Most of them were theologically liberal. By the mid-seventies, almost all were gone. These efforts were begun with rapid starts and high hopes. However, when those who initiated them found the going extraordinarily tough, the city political systems unbending, the problems too complex, and the publicity and glamor gone, the programs blew away. What was absent was a clear-cut theology that ordained faithfulness in serving the interests of the city regardless of success or politics.

Knowledge of the problems, compassion for the people, and a desire for challenge are not sufficient. These elements were present in the hundreds and perhaps thousands who burned out. Moreover, it is easy to rationalize leaving by pointing at different and more soluble problems, other groups in need of ministry, and alternative challenges to confront. However, a person who feels called by his theological commitment to urban service becomes aware that he is where he should be and thus, in that sense, he is succeeding no matter what the external signs of effectiveness may be.

Urban ministry can be an extremely lonely and unrewarding task, as mentioned previously. Hence, as a second point, *having a sense of community and support* is vital. Dr. Gilbert James, of Asbury Theological Seminary, a sociologist who dedicated much of his adult professional life to urban ministry, was asked what bit of advice he would give to aspiring urban pastors. He responded by saying, "Find someone you can track with. You are going to need it." Sage counsel, according to many other enduring pastors.

There is a need for support and reinforcement from others who genuinely understand the nature of the inner-city mission. In Chicago several people who do various forms of Christian urban work get together one Monday each month for a retreat held out of town. This day of fellowship, sharing, and refreshment has become a necessary monthly oasis for many of them. No longer do they feel lonely and unappreciated. There is a place to share trophies and troubles, to exchange ideas, counsel, sympathy, and support.

When the energy fire burns low, there is a special need for support. James Roache suggests that peers in the ministry help sort out the confusions of the pastor who is considering leaving an urban post because of burnout.[19] The intimacy of a support group not only provides a safe haven for blowing off steam and letting out frustration and disappointment, it is also an excellent reality check for denial or rationalization.[20] Ministers need ministering too, and such relationships provide it.

A third factor involves *taking time for individual development.* It is important that the pastor find other activities to provide a sense of progress, satisfaction, and accomplishment. These may be writing, teaching seminary courses, or pursuing a doctoral degree. Most people have a favorite avocation or second career they would like to pursue. Pastors are no different, and they should pursue them; for these second interests serve as necessary pit stops. One pastor spoke of his "toys," referring to his proclivity to teach courses in various seminaries, give speeches, start new programs, etc. Acknowledging that he is probably criticized for spreading himself a bit thin because of them, he stated that he would never have been able to make urban ministry a career without these very constructive diversions.

A pastor pointed out that just after he received his Ph.D. in theology he nearly burned out. He had expected to be filled with energy once the dissertation was over and he was free to pursue his parish charges unfettered, but the opposite occurred. He needed other areas of refreshment.

The reason why these diversions are so important in urban ministry is that so much of the work is cyclical. It is the same set of problems over and over. One has continually to be orienting new members to the mission of the church. Such orientation can be tedious repetition. Sunday after Sunday, poverty case after poverty case, and staff change after staff change—one feels much like Christ must have felt with the multitudes of needy crowding in on Him. He needed to push out into the lake to get His bearings.

Individual development includes spiritual nourishment.[21] Pastors are so often out doing and caring that they never have enough time to pray and meditate. They provide spiritual food and water regularly but fail to replenish their pantry or dig new wells. The result is a barrenness and an inability to minister. Setting aside a day each month or some time each week to work with another spiritual mentor who can refresh one spiritually can be time very well spent. One pastor has gone regularly to another clergyperson for "feeding" and has found that it has revitalized his power to minister.

Leslie presents an interesting formula for spiritual survival in the city.[22] First, it is important to keep uppermost that the primary purpose of life is to seek God's kingdom and will. It is not to horde money, get the most with the least effort, or be concerned with what others may think. Next, a pastor needs a support group—people who are living the same experience and can encourage him. Finally, there needs to be personal communication with God. Leslie paraphrased a former colleague of his who said that if the devil can beat you in having a daily meditation time, he can beat you at anything else.

The fourth factor involves *getting surcease from the city.* The heat and concrete, the pains and the problems, the noises and the nuisances, and the pace and the pressure of the city have a wearing effect. Getting away from the plastic and glass to areas that are grassy and cool is a necessary change of pace. Time for reflection and rest can reenergize a person who takes a week or a weekend or even a day off on a regular basis.

Rewards. Despite all the problems and challenges involved in urban ministry, there are real rewards. One, of course, is that the ministry is taking place where needs are particularly acute. Simply being faithful to the call is a triumph. Any victory—through either a service or stewardship ministry—merits celebration, for it is likely the job would not have been done without the church's involvement.

Living in the city itself is invigorating. Its diversity, stimulation, and opportunities are endless. Although the city may indeed contain the worst elements of life, it also has the best. From culture and the arts to sports and excitement, the city is the place.

For family members, the city can be liberating. The family of an urban minister is not living in a gossip-laden goldfish bowl. There are a myriad of opportunities for each family member to live his own life and pursue personal goals and development. There are many free activities for family entertainment.

Living in the city also has economic advantages. Only one car is needed because urban mass transit is available. Keeping up appearances is less of an issue. Suburban pastors often live in tract homes and thus their children feel enormous peer pressure to dress well and have certain possessions to be "in." Individuality and diversity are much greater in the city, taking such economic and social burdens off the family. The city also abounds with rummage and garage sales, resale shops, and flea markets, further reducing economic stress.

Finally, for the urban church worker a host of professional opportunities abound in the city—seminaries and graduate schools nearby, the finest libraries for research, conferences pertaining to urban ministry. There are many other churches and church staffs for forming relationships and giving mutual support.

Nonetheless, it is important that anyone entering urban ministry work zealously to guard his own sanity and person. This means unflinchingly holding on to time off, hobbies, and family time, so that energy level remains high and enthusiasm for the challenge does not abate. Urban ministry is servanthood personified. Service means giving. If a person does not minister to himself, he may soon be so burned out that there will be nothing to give, no service to render. Soon the servant will be gone. The model of Christ is best here. His ministry was paced. It was spiced with social times, prayer alone, and person-to-person ministry. As such, it was the effective model of what ministry and servanthood is all about.

Notes

NOTES ON PREFACE

[1]David Claerbaut, *Social Problems*, parts 1 & 2 (Scottsdale, Ariz.: Christian Academic Publications, 1976, 1977).

[2]Amos H. Hawley, *Urban Society* (New York: Wiley, 1981), p. 7.

[3]Mark Abrahamson, *Urban Sociology* (Englewood Cliffs, N.J.: Prentice-Hall, 1980), p. 2.

[4]Ibid.

[5]Ibid., p. 8.

[6]George D. Younger, *Church and Urban Power Structure* (Philadelphia: Westminster, 1963), p. 4.

[7]Lewis Mumford, *The Culture of Cities* (New York: Harcourt, Brace, 1938), p. 3.

[8]Ibid., p. 480.

[9]Edwin Eames and Judith Granich Goode, *Anthropology of the City* (Englewood Cliffs, N.J.: Prentice-Hall, 1977), p. 29.

NOTES ON CHAPTER 1

[1]Bill Leslie, "God Loves the Inner City," *Christian Life*, July 1973, p. 27.

[2]Roger S. Greenway, *Apostles to the City* (Grand Rapids: Baker, 1978), pp. 26–27.

[3]Leslie, "God Loves the Inner City," p. 27.

[4]Lewis Mumford, *The City in History* (New York: Harcourt, Brace, and World, 1961), p. 573.

[5]Leslie, "God Loves the Inner City," p. 27.

[6]David O. Moberg, *Inasmuch* (Grand Rapids: Eerdmans, 1965), pp. 51, 75.

[7]John Perkins, "Urban Church/Urban Poor," in *Metro-Ministry*, David Frenchak and Sharrel Keyes, eds. (Elgin, Ill.: David C. Cook, 1979), p. 45.

[8]Roger S. Greenway, *Calling Our Cities to Christ* (Nutley, N.J.: Presbyterian and Reformed, 1973), p. 27.

[9]Greenway, *Apostles*, p. 12.

[10]Raymond Bakke, "A Biblical Theology for Urban Ministry," in Frenchak and Keyes, *Metro-Ministry*, pp. 16–18.

[11]Greenway, *Apostles*, pp. 15–96.

[12]Leslie, p. 27.

[13]David Claerbaut, *The Reluctant Defender* (Wheaton, Ill.: Tyndale, 1978), p. 92.

[14]Roger S. Greenway, "Content and Context: The Whole Christ for the Whole City," in Roger S. Greenway, ed., *Discipling the City* (Grand Rapids: Baker, 1979), p. 96.

[15]Ronald J. Sider, *Rich Christians in an Age of Hunger* (Downers Grove, Ill.: InterVarsity, 1977), p. 85.

[16]Paul S. Rees, "The 'Right to Food' Muddle," *World Vision*, April 1976, p. 23.

[17]Sider, *Rich Christians*, p. 78.

[18]Ibid., pp. 78–79.

[19]Ibid., p. 65.

[20]Ibid., p. 63.

[21]Ibid., pp. 62, 81.

[22]Ibid., p. 73.

[23]Clark H. Pinnock, "An Evangelical Theology of Human Liberation," *Sojourners* (February 1976), quoted in Sider, *Rich Christians*, p. 77.

[24]Harvie M. Conn, "Christ and the City: Biblical Themes for Building Urban Theology Models," in Greenway, ed., *Discipling*, p. 252.

[25]Frank E. Gaebelein, "Challenging Christians to the Simple Life," *Christianity Today*, 21 (September 1979): 24–25.

[26]Sider, *Rich Christians*, p. 88.

[27]Ibid., pp. 96–104.

[28]Ibid., p. 66.

[29]Arthur F. Glasser, "Social Concern and the Gospel," p. 2.

[30]Sider, *Rich Christians*, p. 68.

[31]Ibid., pp. 68–69, 79.

[32]Leslie, pp. 33–34.

[33]Rene Bideaux, "Faith and Obedience for Missional Congregations," *Justice Ministries*, 15–16 (Winter-Spring 1982): 11. Justice Ministries (JM) 621. Note: materials available from *Justice Ministries* are given a JM number.

[34]William Leslie, "The Ministering Church," in Frenchak and Keyes, *Metro-Ministry*, p. 132.

[35]"The Mission of the Church," early position paper of LaSalle Street Church, Chicago, Ill.

[36]Leslie, "God Loves the Inner City," p. 33.

[37]"Mission of the Church."

[38]Howard Rice, "Toward an Urban Strategy," Knoxville: *Cities* (July 1981), pp. 1–9. JM 622.

39"Mission of the Church."

40Ibid.

41Nicholas Wolterstorff, "Peace Workers," address at Wheaton College, Wheaton, Ill., 11 April 1978.

42Jo Anne Moser Gibbons, *Greeting with Peace, Gifting with Hope* (Cincinnati: Verona Missions, 1981). ICUIS 4785. Note: Citations with an ICUIS number can be obtained at a nominal charge by writing ICUIS, Richard Poethig, Director, 5700 South Woodlawn Ave., Chicago, IL 60637. Summaries of the ICUIS materials in Gibbons's book are available in their journal, *Justice Ministries* 15–16 (Winter-Spring 1982).

43Bideaux, p. 11.

44Daniel W. Pawley, "Gifts and Growth: A Case Study," *Leadership*, 3 (Winter 1982): 92–99. JM 658.

45James Hefley and Marti Hefley, *The Church That Takes on Trouble* (Elgin, Ill.: David C. Cook, 1976), pp. 241–42.

46Bryan O. Walsh, "The Church and the City: The Miami Experience," *New Catholic World* (May/June 1982), pp. 107–8.

47Nicholas Wolterstorff, "Families, Children, and Vouchers," *Reformed Journal*, 28 (October 1978): 6.

48"A Joint Urban Policy for the United Presbyterian Church in the USA and the Presbyterian Church in the United States" (New York: The Program Agency, the United Presbyterian Church in the USA, 1981). JM 641.

49Vincent P. Quayle, "The Housing Ministry in Baltimore," *New Catholic World* (May/June 1982), p. 102.

50"Metropolitan Lutheran Ministry of Greater Kansas City" (Kansas City, Mo.: Metropolitan Lutheran Ministry, 1982). JM 652.

51"Toward an Urban Mission Strategy for Presbyterians in Tulsa; One Model for Developing a Metropolitan Missions Strategy" (Tulsa: Presbyterian Urban Ministry Council, 1978). JM 151.

52Bideaux, "Faith and Obedience," p. 12; Connie Myer, *Developing New Churches Is No Easy Task for Experts* (New York: Board of Global Ministries, United Methodist Church, 1976). JM 637.

53Dennis E. Shoemaker, "The Church in the City: A Strategy for Hope," *The Other Side* (October 1978), pp. 26–37. ICUIS 4174.

54John Robert Smith, *The Church That Stayed: The Life and Times of Central Presbyterian Church in the Heart of Atlanta, 1858–1978* (Atlanta: Atlanta Historical Society, 1979). ICUIS 4320.

55Frye Gaillard, "A Congregation Meets Life Head-On in the Inner City," *Charlotte Observer* (28 September 1980). ICUIS 4602.

56Hefley and Hefley, *Church That Takes on Trouble*, pp. 241–42.

57David A. Pollard, "Toward the New City," *New Catholic World* (May/June 1982), p. 117.

58Jere Allen and George Bullard, *Shaping a Future for the Church in the Changing Community* (Atlanta: Home Mission Board, Southern Baptist Convention, n.d.). JM 646.

59James H. Davis, *Strategy Workbook for St. Louis, 1978* (New York: Board of Global Ministries, United Methodist Church, 1978). JM 150.

[60]Keith Olstad, "Outreach Ministry of Our Savior's Lutheran Church" (Minneapolis: Our Savior's Lutheran Church, 1982). JM 657.

[61]Toronto Area Presbytery, Toronto West Presbytery, and Toronto United Church Council, *Directions: A Mission Strategy for the Metro United Church, 1980–1985* (Toronto: Metro United Church, 1980). ICUIS 4541.

[62]Eunice P. Poethig, ed., *150 Plus Tomorrow* (Chicago: Presbytery of Chicago, n.d.).

[63]SCUPE, 30 W. Chicago Ave., Chicago, IL 60610.

[64]Bakke, pp. 15–16.

[65]Tom Finger, "Viability of Alternative Urban Life-styles," in Frenchak and Keyes, *Metro-Ministry*, p. 139.

[66]Perkins, p. 50.

[67]Hefley and Hefley, *Church That Takes on Trouble*, p. 242.

[68]Ibid., pp. 241–42.

NOTES ON CHAPTER 2

[1]Donald L. Benedict, "Toward an Urban Church Strategy," in *Metro-Ministry,* David Frenchak and Sharrel Keyes, eds. (Elgin, Ill.: David C. Cook, 1979), p. 66.

[2]Ibid., p. 67.

[3]Carl Dudley, "Churches in Changing Communities," in Frenchak and Keyes, pp. 79–80.

[4]Jim Newton, "The Challenge of Change: A PACT Report" (Atlanta: Home Mission Board). JM 643.

[5]Anthony Campolo, "The Sociological Nature of the Urban Church," in Frenchak and Keyes, *Metro-Ministry*, p. 37.

[6]Michael Harrington, *The Other America* (New York: Macmillan, 1962).

[7]F. K. Plous, Jr., "Three Reasons for Urban Decline," *Chicago Tribune* (11 September 1982).

[8]Ibid.

[9]Ed Marciniak, address at the Seminary Consortium for Urban Pastoral Education orientation, Latino Seminario, Chicago, Ill., 23 September 1978; Ed Marciniak, *Reviving an Inner City Community* (Chicago: Center for Research in Urban Government, 1977).

[10]Ibid.

[11]Ibid.

[12]John B. Calhoun, "Population Density and Social Pathology," *Scientific American* (1962), in *Population, Evolution, and Birth Control*, assembled by Garrett Hardin, 2nd ed. (San Francisco: Freeman, 1969), pp. 101–5.

[13]Campolo, "Sociological Nature of the Urban Church," pp. 36–38.

[14]Dudley, "Churches in Changing Communities," pp. 82–83.

[15]Stanley Hallett, "Strategies for Urban Reconstruction," in Frenchak and Keyes, *Metro-Ministry*, p. 199.

[16]William R. Brown, Melissa Hoops, and William A. Peterman, "Preliminary Investigations of Redlining in Toledo" (Bowling Green: Environmental Studies Center, Bowling Green State University, 1977). JM 23.

[17]Hallett, "Strategies for Urban Reconstruction," p. 199.

[18]Dudley, "Churches in Changing Communities," pp. 81–82.

[19]Hallett, "Strategies for Urban Reconstruction," p. 200.

[20]Ibid., pp. 200–201.

[21]William Ipema, "Ministry Resources in Community Systems," in Frenchak and Keyes, *Metro-Ministry*, pp. 212–13.

[22]Joint Strategy and Action Committee, "JSAC in Action—The South Bronx Experience," New York: *JSAC Grapevine* (February 1982). JM 653.

[23]Dudley, "Churches in Changing Communities," pp. 83–89.

[24]Ibid., p. 80.

[25]Richard Mell, address at a seminar of North Park Theological Seminary, Latino Seminario, Chicago, Ill., 15 June 1977.

[26]Ipema, "Ministry Resources," p. 217.

[27]Marciniak, *Reviving an Inner City Community*.

[28]Ipema, "Ministry Resources," pp. 213–15.

[29]Philip Amerson, "Consultation for Assistance in Developing Urban Ministry," in Frenchak and Keyes, *Metro-Ministry*, pp. 205–6.

[30]Ipema, "Ministry Resources," p. 217.

[31]Hallett, "Strategies for Urban Reconstruction," pp. 202–3.

[32]P. David Finks, "Parish Churches and Community Organizations," *New Catholic World* (May/June 1982), pp. 121–23.

[33]"The Cleveland Covenant Concept (Papers)" (Cleveland Heights: Cleveland Covenant, 1979, 1980). ICUIS 4730.

[34]Campolo, "Sociological Nature of the Urban Church," pp. 38–39.

[35]Hallett, "Strategies for Urban Reconstruction," p. 202.

[36]Ibid., p. 203.

[37]Vincent P. Quayle, "The Housing Ministry in Baltimore," *New Catholic World* (May/June 1982), pp. 102–3.

[38]John Perkins, "Urban Church/Urban Poor," in Frenchak and Keyes, *Metro-Ministry*, p. 49.

[39]Raymond Bakke, "The Urban Church Revitalization Process," in Frenchak and Keyes, *Metro-Ministry*, pp. 172–73.

[40]Matt Kane, " 'The People Who Built the Wall': Bethel Church—Self-Help Development at Work in a West Side Neighborhood" Chicago: *The Neighborhood Works* (27 February 1982). ICUIS 4784.

[41]Ron Spann, "The Church of the Messiah-Material" (Detroit: Church of the Messiah, n.d.). ICUIS 4428.

[42]Charles Burden, "Greenbacks & Grassroots Marry in Church," New York: *The News World* (6 October 1979). ICUIS 4266.

[43]Quayle, "Housing Ministry," pp. 100–101.

[44]Odessa Elliott, "The Cathedral Ministry to the City," *New Catholic World* (May/June 1982), pp. 113–15.

NOTES ON CHAPTER 3

[1]Ernest W. Burgess, "The Growth of the City: An Introduction to a Research Project," *Publications of the American Sociological Society,* 18 (1924), in Robert E. Park, Ernest W. Burgess, and Roderick McKenzie, eds., *The City* (Chicago: University of Chicago Press, 1967), pp. 47–62.

[2]Kingsley Davis and Wilbert E. Moore, "Some Principles of Stratification," *American Sociological Review,* 10 (1945): 242–49.

[3]Robert F. Kennedy, *To Seek a Newer World* (New York: Bantam, 1968), p. 34.

[4]Robert J. Havighurst and Bernice L. Neugarten, *Society and Education* (Boston: Allyn and Bacon, 1967), p. 12.

[5]*Welfare Myths vs. Facts,* pamphlet published by the Department of Health, Education, and Welfare.

[6]Conversation with Dr. William Pannell, 1 October 1982.

[7]Adapted from Kurt B. Mayer and Walter Buckley, *Class and Society* (1970), pp. 51–55, in David Claerbaut, *Social Problems,* part 1 (Scottsdale, Ariz.: Christian Academic Publications, 1976), p. 53.

[8]Charles Valentine, *Culture and Poverty: Critique and Counter-Proposals* (Chicago: University of Chicago Press, Midway Paperback Text Series, 1969), p. 115.

[9]Sarane Spence Boocock, *An Introduction to the Sociology of Learning* (Boston: Houghton Mifflin, 1972), p. 36.

[10]Paul E. Peterson, *City Limits* (Chicago: University of Chicago Press, 1981), p. 4.

[11]Richard P. Coleman, *Attitudes Toward Neighborhoods: How Americans Choose to Live* (Cambridge: Joint Center for Urban Studies of the Massachusetts Institute of Technology and Harvard University). JM 631.

[12]Harlan Hahn and Charles Levine, *Urban Politics* (New York: Longman, 1980), pp. 36–37.

[13]Roger S. Greenway, *Calling Our Cities to Christ* (Nutley, N.J.: Presbyterian and Reformed, 1973), p. 114.

[14]Keith Olstad, "Outreach Ministry of Our Savior's Lutheran Church" (Minneapolis: Our Savior's Lutheran Church, 1982). JM 657.

[15]Rachelle B. Warren and Donald I. Warren, *The Neighborhood Organizer's Handbook* (Notre Dame, Ind.: University of Notre Dame Press, 1977), pp. 94–112.

[16]David A. Pollard, "Toward the New City," *New Catholic World* (May/June 1982), pp. 118–20.

[17]Stanley J. Hallett, "The High Cost of Disinvestment" (Chicago: Center for Urban Affairs, Northwestern University). JM 629.

[18]Samuel Acosta, "The Transitional Community from an Hispanic Perspective" (Philadelphia: Conferences on Churches in Racial/Ethnic Transitional Communities, 1979). ICUIS 4175.

[19]Hallett, "High Cost of Disinvestment."

[20]Edward C. Banfield, "America's Cities Enter a Crucial Decade," *Chicago Tribune* (23 March 1980).

[21]Ed Marciniak, *Reversing Urban Decline: The Winthrop-Kenmore Corridor in the Edgewater and Uptown Communities of Chicago* (Washington, D.C.: National Center for Urban Affairs). JM 654.

[22]"Metropolitan Lutheran Ministry of Greater Kansas City" (Kansas City, Mo.: Metropolitan Lutheran Ministry, 1982). JM 652.

[23]"The LISC South Bronx Program" (South Bronx, N.Y.: Local Initiatives Support Corporation—South Bronx Program). JM 632.

[24]William Ipema, "Ministry Resources in Community Systems," in David Frenchak and Sharrell Keyes, eds., *Metro-Ministry* (Elgin, Ill.: David C. Cook, 1979), p. 216.

[25]David W. Gagne, "Christian Sharing Fund—A Diocesan Model," *New Catholic World* (May/June 1982), pp. 127–30.

[26]Joint Strategy and Action Committee, "JSAC in Action—The South Bronx Experience," New York: *JSAC Grapevine*, February 1982. JM 653.

[27]Donald S. Brown, "A July Night in Queens: Christians Working Through Broad-based Community Organizations to Improve the Quality of Life for Their Families, Neighborhoods, and Churches" (Buffalo: Presbytery of Western New York, 1978). JM 154.

[28]Stuart E. Whitney and Hans H. Frick, "Linwood United Ministries—Materials" (Kansas City, Mo.: Linwood United Ministries, 1979). JM 135.

NOTES ON CHAPTER 4

[1]Michael Harrington, "The Invisible Land," in *The Quality of Life in America*, A. David Hill et al., eds. (New York: Holt, Rinehart, and Winston, 1973), pp. 140–47.

[2]Elliot Aronson, *The Social Animal*. 2nd ed. (San Francisco: W. H. Freeman, 1976), p. 90.

[3]Oscar Lewis, *The Study of Slum Culture—Backgrounds for LaVida* (New York: Random House, 1968), pp. 4–21, in *Spectrum on Social Problems*, Jon M. Shepard, ed. (Columbus, Ohio: Merrill, 1973), pp. 106–18.

[4]Richard Gary, "Small Congregations," *Justice Ministries*, 15–16 (Winter-Spring 1982): 4. JM 619.

[5]Max Weber, *The Protestant Ethic and the Spirit of Capitalism* (London: G. Allen, 1930).

[6]David Claerbaut, *Social Problems*, part 1 (Scottsdale, Ariz.: Christian Academic Publications, 1976), p. 86.

[7]Karl Marx, *The Communist Manifesto*, trans. Samuel Moore (Chicago: Henry Regnery, 1954); Karl Marx, *Wage-Labour and Capital*, rev. ed. (New York: International Publishers, 1933).

[8]Paul Jacobs, "Keeping the Poor Poor," in Jerome H. Skolnick and Elliott Currie, eds., *Crisis in American Institutions* (Boston: Little, Brown, 1976), pp. 129–39.

[9]Ibid.

[10]David Claerbaut, *The Reluctant Defender* (Wheaton, Ill.: Tyndale, 1978), pp. 211–12.

[11]Jacobs, "Keeping the Poor Poor."

[12]Ibid.

[13]Claerbaut, *Reluctant Defender*, pp. 204–5.

[14]*Current Population Reports*, "Money Income and Poverty Status of Families and Persons in the United States: 1975 (Advance Report," United States Department of Commerce, Bureau of the Census Series P-60: No. 98.

[15]Claerbaut, *Reluctant Defender*, p. 19.

[16]Robert E. Herriott and Nancy Hoyt St. John, *Social Class and the Urban School* (New York: Wiley, 1966).

[17]Claerbaut, *Reluctant Defender*, p. 20.

[18]David Claerbaut, *Black Jargon in White America* (Grand Rapids: Eerdmans, 1972), p. 30.

NOTES ON CHAPTER 5

[1]William Ryan, *Blaming the Victim* (New York: Vintage, 1971), pp. 3–29.

[2]Whitney M. Young, Jr., *Beyond Racism* (New York: McGraw-Hill, 1971), pp. 29–30.

[3]William C. Cockerham, *Medical Sociology* (Englewood Cliffs, N.J.: Prentice-Hall, 1978), pp. 33–42; Ryan, pp. 136–63.

[4]Ryan, pp. 142–54.

[5]Lewis A. Coser, "The Sociology of Poverty," in *The Quality of Life in America*, A. David Hill et al., eds. (New York: Holt, Rinehart, and Winston, 1973), pp. 244–52. For information on the myths of welfare, such as "welfare cadillacs," read *Welfare Myths vs. Facts*, pamphlet published by the Department of Health, Education and Welfare.

[6]Albert J. Reiss, Jr., "Police Brutality—Answers to Key Questions," *Trans-Action* (July/August 1968), pp. 10–19, in Norman Johnson, Leonard Savitz, and Marvin E. Wolfgang, eds., *The Sociology of Punishment and Correction*, 2nd ed. (New York: Wiley, 1970), pp. 54–65; Ramsey Clark, *Crime in America* (New York: Pocket Books, 1971), pp. 133–69; David Claerbaut, *The Reluctant Defender* (Wheaton, Ill.: Tyndale, 1978), pp. 179–200.

[7]*Report of the National Advisory Commission on Civil Disorders* (New York: Bantam, 1968), pp. 35–200, 299–336, 484–93.

[8]Claerbaut, *Reluctant Defender*, pp. 56–65.

[9]Ibid., pp. 15–16.

[10]Ibid., p. 184.

[11]Samuel G. Chapman, "Police Policy on the Use of Firearms," *The Police Chief* (July 1967), pp. 16–32, in Johnston, Savitz, and Wolfgang, *Sociology of Punishment and Correction*, pp. 84–94; Clark, pp. 54–59.

[12]Ryan, *Blaming the Victim*.

[13]Claerbaut, *Reluctant Defender*, pp. 34–35.

[14]Ibid., pp. 188–89.

15*Struggle for Justice: A Report on Crime and Punishment in America*, prepared for the American Friends Service Committee (New York: Hill and Wang, 1971), pp. 124–44.

16The President's Commission on Law Enforcement and the Administration of Justice, *The Challenge of Crime in a Free Society*, A Report, 1967, p. 128; Task Force on Administration of Justice, *Task Force Report: The Courts*, 1967, p. 29; *Report of the National Advisory Commission on Civil Disorders*, pp. 337–57.

17Lee Rainwater, "The Lessons of Pruitt-Igoe," *The Public Interest*, 8 (Summer 1967): 116–26, in *Spectrum on Social Problems*, Jon M. Shepard, ed. (Columbus, Ohio: Merrill, 1973), pp. 119–26.

18Clark, *Crime in America*, pp. 133–45; for an examination of citizen attitudes toward the police, see *Task Force Report: The Police*, President's Commission on Law Enforcement and the Administration of Justice (Washington, D.C., 1967), pp. 145–49, in Johnston, Savitz, and Wolfgang, *Sociology of Punishment and Correction*, pp. 26–33.

19Ryan, *Blaming the Victim*, pp. 207–8.

20Clark, *Crime in America*, pp. 133–69.

21For valuable suggestions (pertinent to dealing with poverty and powerlessness) for church and individual action, see Young, pp. 218–19, 224–36.

NOTES ON CHAPTER 6

1David Claerbaut, *The Reluctant Defender* (Wheaton, Ill.: Tyndale, 1978), p. 22.

2Ibid., p. 24.

3Ibid., p. 229.

4Gwynn Nettler, *Social Concerns* (New York: McGraw-Hill, 1976), pp. 221–47.

5William Ryan, *Blaming the Victim* (New York: Vintage, 1971), pp. 92–98.

6Claerbaut, *Reluctant Defender*, p. 19

7Conversation with Ron Nikkel, National Director, Youth for Christ, Youth Guidance, 30 September 1982.

8For a helpful treatment of values clarification, see Sidney B. Simon, Leland W. Howe, and Howard Kirschenbaum, *Values Clarification*, rev. ed. (New York: Hart, 1978).

9For an excellent discussion of effective, nonmanipulative, low-key evangelism, see Em Griffin, *The Mind Changers* (Wheaton, Ill.: Tyndale, 1976).

10Malcolm Muggeridge, "25 Propositions on a 75th Birthday," *The New York Times* (24 April 1978).

NOTES ON CHAPTER 7

1Peter I. Rose, *They and We*, 2nd ed. (New York: Random House, 1974).

2Gunnar Myrdal, *An American Dilemma*, vol. 1 (New York: Harper and Brothers, 1944).

[3]Based on George Eaton Simpson and J. Milton Yinger, *Racial and Cultural Minorities* (New York: Harper and Brothers, 1953).

[4]The discussion on rights is taken from the film "Mythology of Racism," copyright Dr. Paul Mundy, 1968. Dr. Mundy is a sociologist at Loyola University of Chicago, and an expert on majority-minority relations.

[5]Egon E. Bergel, *Urban Sociology* (New York: McGraw-Hill, 1955), pp. 9–10.

[6]Louis L. Knowles and Kenneth Prewitt, eds., *Institutional Racism in America* (Englewood Cliffs, N.J.: Prentice-Hall, 1969).

[7]David Claerbaut, "Black Students and Christian Colleges," *Reformed Journal*, 26 (December 1976): 17–20.

[8]Anthony Campolo, "The Sociological Nature of the Urban Church," in David Frenchak and Sharrel Keyes, eds., *Metro-Ministry* (Elgin, Ill.: David C. Cook, 1979), p. 39.

[9]Knowles and Prewitt, *Institutional Racism*, pp. 22–24.

[10]Ibid., pp. 31–57.

[11]Adapted from a variety of materials by Dr. Paul Mundy, Loyola University of Chicago; see also Robert Ezra Park, *Race and Culture* (Glencoe, Ill.: Free Press, 1950).

[12]George Eaton Simpson and J. Milton Yinger, *Racial and Cultural Minorities*, rev. ed. (New York: Harper and Brothers, 1958), pp. 25–36.

[13]Ibid., pp. 23–25.

[14]James E. Conklin, "Urban Church Evangelism in a Multi-Ethnic Society: A Multi-Congregational Model" (Chicago: Seminary Consortium for Urban Pastoral Education, 1978). JM 35.

[15]For an excellent summary of minority experiences in America see Rose, *They and We;* Donald Keith Fellows, *A Mosaic of America's Ethnic Minorities* (New York: Wiley, 1972); Harry H. L. Kitano, *Race Relations* (Englewood Cliffs, N.J.: Prentice-Hall, 1974). Books helpful in understanding the native-American experience include: Dee Brown, *Bury My Heart at Wounded Knee* (New York: Holt, Rinehart and Winston, 1970); Howard M. Bahr, Bruce A. Chadwick, and Robert C. Day, eds., *Native Americans Today: Sociological Perspectives* (New York: Harper and Row, 1972); Murray Wax, *Indian Americans* (Englewood Cliffs, N.J.: Prentice-Hall, 1971).

[16]Works treating the experiences of Japanese Americans include: Harry H. L. Kitano, *Japanese Americans* (Englewood Cliffs, N.J.: Prentice-Hall, 1969); Leonard Bloom and Ruth Riemer, *Removal and Return* (Berkeley: University of California Press, 1949).

[17]Books of value in reviewing the Chinese-American experience include: Stanford M. Lyman, *Chinese Americans* (New York: Random House, 1974); Rose Hum Lee, *The Chinese in the United States of America* (New York: Oxford University Press, 1960).

[18]For additional reading on Mexican Americans, see John Burma, ed., *Mexican-Americans in the United States* (New York: Schenkman, 1970); Ellwyn Stoddard, *Mexican Americans* (New York: Random House, 1973).

[19]For an excellent discussion of black experience in America from a Christian perspective, see Ronald Behm and Columbus Salley, *Your God Is Too White* (Downers Grove, Ill.: InterVarsity, 1970).

[20]David Claerbaut, *Black Jargon in White America* (Grand Rapids: Eerdmans, 1972), p. 46.

[21]Ibid., pp. 46–47.

[22]Paul Mundy, "The Rural Past of Our Urban Present: A Sociologist Sketches the Chicago Personality," in *Leadership, Localism and Urbanism: Components in Search of a System,* monograph 10 (Chicago: Loyola University, Center for Research in Urban Government, 1968), pp. 20–24.

[23]James Coates, "Latin, Black Population Boom Predicted Here," *Chicago Tribune* (12 September 1982).

[24]Ibid.

[25]Crosscultural work by Mayers and the study of minorities by Greeley deal with this assimilation twist. See Marvin K. Mayers, *Christianity Confronts Culture* (Grand Rapids: Zondervan, 1974); and Andrew Greeley, *Why Can't They Be Like Us?* (New York: Dutton, 1971).

[26]Nicholas Wolterstorff, "Peace Workers," address at Wheaton College, Wheaton, Ill., 11 April 1978.

[27]James White, "Developing Black Leadership in White Denominations," in Frenchak and Keyes, *Metro-Ministry,* p. 54.

[28]James Conklin, "Urban Church Evangelism in a Multiethnic Society," in Frenchak and Keyes, *Metro-Ministry,* p. 189.

[29]Leonard P. Rascher, "Ministry Among the Urban Indians," in Frenchak and Keyes, *Metro-Ministry,* pp. 185–86.

[30]Ibid., p. 186.

[31]Bryan O. Walsh, "The Church and the City: The Miami Experience," *New Catholic World* (May/June 1982), p. 110; for an excellent review of Puerto Rican life, see Adalberto Lopez, *Puerto Rico and the Puerto Ricans* (Cambridge, Mass.: Schenkman, 1974).

[32]Robert L. Stern, "The South Bronx Pastoral Center," *New Catholic World* (May/June 1982), pp. 111–12.

[33]Whitney M. Young, Jr., *Beyond Racism* (New York: McGraw-Hill, 1971), pp. 218–19, 224–36.

NOTES ON CHAPTER 8

[1]Goodwin Watson and David Johnson, *Social Psychology,* 2nd ed. (Philadelphia: Lippincott, 1972), p. 108.

[2]James W. Vander Zanden, *Sociology: A Systematic Approach,* 3rd ed. (New York: Ronald, 1975), pp. 48–50.

[3]Ibid., pp. 51–52.

[4]Jerome G. Manis and Bernard N. Meltzer, *Symbolic Interaction,* 3rd ed. (Boston: Allyn and Bacon, 1978), pp. 35–36.

[5]Metta Spencer, *Foundations of Modern Sociology,* 2nd ed. (Englewood Cliffs, N.J.: Prentice-Hall, 1979), pp. 55–56.

[6]David Claerbaut, "Black Students and Christian Colleges," *Reformed Journal,* 10 (December 1976): 17–20.

[7]H. H. Hyman, "The Value Systems of Different Classes: A Social Psychological Contribution to the Analysis of Stratification," in R. Bendix and S. M. Lipset, eds., *Class, Status and Power* (Glencoe, Ill.: Free Press, 1953), pp. 426–42; B. C. Rosen, "The Achievement Syndrome: A Psychocultural Dimension of Social Stratification," *American Sociological Review,* 21: 203–11.

[8]James S. Coleman et al., *Equality of Educational Opportunity* (Washington, D.C.: United States Department of Health, Education and Welfare, Office of Education, 1966); Sarane S. Boocock, *An Introduction to the Sociology of Learning* (Boston: Houghton, Mifflin, 1972), pp. 75–76.

[9]Elliot Liebow, *Tally's Corner* (Boston: Little, Brown, 1967), pp. 29–71.

[10]Louis L. Knowles and Kenneth Prewitt, eds., *Institutional Racism in America* (Englewood Cliffs, N.J.: Prentice-Hall, 1969), pp. 37–39.

[11]Henry Clay Lindgren, *An Introduction to Social Psychology,* 2nd ed. (New York: Wiley, 1973), p. 90.

[12]William Ryan, *Blaming the Victim* (New York: Vintage, 1971).

[13]Ibid., p. xii.

[14]Knowles and Prewitt, *Institutional Racism.*

[15]David Claerbaut, *Social Problems,* part 2 (Scottsdale, Ariz.: Christian Academic Publications, 1977), pp. 122–25.

[16]Boocock, *Introduction to the Sociology of Learning.*

[17]Robert Rosenthal and Lenore Jacobson, *Pygmalion in the Classroom* (New York: Holt, Rinehart and Winston, 1968).

[18]Michael Harrington, "The Invisible Land," in A. David Hill et al., eds., *The Quality of Life in America* (New York: Holt, Rinehart and Winston, 1973), pp. 140–47.

[19]Elizabeth B. Drew, "Going Hungry in America: Government's Failure," *Atlantic Monthly* (December 1968), pp. 53–61, in Hill, *Quality of Life,* pp. 154–65.

[20]Ramsey Clark, *Crime in America* (New York: Pocket Books, 1971).

[21]Ryan, *Blaming the Victim,* pp. 185–210.

NOTES ON CHAPTER 9

[1]Adapted from Anthony Campolo, "The Sociological Nature of the Urban Church," in David Frenchak and Sharrel Keyes, eds., *Metro-Ministry* (Elgin, Ill.: David C. Cook, 1979), pp. 27–35.

[2]George W. Baybrook, "Six Churches: Thriving on Common Ground," *Christianity Today* (18 June 1976), pp. 18–19.

[3]Dennis Bakke, "Churches and Energy Conservation," in Frenchak and Keyes, *Metro-Ministry,* pp. 104–6.

[4]William Bentley and Willie Jemison, "Church Growth in Black Congregations," in Frenchak and Keyes, *Metro-Ministry,* pp. 61–64.

[5]Donald L. Benedict, "Toward an Urban Church Strategy," in Frenchak and Keyes, *Metro-Ministry,* pp. 70–76.

[6]William Leslie, "The Ministering Church," in Frenchak and Keyes, *Metro-Ministry*, pp. 126–34.

[7]Michael Roschke, "The Gifted Urban Lay Person," In Frenchak and Keyes, *Metro-Ministry*, pp. 153–63.

[8]James Conklin, "Urban Church Evangelism in a Multiethnic Society," in Frenchak and Keyes, *Metro-Ministry*, pp. 189–91.

[9]David Wilkerson, *Urban Heartbeat, the Human Touch in Metropolitan Missions—"Chicago"* (Atlanta: Home Mission Board, Southern Baptist Convention, 1981). JM 651.

[10]Denver Core City Mission Study Supervisory Committee, *A Summary Report of the Core City Study for the Presbytery of Denver* (Denver: Department of National Mission, Presbytery of Denver, 1979). ICUIS 4387.

[11]Ron Spann, "The Church of the Messiah–Material" (Detroit: Church of the Messiah, n.d.). ICUIS 4428.

[12]Lyle E. Schaller, "Twenty Questions for Self-Evaluation in the Downtown Church," *Church Management*, July 1976, pp. 17–18, 27, 29.

[13]His story and that of LaSalle Street Church is chronicled in James Hefley and Marti Hefley, *The Church That Takes on Trouble* (Elgin, Ill.: David C. Cook, 1976).

[14]Raymond Bakke, "The Urban Church Revitalization Process," in Frenchak and Keyes, *Metro-Ministry*, pp. 168–73.

[15]David I. Frenchak, "Urban Fatigue," in Frenchak and Keyes, *Metro-Ministry*, pp. 115–16.

[16]Ibid., p. 120.

[17]David Claerbaut, *The Reluctant Defender* (Wheaton, Ill.: Tyndale, 1978), pp. 222–23.

[18]Harvey Cox, *The Secular City*, rev. ed. (New York: Macmillan, 1966).

[19]James P. Roache, "Anglo Minister in Black/Hispanic/Ethnic Communities," *New Catholic World* (May/June 1982), p. 126.

[20]Frenchak, "Urban Fatigue," p. 122.

[21]Ibid., p. 123.

[22]William Leslie, "Key to Living in the City," sermon at LaSalle Street Church, Chicago, 10 June 1979.

Index

Peterson, Paul, 61
Philadelphia, 45, 64, 124
Pinnock, Clark, 22
Plous, F. K., Jr., 33
Poverty
  effects of justice system on,
    102–4
  health care in, 97–98
  in institutions, 70–81
  insecurity of, 93–106
  ministry to insecurity of,
    106–11
  ministry of institutional, 81–88
  perpetuation of, 69–70
  police brutality and, 99–102
  Protestant work ethic and, 73
  psychological impact of—para-
    noia, 93
  responses to insecurity, 104–6
  school desegregation and, 96–97
  sources of insecurity, 94
  urban renewal and, 95–96, 176
  and welfare, 98
Prejudice. *See* Racism and
    Prejudice.

Quayle, Vincent, 45

Racism and prejudice
  and the church, 194
  defined, 130
  European and American concept
    of rights and, 132–34
  historical and sociological fac-
    tors in, 131–43
  majority-minority relations and,
    136–43
  pervasiveness of, 129
Rainwater, Lee, 104
Rascher, Leonard, 158
Rice, Howard, 24

Roache, James, 208
Rome, 18
Roschke, Michael, 195
Rose, Peter, 129
Ryan, William, 174, 187

St. Louis, 203
  United Methodist Church, 29
St. Paul
  Archdiocese of, and Min-
    neapolis, 67
  Christian Sharing Fund, 67
San Diego, 15
San Francisco, 15
Schaller, Lyle, 196
Scott, Arthur, 100
Seattle, 16
Seminary Consortium for Urban
    Pastoral Education (SCUPE),
    29
Shoemaker, Dennis, 28
Sider, Ronald, 19, 23
Social concern, 16–17, 24, 25, 29
Socialization
  defined, 163
  of middle class pastor, 165–67
Sodom, 29
Southern Baptist Convention, 28
Stratification
  bases of, 50–51
  concentric zone model of, 49–50
  defined, 49
  dysfunctions of, 51–52
  functions of, 50
  perpetuation of, 57–61
  poverty within, 55–57
  social classes and, 52–57

Toledo, 38
Toronto: United Church of Canada
    Task Group, 29